He Gave the Order

The Life and Times of Admiral Osami Nagano

F.J. Bradley

NAVAL HISTORY 2

BENNINGTON, VERMONT

2014

First Edition published in 2014 by the Merriam Press

First Edition

Copyright © 2014 by F.J. Bradley
Additional material copyright of named contributors.
Design by Ray Merriam

All rights reserved.
No part of this book may be used or reproduced in any manner whatsoever without written permission, except in the case of brief quotations embodied in critical articles or reviews.

WARNING
The unauthorized reproduction or distribution of this copyrighted work is illegal. Criminal copyright infringement, including infringement without monetary gain, is investigated by the FBI and is punishable by up to five years in federal prison and a fine of $250,000.

ISBN 9781576383711
Library of Congress Control Number: 2013949827
Merriam Press #NH2-PG

This work was designed, produced, and published in
the United States of America by the

Merriam Press
133 Elm Street Suite 3R
Bennington VT 05201-2250
USA

E-mail: ray@merriam-press.com
Web site: merriam-press.com

The Merriam Press publishes new manuscripts on historical subjects, especially military history and with an emphasis on World War II, as well as reprinting previously published works, including reports, documents, manuals, articles and other materials on historical topics.

FRONT COVER

Osami Nagano. Via Narodowe Archiwum Cyfrowe (National Digital Archive) of Poland.
Inset: View of Battleship Row during Pearl Harbor attack. From Wikipedia.

BACK COVER

Top: IJN battleship *Nagato* and all her crew members, 1937. From Wikimedia.

Bottom Left: Portrait of Osami Nagano. Via Misako Nagano, Everlasting Ocean,
Minami-No-Kaze Publishing Company, Kochi City, 1995.

Table of Contents

Chapter 1: Early Years of Osami Nagano, 1880 – 1900 5

Chapter 2: Early Career and Marriages, 1900 – 1920 12

Chapter 3: Diplomat and Traveler, 1920 – 1930 19

Chapter 4: Diplomat, Sailor and Politician, 1930 – 1941 33

    Part 1: Diplomat: Geneva Disarmament Conference 1932-1933 33
    Part 2: Sailor: Commandant, Yokosuka Naval Base 48
    Part 3: Diplomat: Second London Naval Conference 1935-1936 53
    Part 4: Politician: Naval Minister 63
    Part 5: Sailor: Commander in Chief of the Combined Fleet 76
    Part 6: Retiree and Celebrity 84
    Part 7: Concerned Warrior, 9 April to 8 December 1941 90

Chapter 5: Post Script 130

Glossary 141

Significant Individuals 144

Appendix A1-A8: Postcards 146

Appendix B: Nagano Family Tree and Osami Nagano's Wives and Children 174

Appendix C1-C4: Naval Treaties and Naval Ship Estimates 1941 176

Appendix D: Meiji Constitution 183

Appendix E: Nagano Medals, Orders, Decorations 184

Appendix F: Soviet Japan Neutrality Treaty, April 13, 1941 190

Appendix G: Summary of IMTFE Trial Results 192

Acknowledgements

MANY persons, both in the United States and Japan, have assisted me in writing this profile of Admiral Osami Nagano. I have avoided the use of the term biography – the document is not a complete biography of Nagano's life. I have written material regarding Nagano from documents available to us. I have attempted to avoid any "what if" scenarios.

The persons who have assisted us in this profile are the Nagano children and grandchildren.

Masako Sakaguchi, attorney at law in Tokyo and also in New York, has been invaluable in her accessing the Nagano papers in Japan to provide historical photographs.

The important translators were Nobuo Kohyama, Hisako Izutsu, Naomi Pudvah and also translators from the Japan Society and Columbia University.

I am grateful to my wife Rose Marie Pratt, for enduring long hours researching, reviewing data and typing myriad drafts of the document. Ray Merriam shaped the manuscript into final format fit for publishing.

Chapter 1

Early Years of Osami Nagano 1880-1900

Overview

OSAMI Nagano was born in 1880, a time and place of great transformation in Japan. The Shogun era was giving way to the Meiji Empire and political power was centralized in the new capital of Edo (now Tokyo). The samurai system of warlord rule was ending and Japan was forced to look beyond her borders to shape her future. Nagano, with a strict but loving father and persevering mother, started out with a solid background. He attained great achievements in his military and political careers, but his involvement in Japan's entrance into World War II on 8 December 1941 led to his ultimate downfall. He died in 1947, in Sugamo Prison in Tokyo during the International Military Tribunal for the Far East under U.S. occupation, following Japan's defeat.

Events during this era included:

- Japan's modern era emerged with the re-establishment of an Emperor regime. Emperor Meiji, formerly residing in Kyoto, was relocated to Edo (now Tokyo) in 1877. He was not only a spiritual monarch but a political leader as well. Emperor Meiji's lineage – so the legend goes – goes back about 2000 years to era of the Sun Goddess.
- The Meiji Constitution was signed in 1889 and took effect in 1890.
- The Tokugawa Shogunate, which ruled from 1600, was in its ending stages due to infighting.
- Japan turned outward to engage in the Sino-Japanese War of 1894-1895, which ended with the Treaty of Shimonoseki. The Shimonoseki Treaty gave Formosa (Taiwan) to Japan and, most importantly, the Liaotung Peninsula. But in 1897, Russia, Germany and France ganged up on Japan and she had to cede the peninsula back to China.
- In the western world, America was engaged in a war with Spain and ended up with the Philippines, which took some battling to subdue (1898).
- Britain was fighting the Crimean War and France opposed Germany in the Franco-Prussian War. This was the first in a series of wars between France and Germany.

Shogun Era Transformation

The Tokugawa Shogunate political rule, known as the Edo Era, lasted from 1600 to 1867, approximately. The ruling philosophy was of strict isolationism for Japan and disdain for foreign notions and influence. Tokugawa feared the overpowering alien influence circulating among the Japanese population. To keep the Japanese race pure, he initiated a program to stamp out "foreign diseases" such as Christianity. In 1640, all ports were closed to foreign vessels and visitors, except for the trade port of Nagasaki on Kyushu Island, which provided the only window outward. Commerce through this port was primarily from Europe and China.

The Shogun instituted thought-control which included secret police. The only tolerated overseas literature was Dutch publications on geography and, of course, extremely few Japanese people could read the Dutch language. So the populace was isolated in their thinking over this period and very few traveled outside Japan. The war between Britain and China introduced many publications written in Chinese and these were disseminated to a much wider Japanese audience. These writings described the world in a much broader sense and to a wider audience than was available through geographic publications.

Mistreatment of stranded American sailors shipwrecked along the Japanese coastline in the 19th century worked against the bastion of isolationism. It prompted President Millard Fillmore, 13th American president, to order Commodore Matthew Perry to sail a fleet of warships to Japan in 1853. He returned in 1854 and ultimately signed a treaty with Japan which granted American sailors and vessels certain rights. In 1858 Townsend Harris signed a treaty with Shogun Tokugawa to open up certain ports to American vessels. Japan gradually unlocked additional ports and granted similar rights to other maritime powers, such as Britain, France, and Russia.

The transformation from the Shogunate system to Emperor rule evolved over a period of years starting with the Anglo-Sino war – 1839 to 1842. In this war, the Chinese were defeated and, thus, alerted the Japanese that they must look outside the feudal system or they would also be defeated, like China. Japan slowly embraced the outside world.

In the south, the Choshu, Satsuma and Tosa clans were anti-Tokugawa. In particular, the Choshu and Satsuma clans wanted to remove Shogun Tokugawa by force. The Tosa clan came up with a compromise plan in which Shogun Tokugawa Keiki would resign and relinquish power to Emperor Meiji. Tokugawa signed his resignation on 8 November 1867 and a budding constitutional government was established. Emperor Meiji put his signature to the agreement on 10 November 1867, thus ending the approximately 260-year reign of Shogunate rule in Edo. (Ref. 1.1) Laws were enacted by a bicameral legislative body composed of two houses. The upper house was of the nobility while the samurai comprised the lower house. A method of qualification and selection of legislative officials evolved over the next 20 years and was finally imbedded in the Meiji constitution, which was signed in 1889 and took effect in 1890.

The Shogun expected that he would have some political power in the new government but he was mistaken. Eventually, the samurai class was eliminated and compulsory conscription was instituted in 1875. Japan dreaded a takeover by a foreign power and, therefore, a trained military was essential. The naval academy opened in 1872 and the army's military academy was established in 1875.

Osami Nagano's Parents

Harukichi Nagano was born about 1835, nearing the end of the Tokugawa Era (see Figure 1.1 as an elder). He was a member of the *Bushi* (samurai warrior) class and gave his allegiance to the Tosa clan in the city of Tosa (now Kochi) on Shikoku Island (Figure 1.2). At the time, there were over 40 clans in Japan spread out over the islands of Kyushu, Shikoku, Honshu, and Hokkaido. In his later years, Harukichi lived in the town of Minamishinmachi, Kochi City (now Sakurai-cho) (Ref. 1.2). Harukichi's wife, Saki, was estimated by Osami Nagano to be in her 70s at her death in 1914; therefore she was born in 1840. Her place of birth is unknown. The Nagano family tree is given in Appendix B.

Harukichi was well trained in the martial arts, presumably the ways of the sword and jujitsu. It is uncertain if he was schooled in modern weaponry. As recounted in Osami Nagano's memoirs (Ref. 1.3), Harukichi, was able to read classicial Chinese writing and was well versed in Confucianism. He shared his knowledge of the Chinese language and philosophy with the local youngsters in his village. This philosophy was based on filial piety (ancestor worship) and maintenance of peace and justice. Such a code of conduct would appear to be at variance with the Emperor Meiji's philosophy in which individuals owed their allegiance to the Emperor-State and the State dictated morality. Another aspect of the Meiji philosophy was that the Japanese people were the superior race in Asia.

His father was very strict and Osami related that at meal time there was little grumbling about the food. If he complained, Harukichi would scold—"Then do not eat!" Throughout his life, Osami ate what was placed in front of him, as he recalled that his childhood training left him no choice. But as noted in Figure 1.3 Nagano brothers and Harukichi seem to be relaxing in martial arts garments. So, while strict, Harukichi seemed to engender a collegial relationship with his family.

Saki, Osami's mother married Harukichi in about 1862 and their first child, a daughter, arrived in 1864. Osami was born on 15 June 1880, the youngest of five siblings. It was a very difficult birth for Saki. Osami admired his mother greatly and described her as strong-willed yet broadminded. She endured a hard life with patience, perseverance and optimism. Her one enjoyment was smoking and Osami bought her a bamboo smoking pipe with his first paycheck he earned as an Ensign. While her education was limited, she listened attentively to her husband's lectures on Confucian philosophy.

Kochi Prefecture on Shikoku Island, in the 19th century, was an isolated area bordered on one side by the Pacific Ocean and on the other side by the Inland Sea. Growing up, Osami loved the outdoors surrounded by water and fished in the local streams. But, when Osami told his father he was going to the Naval Academy, Harukichi remarked that the navy may not be the best choice for a person with poor boating skills. Figures 1.4 and 1.5 shows Osami in traditional garb as a youngster.

Harukichi retired at age 40, about 1875, presumably because the Emperor's new orientation of the state made little work for an ex-Samurai. He died at age 70 while Osami was away fighting in the Russo-Japanese war.

EARLY SCHOOLING

Osami Nagano attended the local Kainan Middle School in Tosa. He recalled that in his fourth year (approximately 10th year in the U.S. high school system), a former student was attending the Naval Academy on the island of Eta Jima in Hiroshima Bay, which is approximately 50 miles from Tosa as the crow flies. Osami was sufficiently impressed that he decided to sit for the Naval Academy's entrance exam. If he did not get in, he would try law or engineering – so his sights were set high even as a youngster. Many of the applicants from local schools had attended prep schools in Tokyo to better prepare themselves for the entrance exam. In reflection, Osami related some traits in math, science and language that he believed were necessary for success. Those qualities he received at Kainan Middle School were as good as those provided by the big city prep schools

Principal Kazuma Yoshida at Kainan taught that, in spite of poor facilities and low budget, one can achieve excellence by extra effort to offset physical shortages. Osami's extra effort meant studying independently. For foreign languages he used memory power, reading and writing abundantly to simply get used to the language rather than trying to analyze it. He wanted to put as many words as possible into his vocabulary. Later he recalled making up a word index of six hundred words per month while in Washington DC as a Naval Attaché. This index remained useful many years later. For math and science he advocated the ability to think through and analyze a problem to arrive at the solution. Nagano recalled that, at one point in his life, it took him several months to resolve a problem and this was what he urged his children to do. In his words: "Use your own facilities to arrive at a solution without asking for a solution or looking at the answer."

Nagano was proud of his local school and he returned the honor by achieving second place in the country-wide Naval Academy entrance exam, beating out all the Tokyo prep school students. His one weakness was in the oral part of the English exam. He related that his local school had no native English-speaker and hearing words spoken by an Englishman was difficult to interpret. Eventually he mastered the phonetics of the English language. Osami was very proud of his success on the Naval Academy entrance exam, as was Principal Kazuma Yoshida.

IMPERIAL JAPANESE NAVAL ACADEMY, ETA JIMA

In 1897, Osami Nagano entered the Imperial Japanese Naval Academy at Eta Jima. The Academy's spartan life did not seem to have made a lasting impression or phase Midshipman Nagano. His upbringing in Tosa under his strict father prepared him well for the ardors of military regimentation and he continued to excel academically.

In his first year at the Academy, Nagano became close friends with upperclassman Kichisaburo Nomura, who ultimately became the Japanese ambassador to the USA at the time of the Japanese attack on Pearl Harbor in 1941. Both Nomura and Nagano won binoculars in recognition for their achievements at the academy – Nagano's was for his exemplary conduct. A cadet's accomplishments at the Academy would go on to influence his status and promotion throughout his naval career (Ref. 1.5). The later heights to which Nagano climbed were predestined by his second-place position of 105 midshipmen graduated in the Academy's 28th class of 1900. By 1945 there was one admiral of the fleet, eight vice admirals and 18 rear admirals from Nagano's class. As a desperately poor nation with no natural resources, Japan did very well with its navy up to 1942.

A contemporary of Nagano, Isoroku Takano (later adopted by a local prominent citizen with the name Yamamoto), grew up in a far-off village called Nagaoka on the west side of Honshu. His father was the school master but he grew up in relative poverty, not unlike Nagano's youth. He had one interest that he shared with Osami, which was calligraphy. Yamamoto applied for entrance to the Naval Academy in 1900 and placed second on the exam. In 1904, he graduated in the 11th position of 192 midshipmen and was commissioned just in time for the Russo-Japanese War.

The physical rigors of military training honed Nagano into shape. As described by Potter (Ref. 1.4) midshipmen had to swim across Hiroshima Bay from Miyajima to Eta Jima — an ordeal of 8 to 10 arduous hours. Photos of Nagano from his early naval career to his later years show that as his career expanded, his profile expanded as well. Note Osami as a midshipman (Figure 1.6) and as an ensign (Figures 1.7 and 1.8). The last picture shows that the difference in weight was dramatic.

The history of the naval academy is of note. As an island nation, Japan looked to Great Britain, another island nation, for assistance to establish its national academy for the Imperial Japanese Navy. The Academy at Eta Jima was staffed by British naval officers from its start in 1872, Britain having contributed the red brick to construction of the main academy building (See Figure 1.9). On the other hand, the Imperial Japanese Army looked to the German-Prussian model to establish the army's military academy in Kyoto. It was later moved to Tokyo. As is common in many nations, the army and navy were rivals and did not coordinate their actions very well. Nagano was an exception in that he encouraged cooperation between the army and navy. Later, as a young naval lieutenant, he commanded a special naval task force with special field artillery pieces that were used to fire on the Russian fleet in Port Arthur. Nagano's company was part of the Japanese Army Group 2 for its attack on Port Arthur on the Liaotung peninsula in 1904.

Nagano's early life and military training shaped him for the new century where he traveled the world representing the best aspects of Japanese culture and tradition. He fully enjoyed his journey, until the beginning of the end in 1942.

Chapter 1 References

1.1 Ike, Nobutaka, "Western Influences on the Meiji Restoration," *The Pacific Historical Review*, Volume XVII, Number 1, February 1948

1.2 Nagano, Misako, Everlasting Ocean, Minami-No-Kaze Publishing Company, Kochi City, 1995

1.3 Nagano, Osami, Sugamo Prison Diary, April 1946 translated by Nobuo Kohyama

1.4 Potter, J. D., Yamamoto: The Man Who Menaced America, Paperback Library Edition by arrangement with The Viking Press, Inc., New York, 1965

1.5 Mauch, Peter, *Sailor Diplomat: Nomura Kichisaburo and the Japanese-American War*, Harvard University Press, Cambridge, MA, 2011

Figure 1.1 Harukichi Nagano

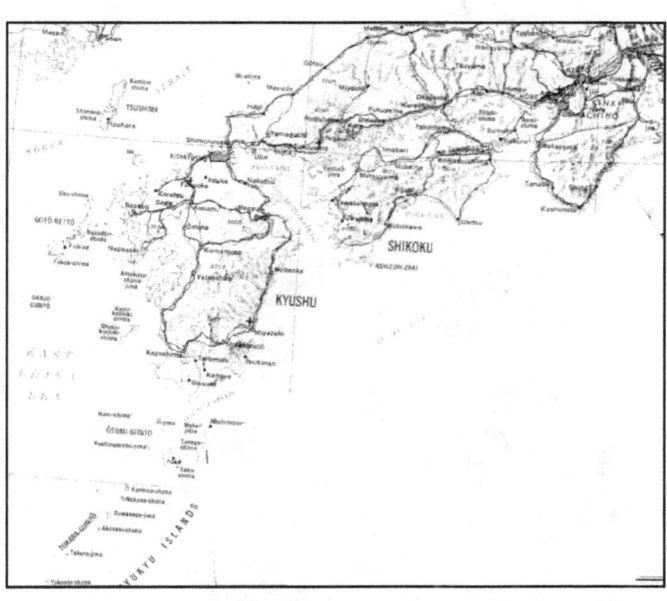

Figure 1.2 Map of Shikoku, birthplace of Osami Nagano in Kochi City, 1880

Figure 1.3 Young Nagano and friends

Figure 1.4 Osami Nagano in traditional Korean garb. (Photo taken at Inchon, Korea)

Figure 1.5 Osami Nagano in traditional Korean garb. (Photo taken at Inchon, Korea)

Figure 1.6 Midshipman Osami Nagano

Figure 1.7 Ensign Osami Nagano, Naval Academy, Eta Jima 1900

Figure 1.8 Ensign Osami Nagano, Naval Academy, Eta Jima 1900

Figure 1.9 Naval Academy at Eta Jima

Chapter 2

Osami Nagano: Early Career and Marriages, 1900-1920

Overview

THROUGH his twenties and thirties, Osami Nagano ambitiously pursued his calling to the Imperial Japanese Navy. Through these same years he began family life. During these years he fathered four children with three wives, two of whom tragically died in childbirth. The backdrop of world events during his early career included:

- The Russian-Japanese war raged from 1904-1905. It was ultimately settled by the Treaty of Portsmouth in New Hampshire, aided by President Theodore Roosevelt.
- World War I began in August 1914 with the assassination of Archduke Ferdinand in Serbia.
- Britain declared war on Germany, Austria-Hungary and the Ottoman Empire.
- Japan, as Britain's ally, took over German concessions in China and the German colonies in the Caroline and Marshall Islands (Figure 2.1).
- The Russian Revolution erupted resulting in the collapse of the Czarist regime in May 1917.
- America entered the "Great War" in April 1917 – the "war to end all wars."
- The Armistice, ending World War I, was signed in November 1918 following the collapse of the Kaiser regime in October 1918 in Berlin.

All the while, the expansion of the Japanese Empire across Asia allowed Japan to consider herself a world power, at least in the naval sense. At the same time and most importantly the Meiji Era (1867-1912) ended and the Taisho Era (1912-1925) began.

Graduation and Specialization 1900-1906

In 1900, Osami Nagano was graduated from the Naval Academy in Eta Jima in second place of 105 cadets. Many of these midshipmen from the 28th class ascended to very high ranks in the Imperial Japanese Navy, and Nagano achieved the highest military rank of them all—that of Gensui in 1943. It is sometimes translated in western literature as Fleet Admiral, but to native Japanese the term Gensui has a more honored connotation. As an Ensign, Nagano was stationed on several ships – the Hashidate and the Asahi and then as Sub-Lieutenant on the Asama. He was assigned to the Yokosuka Naval District and attended Gunnery School. As a lieutenant (see Figure 2.2) Nagano was placed in charge of special naval artillery units. For the next several years, he was assigned to troop transfer ships, Ariake-maru and Hongkong-maru in the First Fleet.

Lieutenant Nagano saw combat on Liaotung Peninsula in the Russo-Japanese War (1904-1905) and described how he went ashore with the 2nd Army. The thrust of the Japanese forces was to blockade the northern land escape route for Russian forces stationed in Port Arthur (Figure 2.3). Meanwhile, Admiral Heihachiro Togo, Commander of the Japanese Combined Fleet, blockaded the sea entrance outside Port Arthur. The combination of the army's land fire assisted by naval ground units and battleship fire defeated the Russian Pacific fleet in 1904.

In his diary (Ref. 2.1) at Sugamo Prison in Tokyo, Nagano wrote: "I recall this very date—7 August, 42 years ago (1904)—we advanced our two 12 cm naval guns to the back of our forces assaulting Port Arthur. Then our first indirect shelling of the fort with great impact on the Russians until the day Port Arthur fell. I continued directing our bombardment as commander of the naval battery. The naval battle outside Port Arthur on 10 August 1904 was the result of our continued shelling by the navy company that drove the Russian vessels out of the port." Note in Figure 2.4 Nagano with three comrades—all decorated with medals from the Russo-Japanese War. Several Japanese major generals who were directing the ground forces against the Russians were demoted after the battle of Port Arthur. Their use of antiquated tactics against modern weaponry resulted in excessive casualties. One of these generals was General Hideki Tojo's father.

The Russian Baltic fleet rushed 8500 miles to rescue their Pacific fleet, but was diverted to Vladivostok after Port Arthur fell to the Japanese. Steaming up the Tsushima Strait between Kyushu and Korea, Admiral Togo's fleet sank or captured all eight Russian battleships on 27 May 1905. This was the first naval battle fought with steam ships in the modern era (Ref. 2.2). In this naval battle Ensign Isoroku Yamamoto was stationed on the cruiser Nisshin which was hit by Russian fire. He was wounded in his right leg and lost two fingers from his left hand (Ref. 2.3).

In his writings, Nagano reminisced of a letter his mother, Saki, sent to him when he shipped off to the Russian-Japanese war. She told him: "I consider your life was already given to our country – then regardless of what may happen to you; this mother will not make any disgraceful scene. Go for broke, my boy, and dedicate your life to our country." Nagano commented that the letter was written in rather elementary penmanship with approximately the above content. Her letter contained a couple of talismans traditionally wrapped in paper. "Well, after telling me not to hesitate to die for the nation" he recalled "she prays for me and my safe return, protected by the talisman. I felt her affection, her love and her prayer for me. I just love this mother. Unfortunately, in going ashore in Endaioh as company commander of a special naval landing force in water up to my waist, the letter was lost."

SCHOOLING, GUNNERY OFFICER AND MARRIAGES 1906-1916

Firing artillery guns accurately on land or sea is a complex process involving math, science and engineering and Nagano excelled in all these subjects. He attended Gunnery Training School from September 1905 to January 1906 and, upon completion, he was appointed to the position of Gunnery Instructor at the Naval Academy until September 1906. He served as Chief Gunnery Officer on the Cruiser Itsukushima from September 1906 to September 1908.

With his battlefield achievement and academic capabilities, the IJN continued to invest much toward Nagano's education. Following Gunnery School and sea service, he was sent to the Japanese Naval War College in Tokyo (25 May 1909 to 30 November 1910). He was then assigned as Resident Scholar at Harvard University in America (January 1913-April 1915). Figure 2.5 shows Nagano with several friends in America. From November 1913 to June 1914, he was enrolled in three courses in the Graduate School under Professor Wilson: Elements of International Law, International Law and Selected Cases in International Law.

While at Harvard he lived with the Wheeler family in Brookline, Massachusetts and also spent some time at the U.S. Naval War College at Newport, RI. Nagano was getting well-rounded training in naval strategy from various view points. He was impressed with teaching methods used in America and later employed them at Eta Jima when he became Director of the Naval Academy.

Family Life

As a young naval lieutenant, Nagano was likely the focus of many young women. In 1907 he met and married Ritsu (Figure 2.7). Three years later they had their first child – a daughter, Tazuko (Figure 2.6). Sadly, Ritsu did not survive the delivery and Nagano had to care for his daughter as a single parent while he attended the War College in Tokyo. He had the support of his sister and three brothers, but, at the same time, he also had to think of his mother who was widowed in 1905.

In 1913, Nagano married Nobuko, who was about 23 years of age and he was 33. This was just prior to his departure for the United States to attend Harvard University and, since Tazuko needed a mother, it may have been a marriage of convenience. It was not in the culture of the Imperial Navy to send wives with their husbands when they were posted to a foreign country and Nagano would not return until early 1915. It is unclear how he traveled to America and back to Japan, but World War I had broken out and sea transportation could be dangerous. In any case he returned home in April 1915 and Nobuko became pregnant with his daughter, Kimiko, who was delivered in January 1916. But, again Nagano was widowed when Nobuko, his second wife, died in childbirth. The infant, Kimiko, survived only six months. It was a time of great sorrow for the young navy man advancing in his career yet trying to keep a stable home for his family.

Fleet Duty and Desk Jobs 1915-1920

Upon his return from America, Nagano shipped out to fleet duty. He served as Deputy Commander on the cruiser Nisshin from May to December 1915. The Nisshin was the same vessel on which Yamamoto was injured in 1905 by Russian fire. Nagano also served as Deputy Commander on the Iwate from December 1915 to August 1916. The Iwate was an Izumo-class cruiser in the Allied effort (Britain and Japan) in World War I, initially dispatched to Tsingtao on the Yellow Sea during his deployment. It was then assigned to convoy duty protecting ships plying from Singapore to the Suez Canal in the Indian Ocean. After the war, she was used as a training vessel which made long training deployments from her home port in Yokosuka. The Iwate was part of Nagano's trans-Pacific training cruise in 1927 (see Chapter 3).

In August 1916, he was assigned to the Personnel Bureau of the Navy Ministry in Tokyo. He later rose to Chief of the Bureau in October 1918 and was promoted to the rank of Captain. With a desk job in Tokyo, Nagano set up house in the city with his infant daughter, Tazuko. He married Yu, who was nearly his own age (Figure 2.8). In rapid succession, his daughter Hisako and son Hiroshi were born in 1918 and 1919 respectively.

In November 1919, he again shipped out, this time as Commanding Officer of the Chikuma-class cruiser Hirado. She was part of a protective patrol along the Siberian coast to provide protection for convoys of troop and supply ships for Japanese and American forces, which were assigned as a stabilizing force in Siberia. Nagano served at sea until 1920, when he was assigned again to America as Naval Attaché at the Japanese Embassy, Washington, DC.

Although duty forced Nagano to be away on many lengthy deployments from 1920 to 1936, he was generous with his communication to his family through postcards, expressing his caring for them and to show them ports of call and sights in America, Asia and Europe (Appendix A).

Chapter 2 References

2.1 Nagano, O., Sugamo Prison Diary, April 1946, translated by Nobuo Kohyama
2.2 Harries, M., Harries, S., Soldiers of the Sun, Random House, New York, 1991
2.3 Potter, J. D., Yamamoto: The Man Who Menaced America, Paperback Library Edition by arrangement with The Viking Press, Inc., New York, 1965

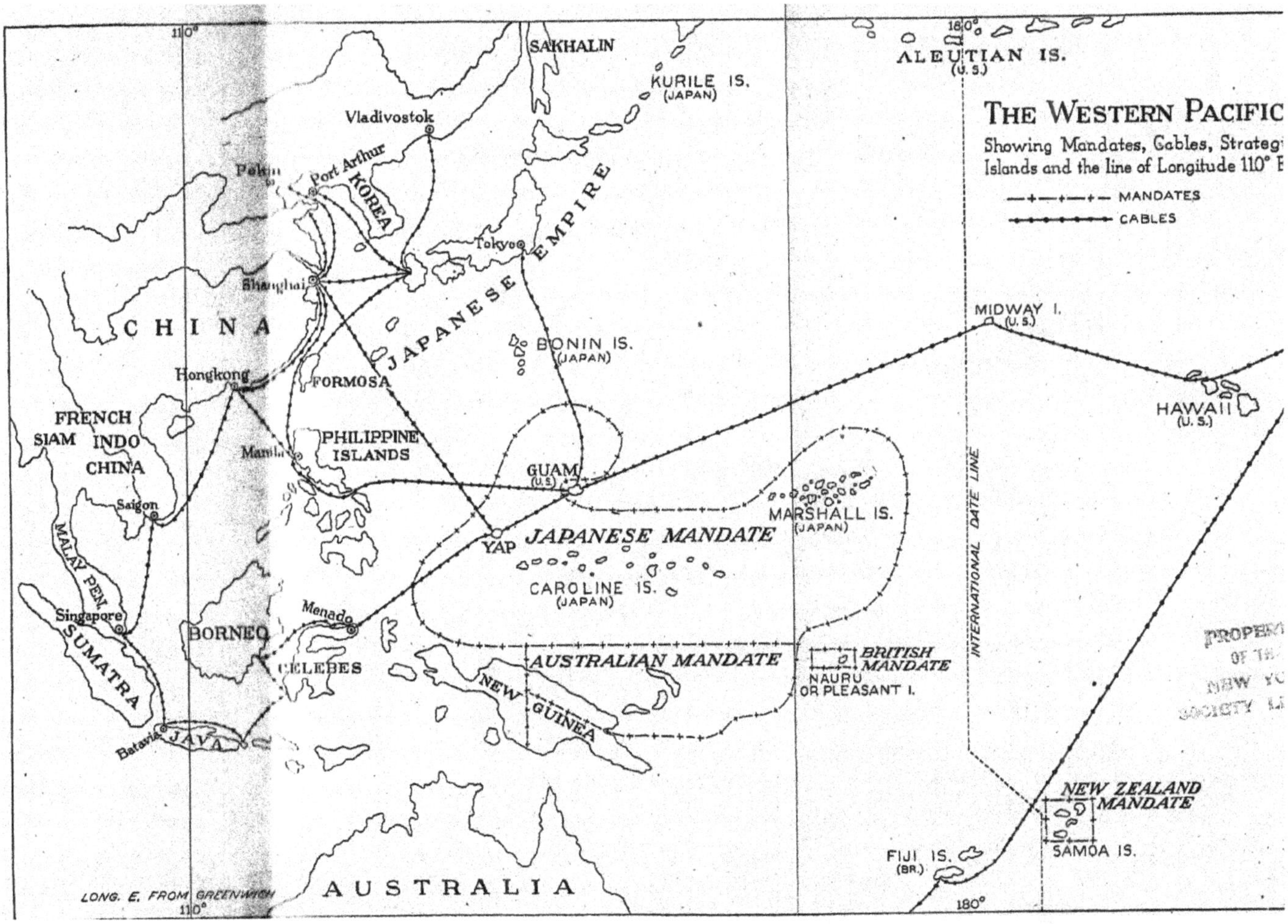

Figure 2.1 Japanese Empire 1920

Figure 2.2 Lt. O. Nagano 1903

HE GAVE THE ORDER

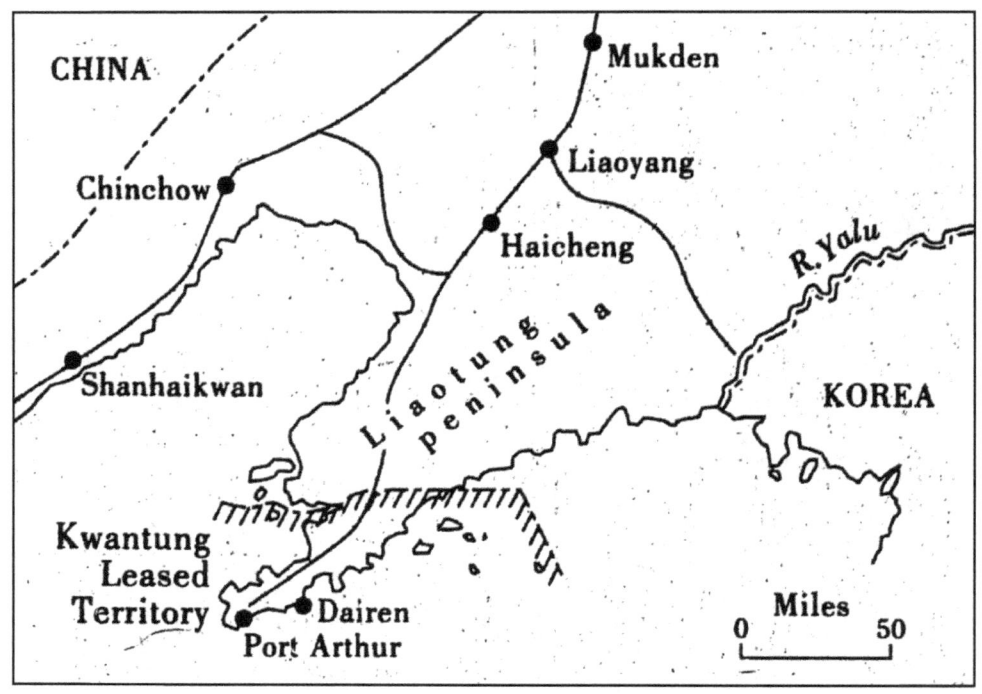

Figure 2.3 Liaotung Peninsula

Figure 2.4 Lt. Osami Nagano with comrades following Russo-Japanese War 1907

Figure 2.5 Nagano with friends in America

Figure 2.6 Tazuko Nagano ~ 1916

Figure 2.7 Osami, Ritsu and friends at wedding, 1907

Figure 2.8 Nagano with Yu and daughter, Tazuko

Chapter 3

Osami Nagano: Sailor, Diplomat and Traveler 1920-1930

Overview

- Hirohito became Emperor of Japan in 1925 upon the death of his father, Taisho
- American constitution was amended to prohibit production, transportation and sale of alcohol. The prohibition lasted from 1920 to 1933 when the amendment was repealed
- Three republican presidents were elected in America in succession – Warren G. Harding 1921-1923, Calvin Coolidge 1923-1929 and Herbert Hoover 1929-1933
- Post-war economic prosperity gave way to economic chaos and the stock market crash in 1929 leading to a global Great Depression

Osami Nagano the Diplomat

DECEMBER 1920 found the young Captain Osami Nagano assigned to Washington DC as the Naval Attaché in the Japanese Embassy. He was to interact with other military personnel in the nation's capital and become skilled in the language and customs. It was a most civilized assignment as he was listed in the Washington Social Register and mingled with the elite of the American capital. It was unfortunate that he had to leave his family at home. Figure 3.1 shows Nagano with his wife, Yu, and three children in early 1920 before he left for Washington DC.

One of his duties as a military envoy was for Nagano to personally extend sympathy to Admiral William Moffet, U.S. Navy, following a tragedy that occurred in England with a significant loss of life, both American and British. It was the crash of the dirigible ZR-2 (Ref. 3.1). General Billy Mitchell, U.S. Army, also telephoned his condolences to Moffet, who was Chief of the Bureau of Aeronautics and an airship enthusiast. The airship had been purchased by U.S. Navy and was undergoing flight trials over Hull, England prior to its trip to Lakehurst NJ in America. The ZR-2 was on its final trial 36-hour run before its transatlantic passage.

The cause of the crash was in dispute until investigation revealed that one of the maneuvers involved sharp rudder turns. This split the ship in two with violent hydrogen-oxygen explosions that spread debris over the city of Hull. As the airship buckled, it dropped toward the Humber River killing 44 of 49 on board, mostly British and American seamen. Among the survivors there was one American and four British.

There was some confusion regarding ownership of the dirigible. A short paragraph in the New York Times incorrectly reported that the dirigible was on loan to the British Air Ministry. It did not tell the full story of the ZR-2, which was designated K-3 by the British admiralty. This was of importance because of liability. It was finally agreed that the costs would be equally shared by the U.S. and British governments. Condolences were exchanged between President Warren G. Harding, King George V and Prime Minister Lloyd George.

On 21 July 1921, Captain Nagano was aboard the USS *Henderson* to witness a demonstration of airpower given by General Billy Mitchell, America's foremost air enthusiast, who believed that aircraft would revolutionize warfare in the future. Mitchell proved his point by the sinking of the German Battleship *Ostfriesland* off the coast of Hampton Roads, VA. This was a common technique by the military at the end of a war to demonstrate the effectiveness of new weapons, such as was carried out at Bikini Atoll with atomic weapons at the end of World War II. Mitchell's success of air power was an eye-opener for Captain Nagano and his future interaction with Yamamoto, who was Mitchell's Japanese counterpart. For Nagano, there was "much to be learned here." (Ref. 3.2)

WASHINGTON ARMS LIMITATION CONFERENCE

On 19 October 1921, Captain Nagano was appointed as assistant to Baron Tomosaburo Kato, the Chief Japanese delegate to the Washington Arms Limitation Conference. The Conference was to address the arms race between the European powers from 1900 to 1914, which many believed to be a major cause of World War I. As a reminder of the war's devastation, the Conference was opened on the third anniversary of the Armistice, 12 November 1921, by President Warren G. Harding. Charles Evans Hughes, U.S. Secretary of State, was the conference chairman.

The major reason for United States initiating the arms limitation conference was to avoid an arms race with other nations, such as Japan and the British Empire. The mediation mechanism under the League of Nations was unavailable to the United States because the U.S. Senate had refused to approve the Treaty of Versailles in 1919 and its potential demands. America had hesitantly entered the war on 6 April 1917 but fought with a vengeance to make the world "safe for democracy." In the post war world, America was finding that Europe was not all that friendly to many of President Woodrow Wilson's ideas, although many had been adopted at Versailles.

The original agenda was to address all armaments – land, sea and air. However, the only agreement reached among the attending nations was with regard to naval arms, thus, ratios of warships became the focus of the Conference. At the time, America was building up its already large navy and there was a lag of at least three years between ship authorization and a finished vessel.

In the case of land armaments, French Prime Minister Aristide Briand stood firm. He said "there was no use in wasting time in platonic expressions. If the Powers were willing to share the burden of guarding France's frontiers, she would consider the reduction of armies." But he heard no such offer. "Consequently, I must insist that the limitation of land armaments, the third subject on the agenda, be dropped. As for the rules for control of new agencies of warfare – the second subject – France would agree to the appointment of three sub-committees, one on aircraft, one on gases, and a third on subjects relating to the rules of war." After this pronouncement, M. Briand left Washington, the object of his coming having been fulfilled. (Ref. 3.3)

Chairman Hughes made a startling recommendation that the Powers freeze their naval construction as of 11 November 1921. In addition, his proposal would set a warship ratio of 1:1:0.6 for America, Britain and Japan respectively. This was supposed to keep everyone happy. A surprising result was that America would scrap 28 battleships. Despite Japanese plans to embark on building additional ships, Baron Kato agreed to scrap 16 battleships. Captain Nagano eventually agreed with these decisions. The reason was that the Japanese infrastructure could not in any way compete with America in ship building and access to raw materials. It would have bankrupted Japan. Of course, Japanese jingoists propagated the false impression that the ratios humiliated the Empire, but they neglected to mention America's sacrifice.

The Washington Naval Treaty, also known as the Five-Power Treaty, was agreed to and signed by United States, Britain, Japan, France and Italy on 6 February 1922. The Treaty covered more than just the number of ships, the data of which are given in Table 1. It included provisions which covered two moratoriums, one on ship construction and the other on fortifications in the Pacific islands. These will be covered in Chapter 4. Later in his career, Admiral Nagano acknowledged that Japan was better off operating under the limits than she would be outside the Treaty.

CAPITAL SHIP NUMBERS

	Capital ships		Capital ships			Replacement (tons)	Aircraft Carriers (tons)
	Retained	scrapped	old	new	total		
USA	18	28	15	3	18	525,000	135,000
Britain	22	20	21	1	22	525,000	135,000
Japan	10	16	8	2	10	315,000	81,000
France	7	0	7	0	7	175,000	60,000
Italy	6	0	6	0	6	175,000	60,000

Table 1: Consensus of ship data, Washington Naval Treaty 1922

Vacation in America

Captain Nagano wrote to his children that he needed a rest from the hectic pace in Washington DC, especially after the time he was assigned as delegate to the Washington Conference of 1921-1922. He enjoyed the outdoors and as part of his vacation he traveled out west. Nagano was a prolific writer of postcards, which he sent home to his children (See Appendix A). He was also an amateur photographer and took many snapshots of his travels for his family.

He explored the Multnomah Falls in Oregon in the Cascade Mountains. On 2 August 1922, he visited the Crown Point Chalet on the Columbia River in the mountains of Oregon. His signature in the Chalet's guestbook was accompanied by those of Japanese Consul Yenji Takeda and J. Nakagawa who listed their addresses as Portland. The guestbook signatures also included William Cornfoot of Portland, as well as T. Inui and S. Inui of Kobe, Japan. Mr. Cornfoot was a prominent local business man.

Nagano's travels from Tokyo to Washington DC via the Suez Canal and Europe are depicted in postcards in Appendix A3. Also, his travels on vacation in North America in the summer of 1922 are included Appendix A3.

The Great Kanto Earthquake

On 1 September 1923 the Great Kanto earthquake (7.9 on the Richter scale) shook Tokyo, resulting in widespread fires that damaged vast acreage. One of the casualties in the city was the Navy Ministry building housing the Hydrographic office and, consequently, significant documents and charts were destroyed. In his capacity as Naval Attaché, Captain Osami Nagano responded to this significant loss. He held daily conferences with Captain F. S. Bassett of the U.S. Naval Hydrographic Office concerning rehabilitation of Japan's Hydrographic Office in Tokyo. Hence, U.S. Navy Secretary Edwin Denby ordered Bassett to supply copies of all charts, sailing directions, light lists and miscellaneous publications to the Japanese navy. Denby pronounced that the American navy would play an important role in *"cementing the bond of friendship which so happily exists between American and Japanese navies"* (Ref. 3.4).

NAVAL TRAINING CRUISES 1924 TO 1928

Osami Nagano's stint in Washington was fruitful and his diplomacy helped establish friendly relations between Japan and the United States. He was ordered to return to Japan in November 1923 where he was promoted to Rear Admiral. For the next few years he served in the Navy General Staff; commanded the Third Battleship Division and the First Expeditionary Fleet. On 1 February, 1927 Rear Admiral Nagano shipped out as Commander of the Training Fleet on a voyage for midshipmen from the Naval Academy. He sent home a commemorative postcard showing the training cruise itinerary (Figure 3.3).

On 21 September 1927, Nagano, on the flagship Asama alongside the cruiser Iwate, arrived off Boston Harbor from Havana, Cuba. They were welcomed by federal, state and city officials and representatives of the Japanese embassy in Washington DC, including Naval Attaché Captain Isoroku Yamamoto (Ref 3.5). American naval crews and staff visited the Charleston Navy Yard to greet their Japanese counterparts. It was obvious that America wanted to maintain good relations with Japan. There was a special performance given by IJN midshipmen on the Boston Commons and later a concert was given by the Imperial Japanese Navy band. Midshipmen were invited to lunch in the homes of Boston families by Japan Society members. They were obviously getting a close look at American culture. Admiral Nagano called on Mayor Malcolm E. Nichols of Boston and, no doubt, reminisced about his Harvard days (Ref. 3.6). On 5 December 1927, Admiral Nagano sent a vase to the Japan Society of Boston to express his gratitude for hospitality shown to him, his staff and midshipmen during their September visit.

The next port was New York City. The squadron arrived in the Hudson River in time to be taken to Yankee Stadium to see Babe Ruth in one of the last games of the baseball season on 29 September 1927 (Ref 3.7). "The Bambino" did not disappoint, he hit a home run in one of the early innings and then, with bases loaded and the count 3 balls, 2 strikes, he smashed another home run. The crowd went wild. The Japanese sailors witnessed history in the making as The Babe broke the record with his 60th home run on the following day, 30 September 1927.

One reported incident took place in the Hudson River that September. The crew's launch for transporting personnel from ship to shore suffered a man overboard event. The pilot of the launch was rescued from the river by a cruise boatman who responded and was able to return the Japanese sailor to his ship. The press reported that he suffered a few broken ribs (Ref. 3.8).

Before the game, Admiral Nagano and his staff were guests of honor at a luncheon given by Japanese Consul General K. Uchiyama at the Lawyers' Club. The Consul General gave a brief presentation citing Nagano's fondness for America, his relish of American humor and possible desire to retire to a place "not very far from Fifth Avenue." Uchiyama also compared Nagano's visit to Commodore Matthew Perry's opening of Japan in 1853. He noted that Commodore Perry found a civilization isolated from western influence for 2000 years. Rear Admiral Chester P. Plunkett, in his address, dwelt on the acts of Commodore Perry and stated that, as a sailor, Perry dealt with Japan with "everything above board and on the level. We have been friendly neighbors ever since." Admiral Nagano responded and briefly summarized the remaining ports of call for the training cruise. He stated that he would return to Japan with messages of good will from all the Americans they encountered. The impressive list of guests at the affair included Major General James H. McRae, Henry W. Taft, British Consul General Sir Harry Gloster Armstrong, Captain A. Fujiyoshi of the Asama, Captain K. Isumi of the Iwate, French Consul General Maxime Mogendre, and Mexican Consul General J. Garza Zetruche, (Ref 3.7).

America was interested in maintaining good neighborly relations with Japan since she had the Commonwealth of the Philippines in Japan's backyard. Changes were occurring in Tokyo with the new Emperor Hirohito, inaugurated in 1925. Some believed a parliamentary democracy was developing in Japan but, that democracy was fragile as New York Times journalist Hugh Byas wrote "It was government by assassination." He was referring to the assassinations of Prime Ministers and other public officials by rightists (Ref. 3.9).

During their six-month cruise, the midshipmen learned many nautical skills such as approaching a harbor, docking and transporting seamen ashore. They made two stops in Hawaii and visited eight ports of call in the United States. In San Pedro, California, close to Hollywood, they met movie stars and posed for a photo opportunity with Gary Cooper (See Figure 3.4). Shore leave in Cuba gave the staff a chance to see downtown Havana and, as noted in Figure 3.5, the officers enjoyed a drink – possibly at Sloppy Joe's. Admiral Nagano also visited the Havana Yacht Club (See Figure 3.6).

During their anchorage at Annapolis, Nagano and staff probably stayed at the Japanese Embassy in Washington DC. In a formal ceremony, Nagano laid a wreath at the Tomb of the Unknown Soldier at Arlington National Cemetery (see Figure 3.7) (Ref. 3.10). He was flanked by Captain Isumi, Captain Fujiyoshi and Captain Isoroku Yamamoto. Behind Nagano was Lieutenant Commander Paulus P. Powell, Nagano's aide during his visit. On 12 October 1927, Admiral Nagano invited Secretary of the Navy Mr. Curtis D. Wilbur to be his guest at a luncheon on the Japanese flagship Asama. Among the other invited dignitaries were Assistant Secretary of the Navy Mr. Theodore Douglas Robinson, the Assistant Secretary of the Navy for Aviation Mr. Edward P. Warner; Admiral Edward Eberle, Rear Admiral Andrew T. Long, Captain William Leahy and Captain David Le Breton (Ref. 3.11).

On the return leg of the cruise, they made landing in Mexico where Mexican President Plutarco Elias Calles greeted the Asama and Iwate in the port of Manzanillo on 7 November. Nagano and his staff took the opportunity to visit Mexico City. Note in Figure 3.8, Admiral Nagano lunching with Mexican dignitaries at La Grutta, a subterranean cave restaurant near Teotihuacán, the monumental pyramid ruins of the indigenous pre-Aztec people of the region. On 14 November the cruisers departed to spend a few days in Mazatlan, just up the coast, which was considered the "Pearl of the Pacific."

The return voyage from Hilo, Hawaiian Islands took approximately 20 days. The final stop on the cruise was Tateyama Naval Station in Tokyo Bay. The last leg was to Yokosuka Naval Base, the ships' home port.

NAGANO IN NEW ORLEANS

The following article appeared in the *Niagara Falls Gazette* (Ref 3.12) on 26 September 1927 and quotes an interview given by Admiral Nagano on his visit to New Orleans with his training cruiser squadron.

Japan Wants America's Friendship Says Japanese Rear-Admiral Who Deprecates "War In The Pacific"

NEW ORLEANS, La, Sept, 26 1927— Japan likes Americans and wants to be friends; and this nation will meet Japan half-way, no one ever need worry about that "war in the Pacific" that agitates so many statesmen and generals.

This is on the word of Rear Admiral Osami Nagano of the Imperial Japanese Navy, who is in New Orleans in command of the Japanese training cruisers Asama and Iwate, which are touring the world with a party of naval cadets.

First – The Toasts

Stocky, wiry and capable, the Admiral in his quarters on the Asama gave an interview setting forth Japan's position. He was cordiality itself; the reporter had hardly been seated before a mess attendant appeared with two brimming goblets of golden sake, Japan's national drink. Before the interview could begin there must be the toasts to President Coolidge and the Imperial majesty, the Mikado.

The admiral speaks excellent English; he spent five years in America as student at Harvard and naval attaché to the Japanese embassy in Washington.

"Japan's problems" he repeated in answer to a question. "Japan has them. We are a nation of more than 70,000,000 souls on an island which in size may be compared to your state of California, and our population is increasing rapidly. Japan must expand. The same urge and necessity that drove the British out from their small islands across the world are impelling Japan today.

"We are trying to meet this in many ways. Thousands of Japanese are in Korea. Thousands more have gone to Brazil; more thousands have gone to Mexico and Central America. But that does not solve our problem."

Developing Industries

"So we are developing industrial life in Japan. We are building industrial centers to provide work for thousands of men making all sorts of things. Under industrial conditions, a population can live in far less space than when it is spread out to farms. We want to make Japan a great importer of raw materials that Japanese workers can make into finished products. Already we are doing that – from New Orleans alone Japan imports some $80,000,000 worth of cotton every year.

"We are doing everything we can to keep the increasing number of Japanese hands busy. It is a real problem – a problem to which Japan is giving its best thought. It is a problem about which America, too, has reason to think."

"You mean the immigration laws?" asked the reporter.

"Exactly," said the admiral. "I say it in all friendship. But that is a sore spot. Thinking Japanese cannot help feeling that America's immigration laws discriminate against the Japanese as against no other nation on earth. And that hurts our national pride.

Don't Want Trouble

"no intelligent Japanese wants trouble with America, just as no intelligent American wants trouble with Japan. But in America you have what you call your 'jingoes' – and in Japan we have our 'jingoes' too.

"It is a problem for the cool heads and intelligent brains of both nations to settle. Our two nations should be friends, both by ancient tradition and by modern relations. And when you want to do business with a man you don't wave weapons and make war talk; you make friends with him, and when differences arise you try to settle them amicably.

"Why, the difference in Japanese immigration to America between the old 'gentlemen's agreement' and your new immigration law would be less, I understand, than 1000 Japanese a year. Yet I understand, too, some of the American feelings that were behind the drawing of your immigration law.

"Is the heart of Japan changing? On the surface, yes, to a small degree. But on the whole many of the old customs cling to us. I, for instance, recently built myself a home in the American style, with American plumbing. I wear a uniform that, except for the difference in insignia, might be an American naval uniform. Yet when I am at home with my family I remove my American clothes and wear the traditional kimono.

"And up in the interior they are still building houses in the old Japanese way, with bamboo and oiled paper. To be sure, Japan is not what it was when your Commodore Perry first visited it; we have, for instance, our suffragettes, and our little group of – flappers, you call them? – who bob their hair and wear short dresses and try to be like the girls of Paris and New York. But there are not enough of them to form a real problem. The men still rule in Japan."

Not the Married Men

"The married men, too?" asked the reporter.

Admiral Nagano rang for another tray of sake to close the interview. As the mess attendant filled the glasses with the golden liquor which can give an army mule three kicks and still be way ahead, the admiral smiled.

"Maybe you are married yourself" he chuckled.

ADMIRAL NAGANO AT THE PAN PACIFIC CLUB, TOKYO

This was more than a training cruise in that it afforded Admiral Nagano opportunity to exercise his adeptness at diplomacy and finesse. He gave a lecture to the Pan Pacific Club at the Imperial Hotel in Tokyo on 2 February 1928 entitled "Peaceful War Vessels" (Ref. 3.13). Japan had a reputation as an aggressive nation in the Far East. In addition to training, this was a diplomatic cruise to assure the nations of the Pacific Rim that Japan had no intention of expansion into the Americas. The aim was to maintain good relations with its neighbors. As related in the lecture, besides the ordinary citizenry, Nagano interacted with political and military leaders of the nations he visited on the voyage. He quipped, "It was indeed a most strenuous life for us, too, to sail through these tornadoes of entertainments, as it were, while our ships lay safe at anchors. We were simply overwhelmed with their kindnesses..."

"At Washington, President Coolidge kindly took us into his office to talk in a friendly way, and invited us to a *real breakfast* which I took as a great and unprecedented honor, indeed."

He continued "The government of Mexico also showed us warm hospitality... At chief stations along the way, not to speak of the terminals, guards of honor saluted us with bands playing *Kimigayo*, while high officials, both military and civil, came to shake hands with us and crowds of people shouted *Viva Japon, Viva Japon* ... Our reception at Mexico City was also unusual, the President spoke very kindly to us and the Secretary of War and the Congressman entertained us warmly at the military academy and at the congress, respectively."

"The President of Cuba and the President of Panama received us kindly, too, and their government gave us much honor and privilege."

"It is also notable that in these countries we visited, newspapers and magazines demonstrated friendly attitude toward Japan with their editorials and comments of the news and illustrations. We, on our part, did our very best to respond to these expressions of hospitality. In order to entertain our friends in the 'dry land' across the Pacific, on board these floating extensions of Japan we had carried with us 18 tons of *sake* and a corresponding quantity of beer and other liquors. But I believe we have not much spoiled our good friends by doing so."

It was obvious that the Imperial Japanese Navy wanted to paint a different picture than did the Imperial Japanese Army, which was cooking up incidents to take over Manchuria.

COMMANDANT, NAVAL ACADEMY

Following the training cruise with the cadets, now Vice Admiral Nagano was made Director of the Naval Academy from December 1928 to June 1930. At the academy, Admiral Nagano introduced a more open, discussion-type, teaching method that he was exposed to at Harvard University. This style of teaching later became known as the Dalton Method.

Being the consummate navy man, Nagano harbored great affection for the Naval Academy. Later, in 1937, he commemorated the birth place of the Japanese Navy with his calligraphy on a monument (Figure 3.9) installed at the Academy's original site in Tokyo, which is the modern day site of the Tsukiji fish market, the largest of its kind. The Academy was established in 1876 and was moved to Eta Jima in 1888. Nagano's epitaph reads: "During the Tokugawa Period, this location was a part of Shizan Mound within Yokuon-en Residence of Sadanobu Matsudaira. In Meiji 2 (1869) Naval Facilities were built here and, as the Ministry was established in Meiji 5 (1872) with the flag of Naval Minister hoisted on the mound, people started to affectionately call the mound as "HATA-YAMA" (Flag-Mountain). This location thus became the BIRTH-PLACE of our Imperial Navy. During the many years and decades that followed, the Ministry has moved leaving today only a few gates of the bygone days. This monument is solemnly dedicated to commemorate Hata-Yama and the birth of the Navy of Japan. 5 January 1937, Minister of the Navy, Osami Nagano." (Ref. 3.14)

Osami Nagano was in a unique position to show the Pacific Rim nations another face of Japan – not the face that caused Charles E. Hughes to "scold the Japanese" at the end of the Washington Naval Conference. Some Japanese proclaimed that they were "the Sun Goddess's gift to Asia." But the Imperial Japanese Army was not making a good impression on the Asians with their "gift" of aggressive actions. Nagano, with his training squadron, showed a more diplomatic approach through the "peaceful war vessels" that docked in many of the major ports in the Americas. Nagano's congeniality extended his good will toward his western counterparts. Another unique event occurred to Admiral Nagano's family in this period. His daughter, Hisako, attended a Catholic boarding school and converted to Catholicism. Figure 3.10 shows Hisako in her first communion dress. Figure 3.11 shows Rear Admiral Nagano onboard the *Asama* with his staff for the training cruise to the Americas.

Chapter 3 References

3.1 New York Times, "Demby Leaves Inquiry to British Officials," August 26, 1921
3.2 Sieff, Martin, "Defense Focus: Submarines Versus Aircraft Carriers," UPI, Washington DC, April 9, 2008
3.3 Buell, Raymond Leslie, The Washington Conference, D. Appleton and Company, New York, 1922
3.4 Science, Vol. 58, No 1507, November 6, 1923, American Association for Advancement of Science
3.5 Christian Science Monitor, "State and City Join in Greeting to Japanese Naval Squadron," September 21, 1927
3.6 Boston Daily Globe, "Japanese Band Given Ovation: Naval Musicians Play on Boston Common," September 23, 1927
3.7 New York Times, "Japanese Sailors Cheer Babe Ruth," September 30, 1927
3.8 New York Times, "Rescues Japanese Officer, Master of Huron Saves Man Whose launch Hit a Rock at Night," September 30, 1927
3.9 Byas, Hugh, Government by Assassination, Alfred A. Knoff, New York, 1942
3.10 Naval History and Heritage Command, 1999, Photograph #NH 96118, Japanese Delegation at Arlington Cemetery, ca. 1927 (page updated 3 May 2009), Available at www.history.navy.mil/photos/prs-for/japan/japrs-n/o-nagno.htm, accessed February 25, 2012
3.11 The Washington Post, "Naval Heads Invited," October 2, 1927
3.12 Niagara Falls Gazette, "Japan Wants America's Friendship Says Japanese Rear Admiral Who Deprecates 'War in Pacific,'" September 29, 1927
3.13 Pan-Pacific Union, Pan-Pacific Research Institution, "Peaceful War Vessels, Speech Delivered by Vice Admiral Osami Nagano, ex-Commander of the Training Squadron, before the Pan-Pacific Club at the Imperial Hotel," Friday, February 2, 1928, Mid Pacific Magazine, Volume 35, Editor A. H. Ford, June 1928
3.14 Nagano, Osami, calligraphy epitaph on commemorative monument at Tsukiji site of Naval Academy in Tokyo, translation by Nobuo Kohyama, 2012

*Figure 3.1 Captain Nagano and Yu, Tazuko, Hiroshi and Hisako
(Nagano on the right standing and Yu sitting on the left)
with a friend and his family.*

Figure 3.2 Japanese Embassy staff, Washington, D.C. 1922-1923

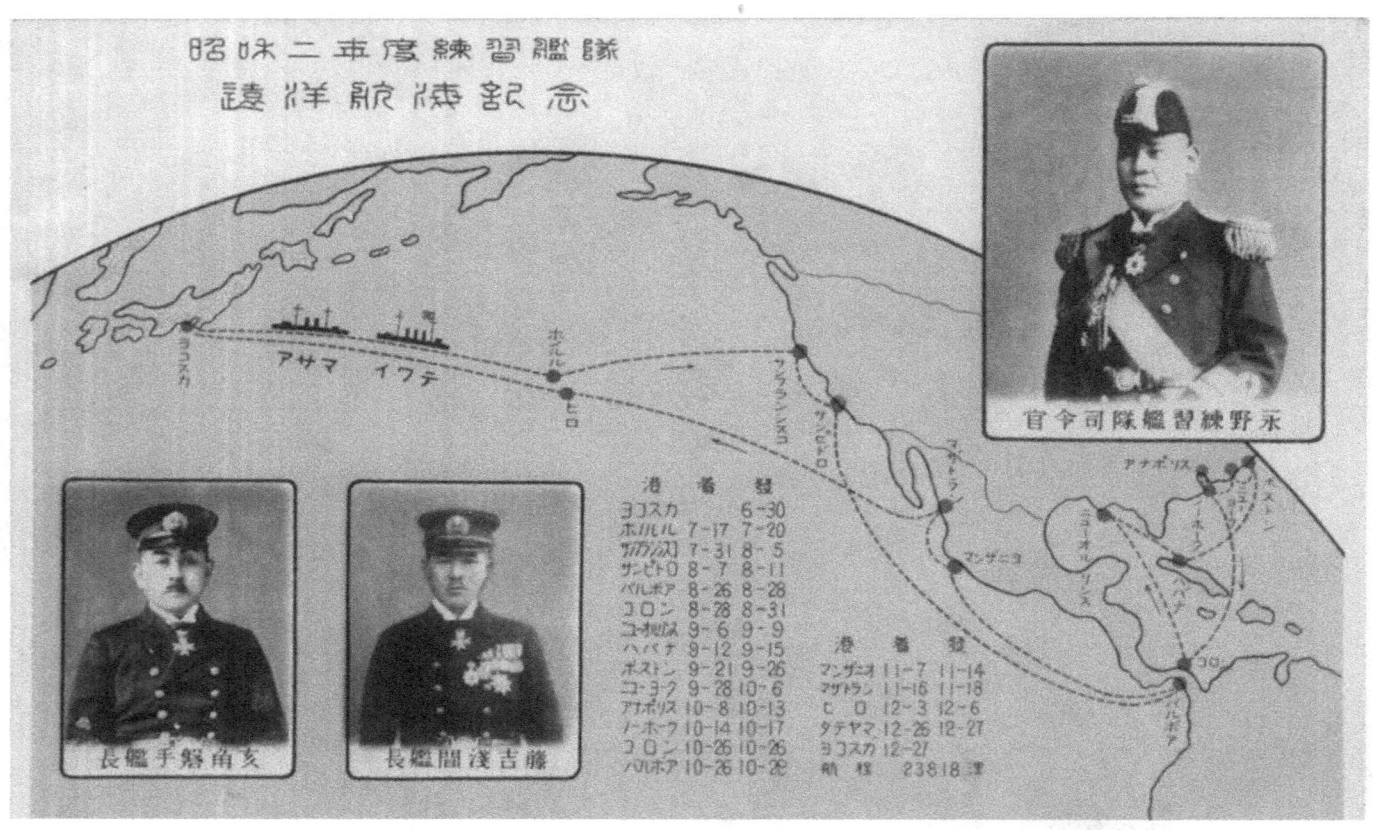

Figure 3.3 Training Cruise Itinerary

Showa 02 (1927) Cadet Training Fleet Overseas Voyage
Photos: Upper right: Commander of the fleet Admiral Osami Nagano
Lower left: Captain Isumi of JNS Iwate
Lower right: Captain Fujiyoshi of JNS Asama

Schedule of the voyage:

Yokosuka	---	30 June 30
Honolulu	17 July	20 July
San Francisco	31 July	5 August
San Pedro	7 August	11 August
Balboa	26 August	28 August
Colon	28 August	31 August
New Orleans	6 September	9 September
Havana	12 September	15 September
Boston	21 September	26 September
New York	28 September	6 October
Annapolis	8 October	13 October
Norfolk	14 October	17 October
Colon	26 October	26 October
Balboa	26 October	28 October
Manzanillo	7 November	14 November
Mazatlan	16 November	18 November
Hilo	3 December	6 December
Tateyama	26 December	27 December
Yokosuka	27 December	---

Total voyage: 23,818 nautical miles

Figure 3.4 Admiral Nagano standing next to Gary Cooper with staff and cadets

Figure 3.5 Good time at Sloppy Joes in Havana, Cuba

Figure 3.6 Adm Nagano at Havana Yatch Club

Figure 3.7 Admiral Nagano lays a wreath at the Tomb of the Unknown Soldier at Arlington National Cemetery, Arlington, VA, 1927. On Nagano's right is Capt. Isumi, to his left is Capt. Fujiyoshi, the next man is Capt. Yamamoto.

At the right end of the Japanese delegation is the Naval Atttache to the United States, Captain Isoroku Yamamoto. The US Navy officer standing hatless just behind them is Lieutenant Commander Paulus P. Powell, aide to Vice Admiral Nagano during this visit. Photo from collection of Rear Admiral Paulus P. Powell.

Figure 3.8 Admiral Nagano with Mexican Dignaries at Luncheon La Grotta subterranean restaurant, Teotihuacán, Mexico

Figure 3.9 Calligraphy by Osami Nagano on monument commemorating the Birth Place of the Japanese Navy in Tsukiji, Tokyo.

Figure 3.10 Hisako Nagano in first communion dress, circa 1930.

Figure 3.11 Rear Admiral Nagano on board the Asama flanked by his ship commanders, Captain Isumi (left) and Captain Fujiyoshi (right).

Chapter 4

Diplomat, Sailor and Politician

1930 to 1941

PART 1:

DIPLOMAT: 9 DECEMBER 1931 – 20 APRIL 1933

Introduction

THE 1930s would be a fateful decade for both Japan and America. Osami Nagano was at the center of many major decisions made during this period, and on 9 December 1931, he was appointed Plenipotentiary (chief Japanese Naval Delegate) to the Geneva Disarmament Conference of 1932. The Conference for the Reduction and Limitation of Armaments was an attempt by the League of Nations to affect arms reduction among the member states. It was a turbulent time in Japan and Nagano was probably happy to get away.

In November 1930, Japanese naval fanatics shot Prime Minister Osachi Hamaguchi (3 July 1929 to 9 April 1931) in an attempted assassination. Just a month earlier, Hamaguchi had signed the first London Naval Disarmament Treaty, which covered auxiliary vessels—defined as heavy cruisers, light cruisers, destroyers and submarines. These vessels were not covered in the original Washington Treaty of 1922 due to strong objections from France among others when the capital ship ratios were applied to auxiliary vessels. This will be covered in more depth in Part 3, Chapter 4.

Nagano was involved in the original Washington Treaty, which set the capital ship ratios for the three major world naval powers at the end of WWI—Britain, U.S. and Japan—at 1:1:0.6 on a per unit basis. This galled other Japanese navy men who wanted a parity of 1:1:1. Debate in the Imperial Japanese Navy over provisions of the Treaty festered long after it was ratified. The divisiveness resulted in two factions within the Navy, i.e. the Treaty faction and the Anti-Treaty or Fleet faction. Allegiance to each faction was fluid. Admiral Isoroku Yamamoto gradually changed his commitment from the Anti-Treaty faction when it was explained to him that the Treaty was to Japan's advantage in the long run. Nagano was a member of the Fleet faction and a disciple of Admiral Mineo Osumi (Ref. 4.1.1), one of the leaders of the Anti-Treaty group. However, reports listed Nagano as a moderate and most who knew him did not consider him to be an ideologue.

Following his appointment, Admiral Nagano started out on the long journey from Tokyo to Geneva. With many stopovers, he used the opportunities to write home (see postcards in Appendices A1 and A2). His first stop was Kobe, a major port on the Inland Sea, where he ascended a local mountain. In a postcard to his children, Tazuko, Hisako and Hiroshi, he wrote "As always, you know I went up the mountain via the famous cable car and prayed at the local shrine on the mountain top. But, since I was by myself it was not as much fun as when we visited the Senzoku-Ike (a pond in Tokyo)." His notes home revealed his attachment to his family. Nagano then traveled from Kobe to Hong Kong on 26 December 1931 and arrived in Singapore on 30 December 1931, from whence he traveled to Penang, Malaysia. He then crossed the Indian Ocean to arrive in Ceylon on 6 January 1932. To amaze his children, he wrote "I will visit the temple which keeps Buddha's teeth and pray." The postcard in Figure 4.1.1 charted the typical itinerary of such a long voyage. Leaving Colombo, Ceylon, the ship crossed the Indian Ocean, up the Red Sea and through the Suez Canal to Genoa, Italy. Figure

4.1.2 shows Nagano with fellow passengers during passage on Tatsuta Maru. Figure 4.1.3 shows Nagano's camel ride to the pyramids in Cairo. He arrived in Geneva to take his position as Chief Japanese Naval delegate to negotiate arms limitation.

The Geneva Conference

Armament races from 1900 to 1914, especially in Europe, made inevitable the clash between nations and power blocks and were among the major causes of World War I. Having been dragged into the European conflict in 1917, the U.S. was acutely aware of the dangers of arms pursuit and, subsequently, led many disarmament conferences from 1920 to 1936. America and other nations were mindful that, under such circumstances, any trigger might lead to war as did the assassination of Archduke Francis Ferdinand on 28 June 1914 by a Serbian revolutionary in Sarajevo. This led to the "Great War" in which the adversaries, Britain, France, Russia, Italy and Japan (The Allies or The Entente) and Austria-Hungary, Germany and the Ottoman Empire (The Central Powers), engaged in a bloody four-year conflict. Except for Austria-Hungary, these powers were not involved in the initiating event.

As background; in November 1920, the League of Nations appointed a preliminary commission, which met periodically to formulate a disarmament agenda. However, these attempts were always coming up against the French delegates' objections. They insisted on security before disarmament and protested "three times in the last 100 years and twice within living memory, France has been invaded and bled white by Germany" (forgetting, of course, Napoleon's rampages). France's demand for security with disarmament was "possibly an impossibility." Finally, in 1931, the one concrete result of the preliminary meetings was a "draft convention," which served as the basis for an agenda.

On 5 May 1931, the League of Nations called for a general disarmament conference to be held in Geneva and British Foreign Secretary in the Labor Government Arthur H. Henderson was appointed President-Elect of the Conference. From a political perspective, this appointment was untimely as the Labor Government had resigned in August 1931. A coalition government came to power with the same Prime Minister Ramsay MacDonald but a different Foreign Secretary, Sir John Simon.

Arthur Henderson was a private citizen when the Conference opened on 2 February 1932, but he was well qualified for the job. From a humble beginning as an apprentice at the Stevens Steel Works in 1875, he rose through the labor ranks and was instrumental in forming the Labor Party to increase political influence of labor unions. For the rest of his life he was a member of the Iron Founders Union. He also had long experience in international congresses involving labor unions. As Foreign Secretary in the aftermath of World War I, Mr. Henderson attempted to ameliorate the effects of reparations on Germany and he became interested in disarmament – probably on moral grounds. America, although not a member of the League of Nations, was interested in disarmament mainly on pragmatic grounds. At the time, with a deepening global economic depression, America was the major creditor nation but was willing to reduce debt payments for arms reduction. Czechoslovakia's President Edward Benes pronounced "A less opportune time for the Conference could not be found."

Henderson's native urbanity and his ability to find a formula for compromise were essential for a conference president. These traits were also attributed to Osami Nagano. Figure 4.1.4 show two drawings that Nagano took back to Japan with him, one of Arthur Henderson and one of himself, sketched at the Geneva Conference.

Preliminary Agenda

International conferences are complex undertakings with many languages, diverse nations and many conflicting agendas. At the Geneva Disarmament Conference, 64 nations were invited and 59 attended. Most attendees were members of the League of Nations, but the United States and USSR were not. The USSR later joined but the U.S. never did. Also roaming the corridors were representatives of Afghan warlords hoping to procure surplus weapons in the wake of disarmament. Sir Samuel Hoare, Secretary of State for India, wrote "We asked the Afghans why, Afghanistan not being a member of the League, they had come to the disarmament conference. They told us that they were short of arms, and that they thought at a Disarmament Conference there would be the chance of picking up secondhand munitions cheap!"

To make the conference function, a bureau of the major states controlled the agenda. All nations were represented in a General Commission and a Technical Commission was composed of three committees for specific land, sea and air considerations. Plenipotentiary Admiral Nagano represented Japan in the Naval Committee.

The only agenda in the preliminary meetings that was agreed upon was the DRAFT CONVENTION. With the Naval Treaties of Washington and London as templates, the naval agenda was relatively easy to devise. The original idea behind the DRAFT CONVENTION was – if states could agree on disarmament in general, then it would be relatively simple to fill in the blanks, i.e.:

- number of soldiers, sailors, marines and airmen
- number of guns
- number of ships
- number of planes

Of course, it turned out to be not quite so simple.

Opening Remarks

The Conference opened on 2 February 1932 in Batiment Electoral with all nations presenting their opening statements. President Arthur Henderson spoke sitting down, which reflected his failing health. Samuel Hoare wrote "After a short interval we adjourned to Batiment Electoral, the grim hall in which the Disarmament Conference was to take place...there are few more dismal buildings in Europe." see Figure 4.1.5. Figure 4.1.6 shows Nagano relaxing in Geneva.

American Statement

Chief American Delegate Hugh Gibson made the following points:

- Consider the DRAFT CONVENTION as a basis for discussion
- Abolish weapons meant for war
- Extend the Washington and London Naval Disarmament Treaties
- Proportional reduction in the figures laid down in these two treaties
- Abolition of submarines
- Abolition of lethal gases and bacteriological weapons
- Computation of the number of armed servicemen needed for internal security and the numbers needed for defense
- Special restrictions on tanks and certain heavy mobile guns of an offensive character
- Consider a limit on the expenditures on war materials

As instructed by the U.S. Secretary of State Henry L. Stimson, Mr. Gibson added the following caveat: "United States will not get involved in political problems in Europe through security guarantees."

French Statement

French Delegate Andre Tardieu favored, first and foremost, sanctions backed by an international police force. As a continental power, France stuck to her philosophy specifying that security must come before disarmament – the exact opposite of the American position. Security was, as ever, the cornerstone of French proposals.

Japanese Statement

Ambassador Tsuneo Matsudaira, remarked that Japan had reduced her army by four divisions, or 35%, since 1913. He proposed the following:

- Adoption of the DRAFT CONVENTION as a basis of discussion
- Limit on the size of submarines by adherence of other nations to the London Declaration on the use of submarines
- Reduction in the size of capital ships and caliber of their guns
- Reduction in tonnage (size) of aircraft
- Abolition of planes landing on ship decks
- Abolition of aerial bombs and use of poison gas and bacteria
- Fair and equitable reduction in armies compatible with national safety

British Statement

Sir John Simon argued that none of these proposals were compatible with Britain's worldwide commitment, forgetting her continental responsibilities. Everyone agreed that Britain fell flat on her face with these remarks that ignored Europe and she only woke up later when Hitler came to power in 1933.

Distraction Number One – Manchuria

Soon after the Conference opened, it adjourned for a special League of Nations Assembly meeting to deal with what the Japanese delegate inadvertently called "the war between Japan and China." For Japan, the term "war" was inappropriate and was hastily erased from the verbatim record of the meeting. The invasion by Japan's Kwantung Army into Manchuria had incensed China. Many believed the Mukden Incident on the evening of 18 September 1931 was a ploy for expansion by Japan. China's representative to the League Council, Dr. W. W. Yen, invited the international press to number 18 Rue Charles Galland on 2 March 1932 where he provided background on China's case before it was presented formally the following day (Ref. 4.1.1).

Japan had already presented its case to the international press. Ambassador Tsuneo Matsudaira invited journalists to the Hotel Metropole on 24 February 1932. He analyzed the Japanese and Chinese conflict and gave background on how Japanese and other foreign nationals were being harassed in China. Other foreign governments and agencies, such as the American Chamber of Commerce, also complained that China was incapable of providing adequate protection to foreigners. Matsudaira believed that there should be no appeal to the Committee of Twelve since Japan was acting in self defense, which was allowed by the League Covenant to its members. Vice Admiral Osami Nagano and General Iwane Matsui, attending the Disarmament Conference, helped the Ambassador by citing technical reasons for the intervention such as the long porous northern border with Russia. They maintained that the Far Eastern trouble was a family affair that needed no interference by outside parties (Ref. 4.1.2). The upshot of the 3 March 1932 League of Nations Council Meeting was formation of a Commission under Earl Lytton to investigate Japan's incursion and subsequent actions and to make recommendations to the League. In October 1932, the Commission delivered its report (subsequently called the Lytton Report).

Yosuke Matsuoka was selected by Prime Minister Makoto Saito to go to Geneva to present the Japanese case. He seemed a logical choice. He had already shown his debating skills at a foreign relations symposium in Kyoto in 1929 where he debated with the Chinese delegate, Dr. Welling Koo and received a favorable response from the foreign press. He also had recently, August 1932, engineered a cease fire between Japanese and Chinese armies that had engaged in a bloody and ferocious battle in Shanghai. Before the eyes of the world, Japan's reputation was in tatters for their indiscriminate firing on civilians during the clash.

Shanghai Incident of 1932

The West had little awareness or interest in what was happening in Asia - but Shanghai was different. Foreign nations - Britain, America, France, Germany (initially) and now Japan - had established sovereign enclaves in Shanghai over the centuries for economic and political reasons. They were also permitted to maintain national troops in the enclaves to uphold order. As sovereign ruler, China also had her troops in the city.

The opening clash between Japanese marines and Chinese troops that erupted over a reported insult to a Japanese citizen was played out on the world stage. Japanese army and marines' engaged in indiscriminate bombing and firing at civilians that was widely publicized. The Japanese marine garrison was besieged and 50,000 Japanese reinforcement troops were deployed, escalating the confrontation. The battle raged for several months before Matsuoka was finally able to arrange a cease fire. American public opinion was so aroused that Secretary of State Henry L. Stimson placed economic sanctions on Japan, but these were reversed by President Herbert Hoover. The damage to Japan's image by the Japanese military's behavior remained until well after 1945.

Matsuoka had two directives on his mission to Geneva:

1. Japan would not leave Manchuria
2. Japan would remain in the League of Nations

Matsuoka had two allies in his corner - Britain and France. Both were not overly concerned about Manchuria since they had no vital economic interest there. But, they had major strategic concerns in Southeast Asia and Southwest Pacific with respect to natural resources - oil, rubber and metals. If Japan remained in the League of Nations, Britain and France could exert some influence on Japan's behavior. The wild card was America. In particular, Secretary Stimson viewed the capture of Manchuria and subsequent behavior of Japanese troops in Shanghai and north China (January 1933) as an aggressive attitude that, if not stopped, might alter the dynamics in the Far East. Furthermore, it violated various League of Nations tenets and treaties to which Japan was a signatory.

Prodded by Stimson, the League condemned Japan's actions. Stimson was so incensed that his oratory and writings aimed at Japan were likened to Hitler's bullying of Dolfus of Austria. Matsuoka did not help his own cause by comparing the West's condemnation of Japan to Christ's crucifixion. Emotions were raw on both sides when Matsuoka, leading a procession of Japanese delegates, made a theatrical exit from the meeting on 23 February 1933.

In time, Japan withdrew from the League of Nations - but she was anxious about her claims to German possessions acquired in the Pacific (Carolines and Marshall Islands) and concessions on the Asian mainland that were granted as spoils of WWI. These territories were in protectorate status and Japan's rights to them were in doubt. Japan's falling out with the League brought to an end Admiral Nagano's sojourn in Geneva - he was recalled in February 1933.

Distraction Number Two – Debts, Reparations and Economic Depression

The Great Depression that gripped the globe diverted attention from the business at hand in the Geneva Conference, i.e. disarmament. The world's focus was on debt and unemployment.

In 1932, the United States was the world's major creditor nation. Everyone owed America money, but strapped by the economic depression, few nations were in a position to repay their loans. America took a practical approach – if nations did not spend on arms, they could repay their loans. America not only talked disarmament – she disarmed, so much so that many thoughtful persons were quite concerned. Reportedly, after meeting with FDR, General Douglas MacArthur, Army Chief of Staff, was so upset that he vomited. There was an isolationist sentiment in America with lack of concern about rearmament in Europe and Asia.

The major debtor nations – Britain and France – having borrowed heavily for arms purchased during World War I were now looking for relief. By December 1932, Britain paid the interest on her loan ($900 million in gold), but France never paid up. For Germany and Austria on the losing side of the Great War, reparations were especially burdensome and attempts were made to tie arms limitation to a reduction in reparations. This worked until 1933 when Hitler came to power with his own agenda.

Focus on the depression effected proposals in Geneva aimed at encouraging nations to disarm by redirecting spending to reduce debt.

Naval Committee

In disarmament talks, the terms offense and defense as applied to weaponry carry great weight. Everyone wanted to reduce or eliminate offensive weapons, but there was more acceptance of defensive weapons. So the battle raged over semantics. Initially, the British and American naval delegates took the position that battleships are primarily defensive, being used to protect convoys. Italy and Germany urged abolition of aircraft carriers, submarines and ships weighing greater than 10,000 tons. Germany defined battleships as offensive, citing those that blockaded German ports. Japan was noncommittal, but quipped "When is a battleship a defensive weapon? When it flies an American or British flag?" United States and Britain finally agreed that no individual ship was offensive or defensive, but it was dependent on their use.

Ultimately, the Committee came up with the following recommendations:

- Britain wanted all nations to sign the London Naval Treaty of 1930 or she would have to build in excess of treaty limits
- U.S. and Britain urged abolition of submarines on the basis that they are inhumane and expensive
- The Japanese delegate claimed that aircraft carriers were offensive weapons and should be abolished, but submarines were defensive weapons and, therefore, should be retained.

Of all the technical committees, (land, sea and air) the Naval Committee appeared to work the hardest at finding common ground for discussion, compromise and possible agreement.

President Herbert Hoover's Disarmament Proposal

The Disarmament Conference was floundering in a sea of words when President Herbert Hoover – up for re-election in November of 1932 – made a bold disarmament proposal in June. It was against the advice of many in his administration who feared that his terms would simply be dismissed. Secretary of War Patrick Hurley stated "Let them go forward and they will soon be forgotten" – which they were.

Hoover's ideas sprang from his Quaker upbringing, according to some reports. His recommendations were:

- Reduce land armies by half
- Eliminate tanks and large mobile weapons
- Eliminate aerial bombardment
- Eliminate chemical and biological weapons
- Reduce the number of capital ships by one third of those permitted under Washington Naval Treaty
- Reduce tonnage of capital ships by one third
- Reduce total Treaty tonnage of aircraft carriers, cruisers and destroyers by one quarter.

Hoover declared that the U.S. was scrapping a million tons of shipping. The response from the delegation in Geneva was as follows:

- The British were cautious
- The French were suspicious, referring to the simple character of Hoover's plan
- The Japanese were hesitant. Hoover's plan took no account of her security in the Far East against China's millions and Russia's uncertain future. Japan claimed that the plan strengthened the U.S. fleet over Japan's fleet. (In reality, this weakness was only "on paper.")

After the delegates responded, the Conference was adjourned until January 1933. That put an end to Hoover's ideas.

Admiral Nagano's Dénouement

During the recess, Admiral Nagano returned to Japan via the Trans-Siberian Railroad and the Southern Manchurian Railroad. He wrote to his family that he ascended the five peaked sacred mountain "Taizan." He was carried in a sedan chair along a treacherous trail on a very hot August day in 1932. Continuing his trip, he stopped in Changchun (former capital of Manchurian Province) and had his photo taken with local Japanese dignitaries (Figure 4.1.7).

Nagano returned to the Conference in December 1932 but Matsuoka's abrupt exit from Geneva with the Japanese delegation in tow brought an end to Nagano's position as Plenipotentiary. In February 1933 he was summoned back to Tokyo ending his efforts to promote Japan's naval interests.

In a December 1932 Time Magazine article (Ref. 4.1.3), Admiral Osami Nagano was described as "a broad faced, oriental sea dog with quarterdeck manners and likeable grin" who brought Japan's naval disarmament plans to Geneva. He had presented Japan's aims as follows:

- Abolish aircraft carriers and flying decks on capital ships
- Scrap long-range cruising submarines and retain short-range, coastal defense submarines
- Reduce maximum tonnage of each type of surface war boats
- Reduce maximum caliber of naval guns to 14 inches

Nagano was quoted as saying; "We stand for a sharp distinction between offense and defense naval weapons. Our principal is to reduce the means of attack while strengthening the means of defense...aircraft carriers are the most offensive of all naval weapons because, by means of their planes, they can not only attack the coast but carry destruction far inland..."

"Japan and the United States are each other's good customers. I see no reason why – especially with the vast Pacific Ocean between us – any differences in our naval views should not be reconciled in a satisfactory manner."

"Such difference will notably arise over the question of naval ratio in capital ships. The U.S., Great Britain and Japan are now limited to the ratio 5:5:3 under the Washington Naval Treaty. The U.S. and Britain would like to extend the ratio to all classes of naval weapons, thus keeping Japan permanently inferior."

At the Conference, Nagano touted the Anti-Treaty line and flatly refused to discuss ratios. This had aroused such passion between Japan's naval ideological factions, as well as the Japanese populace. Hence, he appealed to U.S. and British citizens to ponder Japan's proposal. The U.S. and British delegations believed that, under the Japanese recommendations, Japan would feel supreme in East Asia. She would feel safe to defend herself and be free to operate at short-range against her neighbors.

Nagano commented retrospectively that it was difficult to get a meaningful naval disarmament agenda presented and acted upon at the Conference. Figure 4.1.5 shows the assembly of 59 delegations in Conference Hall. What, if any, impact Nagano had on the Conference was not recorded, but certainly among the Asian delegates there was obvious consternation. One of Nagano's proposals for defensive naval weapons had, as an underlying premise, that Japan would be the principle naval power in Asia, replacing the occidentals. Most importantly, Nagano's presentation was principally for home consumption.

Henderson's Dénouement

The disarmament agenda was not a top priority, but negotiations plodded on until 1935. Conference President Arthur Henderson tried valiantly to keep the discussion focused and on track and he traveled to Rome, Berlin, Paris and London to drum up support. However, the attending representatives in Geneva began to drift away and return home from 1933 to 1935. Henderson, for his valiant, if futile, efforts for national disarmament, was awarded the Nobel Peace prize in 1934. On his deathbed in 1935, it was stated that his friends did not mention the closing of the Disarmament Conference that same year.

The Conference failed to enact a treaty and naval arms limitations talks were deferred to the London Naval Conference of 1935.

Trip Home – Osami Nagano

Admiral Nagano traveled home to Japan by way of America and arrived in a time of great economic stress for ordinary Americans. Unemployment was at 25% and there was panic in the banking system. Into this maelstrom, Franklin Delano Roosevelt was inaugurated as the 32nd President on 4 March 1933. He immediately declared a bank holiday to start on Monday, the 6th of March, and end a week later on the 13th. One key factor to end the banking crisis and restore confidence was FDR's first fireside chat broadcast on Sunday, 12 March 1933. With American households gathered around the radio, the President declared that the federal government would guarantee all bank deposits. The next day banks reopened, the public stopped hoarding cash and started to return funds to the banks (Ref. 4.1.4). Matsuoka, echoing FDR sentiment, commented "The economic recession is psychological rather than material and I believe there will be a quick recovery."

Admiral Nagano's trip was a relatively sedate journey compared to that of Yosuke Matsuoka. Nagano visited Washington DC and was the first Japanese person to meet and congratulate President F. D. Roosevelt on 15 March 1933. Nagano probably knew FDR from the time he was the Japanese

Naval Attaché in Washington (1920-1923) and Roosevelt was the Assistant Secretary of the Navy (1913-1920). The President confided to the admiral a cordial message of good will to deliver to Tokyo (Ref. 4.1.5). When he arrived home Nagano met with a number of his countrymen who were interested in American trade, presumably hoping that FDR's sentiments were real. Figure 4.1.8 shows a group of Kochi citizens from Nagano's hometown.

Despite press reports Nagano expressed "The American people's sentiment for Japan has not changed and I still have the same good impression of the United States that I have received on every former visit" (Ref. 4.1.6). Appendix A3 gives Nagano's personal documentation of his travels in postcards to his family.

Trip Home – Yosuke Matsuoka

Mr. Matsuoka, on the other hand, cut a wide swath across Europe and America as he returned home. He never stopped talking to the press. From his early days in America, where he worked with journalists, he well understood how the press could influence public opinion. While he had no official status, he gave his opinion on a wide range of subjects everywhere he went.

In Paris, he suggested that French bondholders should be given the rights to the Chinese Eastern Railroad since they had provided reconstruction money and the Chinese and Russians had defaulted on their bond payments. A deal along these lines was eventually arranged and then Japan purchased the railroad. Matsuoka also thanked the French for not joining the boycott of Japanese goods issued by the League of Nations in response to the Japanese invasion of Manchuria.

Several of his side trips were also reported in the press. Matsuoka traveled to the I. G. Farben plant in Essen, Germany where they were developing a hydrogenation process to convert coal to fuel. He then visited The Hague in Holland and the offices of Royal Dutch Petroleum (Shell Oil), Standard Oil, Imperial Oil Chemical and I. G. Farben Industry, probably looking for oil. Many armaments used by the Japanese army were made in France, e.g. machine guns, tanks and planes, and Matsuoka visited these plants as well.

In London, he was greeted with shouts "Japan is a nation of bandits." But Matsuoka, always looking for a good comment, diplomatically thanked the British for enforcing the boycott equitably on both Japanese and Chinese goods.

For Matsuoka's landing in New York on 24 March 1933, the State Department requested NY City Police Department to provide a large detail to keep demonstrators at bay. The Chinese Student League of Greater New York and the American Committee for the Struggle Against War had their own version of greeting for the man who defended Japan's invasion of Manchuria. Matsuoka claimed that anarchy reigned in China and that Japan was a stabilizing force there. He traveled under police escort to the Waldorf Astoria and Figure 4.1.9 shows him in a regal pose..

Matsuoka was concerned as to whether America would enforce the League of Nations boycott. A boycott enforced by the U.S. would render Japan "dead in the water" economically in that 60% of Japanese exports were sent to America. The irony of the American position was that former Secretary of State Henry Stimson, pushed the League to punish Japan for its behavior in China. But, America, not a League member, was not obliged to enforce the boycott although she was in a position to be most effective. Keeping up his search for oil, Matsuoka visited the Standard Oil offices in Bayonne, NJ.

Matsuoka, the politician, continued to address the American public sometimes in strident tones. "War between the U.S. and Japan would be madness" he warned. Talk of war between the U.S. and Japan involved the Caroline and Marshall Islands, which had been mandated to Japan from Germany following World War I. Although no longer a League member, Japan would nonetheless fight to maintain control of these South Pacific islands.

Another side of Matsuoka was revealed during his visit to Portland, Oregon – the scene of his earliest remembrance of America. The kindness of one Mrs. Isabelle Dunbar Beveridge, who took the young immigrant Yosuke into her home for two years while he attended American schools, would be repaid. While living in Portland, he joined the Centenary Wilbur Methodist Church (1897-1989) and, throughout his life, he listed himself as a Christian despite following Shinto mores at festivals and solemn occasions. He had visited Mrs. Beveridge's gravesite in 1913 and was disappointed that she had no gravestone. He promised to rectify this the next time he was in America. He lived up to his word and in 1933 had a granite monument erected for her with his signature on a commemorative plaque on the back of the gravestone (Figure 4.1.10). He stated that, next to his mother, she was most influential person in his moral development.

Upon his return to Japan, Matsuoka was greeted as a hero, and some pronounced that he would someday be a Foreign Minister or higher. He already had enjoyed careers as a diplomat and politician. Upon his homecoming, he became a businessman as president of the South Manchurian Railroad Company (1935-1939).

Commandant Osami Nagano

Upon his return home, Admiral Nagano was assigned as Commandant of the Yokosuka Naval Base outside Tokyo. Japan had no intention of giving up the former German possessions in the Pacific and China and would defend them militarily if necessary.

CHAPTER 4, PART 1: REFERENCES

4.1.1　Asada, Sadao, *From Mahan to Pearl Harbor*, Naval Institute Press, Annapolis, MD 2001
4.1.2　*Annals of the American Academy of Political and Social Science*, Vol. 162, "National and World Planning, July 1932, Supplement: The Press as a Factor in International Relations," Paul F. Douglas, Carl Bomer, Emil Dovifat
4.1.3　*Time Magazine*, "Japanese Plan," Vol. XX, No. 24, December 12, 1932
4.1.4　Silber, William L, "Why Did FDR's Bank Holiday Succeed," *Economic Policy Review*, Federal Reserve Bank of New York, Vol. 15, No. 1, July 2009
4.1.5　*New York Times*, "Chinese Report Death of Nagano," December 15, 1937
4.1.6　*New York Times*, "Japanese Gloomy On Arms Conference," April 14, 1933

Figure 4.1.1 Itinerary - Tokyo to Geneva

Figure 4.1.2 Vice Admiral Nagano on ship to Geneva

Figure 4.1.3 Camel ride to pyramids in Cairo

Figure 4.1.4 Plenipotentiary Osami Nagano and President Arthur Henderson, Geneva Disarmament Conference

Figure 4.1.5   Conference hall – Geneva Disarmament Conference

*Figure 4.1.6
Vice Admiral Nagano
in Geneva, 1932.*

*Figure 4.1.7
Hero Memorial,
Changchun City,
26 August 1932.*

Figure 4.1.8 "A welcoming dinner for Vice Admiral Nagano – the Chief Delegate Plenipotentiary to Armaments Reduction Conference" by the North American Kochi Prefectural Club at Yamato Hotel, 22 February 1933

Figure 4.1.9 Yosuke Matsuoka

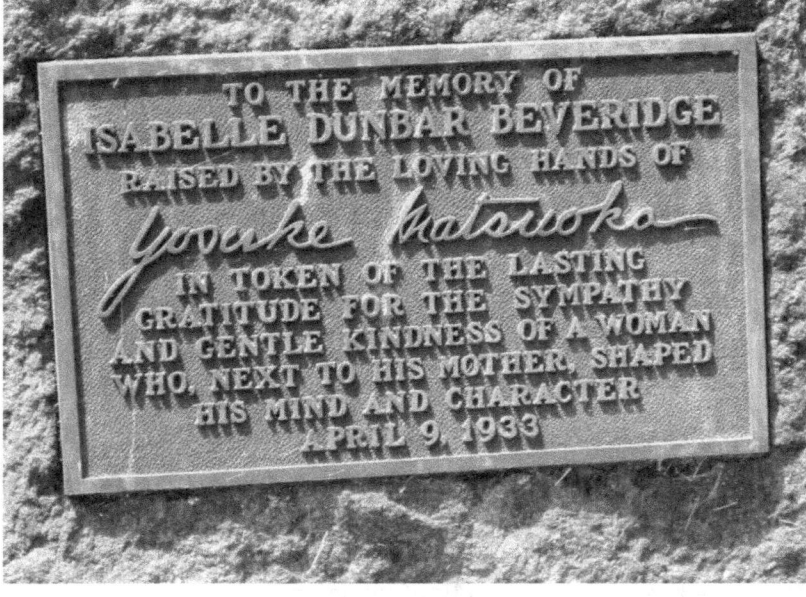

Figure 4.1.10   R. M. Pratt at Isabelle Dunbar Beveridge grave site, Portland, Oregon, July 2007. Plaque placed on tombstone by Yosuke Matsuoka on April 9, 1933

Chapter 4

Diplomat, Sailor and Politician

1930 to 1941

Part 2:

Commander, Naval Maneuvers, 26 April 1933 – 3 November 1935

"THE U.S. should think twice about leaving her fleet in Hawaii" asserted Yosuke Matsuoka in March of 1933 after Claude A. Swanson (U.S. Secretary of the Navy) had just ordered the fleet to remain in Pearl Harbor following Pacific Ocean maneuvers (Ref. 4.2.1). To Matsuoka it was a provocation to which he responded rhetorically "What if the Japanese Navy held maneuvers in the eastern Pacific close to Hawaii?" This sensitivity to mild U.S. "saber rattling" revealed Japan's anxiety over the uncertain status of the Carolines and Marshall Islands. These former German colonies in the Pacific were granted to Japan by the terms of the Versailles Treaty (1919) at the end of World War I. They were held as protectorates by Japan under the League of Nations agreement. But, Matsuoka had just walked out of the League of Nations meeting in Geneva, followed by a formal letter of resignation from the League in March 1933. Nonetheless, Japan had no intention to relinquish the islands even if their legal status was in limbo.

Less than six months later, Emperor Hirohito executed widely publicized Japanese naval maneuvers in these sensitive areas of the Pacific (Ref. 4.2.2). The ships' muster was as follows:

The Red Fleet (defending the Empire) Vice Admiral Osami Nagano, Commander

- 4 battleships
- 2 aircraft carriers
- 4 heavy cruisers, 8 light cruisers
- 27 destroyers and auxiliary vessels
- 11 submarines

The Blue Fleet (antagonist) Admiral Seizo Kobayashi, Commander

- 4 battleships
- 2 aircraft carriers
- 4 heavy cruisers, 6 light cruisers
- 24 destroyers and auxiliary vessels
- 13 submarines

The war games scenario assumed that the Blue Fleet had already seized the Carolines and Marshall Islands and was steaming past the Bonin Islands to invade the Empire. Vice Admiral Osami Nagano, commanding the Red Fleet off the Bonin Islands, opposed the Blue fleet sailing from the Carolines and Marshall Islands. Additional warships protecting Formosa and Korea swelled the armada to 280 vessels – practically the entire Imperial Navy. These war games were implicitly conveying Matsuoka's message to the Americans to "think twice." But, in Washington, President Franklin D. Roosevelt was in his first months in office and confronted with a deep economic depression at home. He had higher priorities than wrestling the former German concessions from Japan.

Ironically, these Pacific war games played out in reality from 1943 to 1945 as the U.S. Navy seized selected islands in the Carolines, Marshalls, Marianas and Bonin Islands at a great cost of American and Japanese lives. One could not close in on the Empire without control of air and sea lanes which required Pacific island bases. Matsuoka's message had been prescient.

In these war games, Vice Admiral Nagano took on the role that he presented at the Geneva Disarmament Conference. The Imperial Navy was a defensive weapon designed to defend the Empire and was not an offensive weapon. Of course, the defensive stance of Japan's navy was not universally held and, historically, when taking on a larger foe, it adopted the philosophy that the best defense was offense.

The Commandant

In November of 1933, Vice Admiral Nagano was appointed Commanding Officer of Yokosuka Naval Base, one of the major bases for the defense of Honshu. Within four months, he was promoted to Admiral. In ordinary times, this would have been the highest rank he would have attained. Figure 4.2.1 shows Nagano as the commanding officer of Yokosuka Naval Base.

Nagano enjoyed having his family with him at the base and Misako was born at Yokosuka in 1933. Figures 4.2.2 and 4.2.3 show Nagano with his wife Kyoko and holding his son alongside his two older children, Hisako (age 16) and Hiroshi (age 15) by his third wife, Yu. (Yu died in 1930 giving birth to their third child, who also did not survive.) Admiral Nagano is shown in Figure 4.3.4 with family and friends in 1935. Present was Kyoko holding Makoto and on the opposite side of the table is Misako who was born at Yokosuka Naval Base Hospital in 1934. Fast forward, Figure 4.2.7 shows Misako and Sakiko Nagano at the Yokosuka Naval Base posing with their father's photograph on display with other former Japanese Commanders at the base. Figure 4.2.5 shows the sisters at the gate to the base in front of the base plaque (the base plaque is in Figure 4.2.6). In 1945, command of the base was turned over to the Americans.

CHAPTER 4, PART 2 REFERENCES

4.2.1   *New York Times*, "Criticizes Our Naval Policy," London, March 11, 1933
4.2.2   *New York Times*, "Japanese Emperor Sails for Naval Battles Vast Maneuvers to Test Nation's Defenses," Tokyo, August 16, 1933

Figure 4.2.1 Vice Admiral Osami Nagano, Commander, Yokosuka Naval Base, 1934

Figure 4.2.2 Admiral Nagano and Kyoko

*Figure 4.2.3 Vice Admiral Nagano and family 1933-1934
(left to right Hisako, Kyoko. Makoto, Nagano and Hiroshi)*

*Figure 4.2.4 Vice Admiral Nagano relaxing with Kyoko,
and her two children, Makoto and Misako, with Hisako and family*

Figure 4.2.5 Frank Bradley, Misako Nagano, Rose Marie Pratt, Noriaki Kataoka, Sakiko Kasai at Yokosuka Naval Base (17 November 2008)

Figure 4.2.6 Yokosuka Naval Base plaque

Figure 4.2.7 Misako Nagano and Sakiko Kasai at Yokosuka Naval Base with Admiral Osami Nagano portrait

Chapter 4

Diplomat, Sailor and Politician

1930 to 1941

PART 3:

DIPLOMAT: SECOND LONDON NAVAL CONFERENCE, 4 NOVEMBER 1935 – 8 MARCH 1936

Introduction

OSAMI Nagano was involved in naval armament and disarmament during his entire navy career, which spanned over 40 years. Throughout this period, he was directly involved in the first and last disarmament conferences; the first in Washington DC (1921-1922) and the last in London, the Second London Naval Conference (1935-1936).

Japanese society had evolved economically, culturally and politically. Since World War I, Japan had two Emperors, Taisho and Hirohito. Culturally they reigned over Taisho Democracy Era and the Showa Restoration Era respectively. Politics evolved and the types of government changed. Finally, this had an impact on Japanese acceptance or rejection of the Naval Disarmament Treaties. At the end of World War I, Japan commanded the world's third largest naval force and by 1936, she wanted to be on par with British and American navies. Obviously, Japan wanted to be supreme in the western Pacific.

As described by Bix (Ref. 4.3.1), during the Taisho Democracy period Japan had Prime Ministers selected by one of the two major political parties, Seiyukai and Minseito. Both were considered conservative, but the Seiyukai Party was the more populist oriented. The Minseito Party was favored by financial and *zaibatsu* (industrial) interests. In this environment, democracy flourished. Disarmament, up to a point, was acceptable, but starting with the Showa Restoration things got bumpier and disarmament became a bad word, especially for the Japanese military. Also, world economic conditions declined which affected all nations. Certain countries began to arm vigorously, e.g. Germany, Italy, Russia and Japan. The poor economic conditions in these countries were partially to blame for arms buildup but it was not the major driving force.

For Japan in 1926, the new Emperor Hirohito was caught up in an evolving government change which was increasingly controlled by the military – following the fascist and Nazi models. Also, for the Japanese military, with an expanding empire in the Pacific and Asian mainland, disarmament was hard to swallow. Starting in 1930, the military, with its own propaganda machines, stirred up the populace against disarmament, which led to political assassinations. As a consequence, politicians tended to be more careful and stayed within narrow political bounds. Only in the Diet was open debate and criticism of military permitted. During the Showa Restoration, the military elevated the Emperor to the status of a god and, according to some, manipulated him for their purposes. More recent studies describe Hirohito as more commanding than merely a figure-head as was supposed by many. One characteristic is obvious – Hirohito wanted to preserve the Meiji image and the Empire he inherited. All these evolving changes meant, from 1926 on, that disarmament in Japan would be a "hard-sell." The resulting arms race led to Pearl Harbor.

The thirties turned out to be a volatile and turbulent time in Japanese political and military life with military expansionism and a naval arms race underway. Much of the unrest could be traced to naval limitation treaties and conferences. These were:

- Washington Naval Conference 1921-1922, ended in treaty signed by Britain, America, Japan, France, and Italy
- Geneva Naval Conference 1927-1928, no treaty
- First London Naval Treaty 1930, ended in treaty signed by Britain, America, Japan
- Geneva General Disarmament Conference 1932-1935 (see Part 1, Chapter 4), no treaty
- Second London Naval Conference 1935-1936, ended in treaty signed by Britain and America, but not endorsed by Japan

Relations between Japan, Britain and America were reflected in the debates of five international conferences to establish arms limitations.

Washington Naval Conference 1921–1922

The Washington Naval Conference was a landmark event for the United States on the world stage in that she initiated international discussion outside of the League of Nations. It was the first international conference hosted by the U.S. and the world's first forum on the concept of disarmament. The talks resulted in agreement for naval arms reduction but failed to reach agreement on limitation of air and land weaponry because of France's objections. While land and air forces might be readily constrained, naval armaments were another story.

At the end of World War I, America was rapidly building up her military arsenal on land, sea and air. America had entered the war late (7 April 1917) and on 11 November 1918 the Kaiser "threw in the towel." Skirmishes continued in the Far East involving Russia and the Allies. American and Japanese troops moved into Siberia to calm the political scene with the understanding that they would withdraw when the situation stabilized.

Most of the naval forces of the Central Powers had been captured or sunk. American naval experts totaled up the Allied naval forces – U.S., Britain, Japan, France and Italy. The U.S. numbers were staggering and the build-up was such that she could easily become the premier world naval power. At the time this was not something that most Americans were interested in – Teddy Roosevelt notwithstanding. Arms expansion aimed to win the war to "end all wars" and make the world "safe for democracy." Such idealism soon ended up on the shoals of political reality. President Woodrow Wilson was unable to persuade America to join the League of Nations, although he helped to remake Europe, and less so the Far East, together with an overarching idealistic League of Nations.

Americans, especially their representatives in Congress, appreciated their isolation and did not like "foreign entanglements." To be tied by treaty to an organization, one might be called upon to get involved where one might not want to get involved. However, President Warren G. Harding, who succeeded Wilson, realized that a mechanism should be established to restrict worldwide arms expansion to a reasonable level in the hope of bringing peace to the world.

So the International Conference on Naval Limitation (Washington Naval Conference) was convened by President Harding and opened in Washington DC on 18 November 1921. Many political heavy weights were in attendance, including Charles Evan Hughes (Secretary of State) from the United States, Earl Arthur J. Balfour (former Prime Minister) from Britain and Admiral Baron Tomosaburo Kato from Japan.

Chairman Hughes, in his opening remarks, stunned the conferees by stating that the battleship tonnage should be stabilized as it currently existed for the British, American, Japanese, French, and Italian fleets. Later reports indicated some collusion between America and Britain (Ref. 4.3.2). This shocked the Allies, especially Britain who was in no position to challenge America's rise. For over 200 years, Britain had ruled the seas from the North Atlantic to the Strait of Malacca, but she was now broke and in debt, as were the other Allies (except for the U.S.). Japan was also astonished since she wanted to keep building ships, at least to the levels of Britain and U.S., but was at their mercy for resources and finance. In the end, Arthur J. Balfour accepted the limits. Admiral T. Kato accepted and spoke "… the conclusion is that a contest between Japan and America is unthinkable… At all costs, Japan should avoid war with America. In view of this, I believe, that the true aim of the nation's defense at present should be to maintain military strength commensurate with national resources and to nurture that strength while using diplomatic measures to avoid war." In his book, Sullivan remarked that this was a "statement of a true statesman" (Ref. 4.3.3). Captain Osami Nagano was part of the Japanese Naval Delegation which was involved in naval evaluation.

Japan had been reliant on Britain to serve as a buffer against western powers in the Far East as was provided by the Anglo-Japanese Treaty of 1901. Culturally, Japan felt more comfortable with the British model of imperialism than with the American idea of open markets and free trade. But, Hughes made it clear in Washington that the U.S. wanted Britain to abrogate that Treaty and sign the Four-Power Treaty regarding trade with China. This so called "open door policy" provided that each signatory was granted equal access to China's markets.

Back in Japan, Fleet Admiral Heihachiro Togo – the admiral who conquered the Russian fleet in 1905 – was in favor of the Washington Naval Treaty. With Taisho Democracy in force, the Treaty was signed and it set the tone of relations between Japan and America for the next 20 years. However, it also spawned division in the Imperial Japanese Navy hierarchy that grew louder through the decade, i.e. the Treaty faction and the Anti-Treaty faction (aka Fleet faction). In reviewing the history, it is simple to place individuals in one faction or the other, but this may not tell the whole story. Admiral Baron T. Kato and Captain O. Nagano were obviously behind the Treaty in 1922 but, later it was claimed that they were of the Anti-Treaty faction.

Provisions of the Treaty

The provisions of the Washington Naval Treaty were straightforward (Ref. 4.3.4). However, since many arguments have arisen around them, the complete Treaty is given in Appendix C. The salient points of agreement between nations were:

- ten year moratorium on capital ship construction
- retention of capital ships
- scrapping capital ships
- moratorium on fortification of Pacific islands

For capital ships, the two most important requirements were the number of ships to be retained and the number to be scrapped. It was obvious that the United States would easily overtake the British Empire in capital ships, but there was no desire to become the dominant sea power. Maintaining a large fleet in stand-by status was not, in America's opinion, cost-effective – unless one had Empire ambitions. Great Britain, the principal sea power for 200 years, wanted to maintain dominance, but it was becoming a costly enterprise; and she was broke (1920). Britain was permitted to complete construction of two capital ships for which the keel had been laid. It would then scrap four ships, bringing their total to 20 capital ships under the Treaty.

To maintain and operate a fleet requires fuel – oil or coal – and that requires bases. Article XIX of the Washington Treaty tended to equalize the three navies in the following passage:

"The United States, the British Empire and Japan agree that the status quo at the time of the signing of the present Treaty, with regard to fortifications and naval bases, shall be maintained in their respective territories and possessions specified hereunder."

Article III prohibited new capital ship construction for ten years and then replacement tonnage would come into effect (see Table 1 of Appendix C). Relative tonnage ratio between the U.S., British and Japanese navies was 1:1:0.6 respectively. All concerned parties believed that the Washington Treaty would stabilize Japan's ambitions in the Far East, especially with regard to China and Russia, both of which were undergoing revolutions. This solution lasted for ten years and was extended for another five years to 1936 as a result of the first London Naval Treaty of 1930. But, thereafter, Japan's empire building took on a more aggressive stance with the creation of the puppet state of Manchukuo and the Marco Polo Bridge Incident of July 1937, which is presented in Part 4, Chapter 4.

American delegates, most notably Chairman Hughes and Admiral William Pratt, were very impressed with Kato's intelligence and vision. Upon his return to Japan, Kato became Prime Minister in June 1922. He would have been instrumental in justifying the ratio and how it was to Japan's advantage in the long run, but he died in August 1923. Unfortunately, the naval hierarchy believed that Japan needed a 1:1:0.7 ratio and they stirred up a propaganda campaign within both the military and civilian population promoting the more favorable ratio.

As Naval Attaché and delegate to the Washington Conference, Captain Nagano must have interacted with Admiral Kato. He surely would have absorbed some of Kato's ideas and world outlook as well as where Japan might fit in the global picture. But, as happened at other international meetings, Japanese naval officers were making a good impression on the westerners, while the Japanese Imperial Army was spreading its wings in East Asia.

At the close of the Washington Conference, Chairman Hughes admonished Japan for not abiding by her international commitments in the joint American and Japanese incursion into Siberia. America withdrew its forces when the situation stabilized, but Japan did not. An outside reporter expressed his surprise that Hughes "scolded the Japs."

Chairman Hughes had wanted to establish the same ratio for destroyers and cruisers but the French delegation objected so vehemently that discussions on auxiliary vessels were not addressed in this treaty. In the end, everyone agreed with the battleship ratio of 1:1:0.6 and signed the Treaty. Auxiliary vessels would be left for another conference.

Geneva Naval Conference 1927

America had taken the lead at the Washington Naval Conference. In 1927, President Calvin Coolidge invited Great Britain and Japan to Geneva to discuss extending naval limitation to include auxiliary vessels. Japanese delegates came prepared to wage a battle for the revised naval ratio of 1:1:0.7. In the interim, Admiral Kanji Kato had become a dominant figure in the Japanese navy as a member of the Anti-Treaty faction. He argued for the increased ratio, and from a political standpoint, made the higher ratio a matter of Japanese pride overshadowing the technical naval logic. Fleet Admiral Heihachiro Togo warned "you don't bring your wife, this is a battlefield."

The major difficulty was between Britain and America who could not come to terms over auxiliary vessels. Britain needed light cruisers to protect worldwide shipping routes. Light cruisers were not as useful to America and she would need to undertake a large building program to achieve parity, if parity were defined in numbers of ships rather than in units of tonnage.

Japan did not engage in broad discussions because of the clash between Britain and America on the ratio for auxiliary vessels. As Admiral I. Yamamoto observed, the difference between the 0.6 and 0.7 ratio in units of tonnage was not significant, especially with new technical developments in aircraft and aircraft carriers (Ref. 4.3.5). The Geneva Naval Conference was a bust. It disbanded with no agreement, but plans were kept open for a future conference to be held in London in 1930.

The First London Naval Conference 1930

The London Naval Disarmament Conference of 1930 opened in January amid regal splendor. King George V welcomed the delegates to England in the Royal Gallery of the House of Lords, from whence conferees proceeded to St. James Palace. A key issue for the conference was a limit on maximum tonnage for cruisers. The American President Herbert H. Hoover, elected in 1928, had immersed himself in the "metaphysics" of equalizing tonnage and ratio of cruisers (light and heavy) between the American and British fleets. In 1929, Hoover personally conferred with British Prime Minister Ramsay MacDonald in Washington to thrash out a verbal agreement on cruisers (also known as auxiliary ships). The Americans and British settled on a parity of 1:1 for the issue of auxiliary ships. At the London Conference, the Americans wanted to keep the auxiliary ship ratio the same as that established for battleships, i.e. 1:1:0.6 for Britain, America and Japan respectively.

Ambassador Tsuneo Matsudaira led the Japanese delegation in London. He was the current ambassador to England, having previously served as ambassador to the U.S. Admiral Isoroku Yamamoto headed the Japanese naval contingent that was aiming for the 1:1:0.7 ratio for cruisers. There was much wrangling on both sides of the discrepancies; however the Americans wanted to maintain the battleship ratio – if only on paper.

The diplomats, as politicians, took over and a compromise was attained in the Reed-Matsudaira Agreement. A middle-ground ratio of 1:1:0.65 was established and endorsed by the Japanese delegation. One possible rationale for the ratio of 1:1:0.65 was that the U.S. defended two ocean fronts; Britain defended the eastern Atlantic, Mediterranean, Indian Ocean and southwest Pacific. Japan only defended the western Pacific Ocean. The justification might have been that Japan would need only half that of the U.S. fleet, plus a little extra. Therefore, the ratio was a reasonable concession for a defensive navy.

The Americans believed that the Conference was a great success with the British parity issue settled, as well as satisfactory auxiliary ship ratio for Japan. The maximum numbers of heavy cruisers were set at 18 for America, 15 for Great Britain and 12 for Japan. The Treaty upheld and extended the provision of the 1922 treaty that prohibited the powers from building new capital ships for five years. The provisions set in both treaties of 1922 and 1930 were to expire in 1936.

The Treaty was ratified by Britain, America and Japan – Italy and France abstained. The Japanese public also believed that they won a victory and Admiral Yamamoto was greeted as a hero upon his return. However, the Anti-Treaty faction, headed by Admiral Kanji Kato, was not pleased and was determined to revise the results or abandon the treaty. Moreover, the Japanese naval brass believed that its prerogatives were violated. As defined in the Meiji Constitution, military services were granted supremacy in military matters and were answerable only to the Emperor. They strongly objected to a diplomat making decisions for the armed services. Consequently, the Imperial Navy would insist that, in the next London Naval Conference to be held five years hence, the delegation would be led by a naval officer.

The Second London Naval Conference 1935-1936

The stage was set for Admiral Osami Nagano to once more step into the role of diplomat and decide the Imperial Navy's future. The disarmament provisions were set to expire on 31 December 1936 so the Second London Naval Conference was convened to determine future arms limitation.

The Imperial Navy sent Admiral Isoroku Yamamoto to the preliminary meeting (1934-1935) to prepare an agenda. Where Yamamoto stood, personally, on the ratio issue is clouded in the literature, but he was staunchly for the 1:1:0.7 ratio at the first London Naval Conference. As was reported, he may have been leaning toward the Treaty faction and public enthusiasm for the Treaty made him broaden his outlook. However, at the preliminary meeting, Navy Minister Admiral Baron Mineo Osumi, an ardent Anti-Treaty official, directed Yamamoto to demand the 1:1:0.7 ratio. If not, Japan would opt out of the naval limitation treaties. Admiral Yamamoto was well-liked and familiar with many of the American and British delegates. They sympathized with his difficult position. He would have preferred to stay in the treaties through compromise and he realized – as some of his compatriots did not – that Japan would lose a naval arms race with America in the long run. It was to Japan's advantage to keep America within the treaty limitations.

Admiral Nagano was called upon to present the Imperial Navy's case to the world. He had just completed his tour at Yokosuka Naval Base and was appointed by Navy Minister Osumi to lead the delegation to London. No civilian diplomat would stand in the way of the Imperial Navy's prerogatives. Japan upped the ante and demanded battleship and cruiser parity, i.e. a ratio of 1:1:1. At the time, the political situation in Tokyo – always a little unstable – was becoming more influenced by military hands and less so by the political parties. The military indirectly dictated the choice of Prime Minister and major government posts, such as Foreign Ministry, Army, Navy and Finance. The navy's propaganda machine advocated that they should have more ships than allowed under the naval treaties since Japan was the major naval power in the western Pacific.

While a Fleet-man, Nagano had a broad understanding of world navies and the Japanese naval situation. He was well familiar with America and knew her capabilities if pressed into a naval arms race. To help him in his dilemma, he asked Admiral Yamamoto to join him; but was refused. Yamamoto had already failed to find a path acceptable to Japan, America and Britain and he knew it would be a wasted trip. Admiral Nagano left Tokyo on 16 November 1935 with Matsuzo Nagai (former ambassador in Berlin). Foreign Minister Koki Hirota and Navy Minister Admiral Mineo Osumi bid their farewell at the railroad station. Following Admiral Yamamoto's failure to obtain a compromise at the preliminary Naval Treaty Conference, the decision was made to opt out of the naval treaties (see Figures 4.3.1. and 4.3.2). Possibly, they were seeking an alliance with the German Navy.

Plenipotentiary Nagano arrived in London looking "grim and inscrutable" (see Figure 4.3.3). He had previously worked with Admiral Baron T. Kato and, presumably, had absorbed some statesmanship. United Press released a dispatch that Nagano personally admired the United States but that the Japanese people were unable to understand why the United States required "such a large navy." And so, on 15 January 1936, Admiral Nagano addressed the Conference with a statement of withdrawal from the previously signed naval treaties. His text stated that the ratios limiting the Imperial Navy relative to British and American navies injured Japan's pride – partially whipped up by naval propaganda.

Time Magazine reported: "In no mood to wait for a royal repast was Japan's Chief Delegate, round-faced and crinkly-smiling but dead-earnest, Admiral Osami Nagano. On the opening day of the Conference he announced that Japan could approve no action which did not begin by setting a 'common upper limit' for the navies of Japan, the U.S. and Britain. It was not, Admiral Nagano said, Japan's demand or desire to build her navy up to parity with those of Britain and the U.S., but instead Japan hoped the 'common upper limit' would be set so low that none of the Great Powers would be in a position to menace another with offensive attack while each would have adequate naval forces to defend itself." Nagano continued "Since the Conference attendees will not agree to eliminate our position of inferiority; we have no other choice than to leave the Conference. But we do not have the slightest wish to embark on an armament race and we are firmly committed to promote the cause of world peace." (Ref. 4.3.6)

The Time article explained that Admiral Nagano was sent to "smash the Conference" and that this might stir the wrath of the great powers to do something to stop Japanese aggression in China starting in 1931. The London papers stated that Japanese pride of race no longer submits to the inferiority imposed by the 1:1:0.6 naval ratios. According to Time "Tokyo newspapers editorialized that Japanese shipyards could build war boats faster than the U.S. shipyards; that Depression has sapped U.S. strength until it no longer overwhelmingly exceeds Japan's; and that not only are most U.S. citizens unwilling to fight but also, in the words of Nichi Nichi 'most American navy men are mere professionals and lack devotion to the state.' Vice-Admiral Sankichi Takahashi, Commander of the Home Fleet cried in Tokyo: 'Put your minds at rest. If we are compelled to use the short sword to control, I am sure we shall win. We have tactics to defeat the Combined Fleet of Great Britain and the United States' ."

When Chief Delegate Nagano walked out of the Second London Naval Conference, Japan, in effect, had abrogated the Washington Naval Treaty and the first London Naval Treaty. U.S. delegate Admiral William H. Standley remarked, "This dealt a death knell to a noble experiment in disarmament."

Nagano Met with Raeder

On his way to London, Nagano had a noteworthy encounter with Grand Admiral Erich Raeder on 1 December 1935 in Berlin. John M. W. Chapman (Ref. 4.3.7) described the clandestine meeting as "one of the most fateful encounters in contemporary history." Nagano wanted to make contact with the German navy, and this could explain why Matsuzo Nagai traveled with him. In addition, Yamamoto's presence would have been advantageous because he had previously met with German Foreign Minister Joachim von Ribbentrop. The point of this Berlin meeting was Nagano's interest in furthering a Japanese-German alliance. The Japanese navy harbored pro-German and anti-German factions. Chief of Naval Staff Prince Hiroyasu Fushimi was in favor of some type of German alliance, but the Anti-German faction was staunchly against such a coalition. Many of them had trained or toured the West and they feared it would alienate America and Britain, which was the last thing they wanted.

As a background: During this period, Italy had invaded Ethiopia (Abyssinia to some) and the British navy was threatening to disrupt the flow of Italian troops and supplies across the Mediterranean. Communication from London to their fleet was intercepted and the Germans knew that the British were bluffing. The British fleet lacked sufficient ammunition for anything but a brief engagement with the Italians. Sanctions were also levied against Italy, but the Americans – not a member of the League – believed in business as usual. Standard Oil and other big oil companies continued to sell oil to anyone with U.S. dollars (gold). The Japanese were very interested in how sanctions would work since they had borne the brunt of sanctions as a result of their adventures in Manchuria and northern China. American neutrality laws had been enacted but how they were enforced was very important to the Japanese. Admiral Nagano had the benefit of Admiral Raeder's perspective.

Nagano realized that the British could be bluffed and that the Americans, private industry at least, ignored the neutrality laws. This was important in Nagano's evolving strategy towards Southeast Asia and southwest Pacific Ocean and access to their resources. He believed that Japan should be less dependent upon the West. This southern strategy would also satisfy the Japanese army – at least some – to settle the China problem and to access resources. The Japanese navy disliked the Japanese army's orientation toward Russia as the principal enemy. The last thing the Japanese navy wanted was Russia at their back and America at their front. With British forces to the south, Nagano believed they could be bluffed.

Nagano's Artistic Side

Nagano was a player on the world stage and his experience in diplomacy gave him opportunities to visit many nations, which rounded his overall make up. His artistic side, though not revealed in his military activities, was demonstrated in London as Time Magazine printed ."..the soul of even most bellicose Japanese is at peace in awe and wonder before marvels of Chinese art. To the white delegates, ...sturdy little (sic) Japanese Chief Delegate Admiral Osami Nagano explained exquisite niceties with elegance and charm" (Ref. 4.3.6). In addition, he was an amateur photographer and some of his prints revealed this part of his nature, see Figure 4.3.4 of his wife bathed in Vermeer lighting. He was also accomplished at calligraphy which was inscribed in stone on monuments still standing today.

Chapter 4, Part 3 References

4.3.1   Bix, Herbert P., *Hirohito on the Making of Modern Japan*, Perennial, Harper, Collins Publisher, New York, NY, 2001

4.3.2   Young, Eugene J., *Powerful America: Our Place in a Rearming World*, Frederick A. Stokes Co., New York, 1936

4.3.3   Sullivan, Mark, *The Great Adventure at Washington*, Doubleday, Garden City, NY, 1922

4.3.4   Burns, Richard D, ed. "Washington Naval Treaty (1922)," *Encyclopedia of Arms Control and Disarmament*, Volume III, Charles Scribner's Sons, New York, 1993

4.3.5   Agawa, S., translated by John Bester, *The Reluctant Admiral*, Hodansha International Ltd., Tokyo 1979

4.3.6   *Time Magazine*, January 25, 1936, Vol. XXVII, No. 4, "Naval Conference Challenge to Hell."

4.3.7   Chapman, John M. W., "A Dance on Eggs: Intelligence and the 'Anti-Commintern,'" *Journal of Contemporary History*, Vol. 22, No. 2, April 1987, pp 333-372

Figure 4.3.1 Meeting for momentous decision resulting in Japan's opting out of naval treaties, 1935. From left to right: Foreign Minister Koki Hirota, Naval Minister Admiral Nineo Osumi, Chief of Naval Staff Admiral Hiroyasu Fushimi, Plenipotentiary Admiral Osami Nagano, Ambassador Matsuzo Nagai.

Figure 4.3.2 Front row 3rd, 4th and 5th from left: Admiral Osami Nagano, Prince Fushimi and Ambassador Nagai in front of naval general staff building, Tokyo, 1935.

Figure 4.3.3 Admiral Osami Nagano and Matsuzo Nagai arriving in London for the Second London Naval Conference (1936)

Figure 4.3.4 Nagano's photo of his wife in a Veermer-like pose

Chapter 4

Diplomat, Sailor and Politician

1930 to 1941

Part 4:

Politician: 4 March 1936 – 2 February 1937

The Deplorable Incident in Tokyo, 26 February 1936

FROM the 1920s onward, Japan was embroiled in a tumultuous period of assassinations and military revolts throughout the home islands. The assassination of Saito Makoto, the former Prime Minister and Lord Keeper of the Privy Seal at his private residence in Tokyo, initiated the "February 26 Incident" of 1936. It was a revolt of the Imperial Japanese Army, which had hoped to establish a military dictatorship (Ref. 4.4.1). The insurrection struck at the heart of the Japanese government structure and posed a threat to the political system envisaged in Meiji Constitution. The change in government provided an opportunity for Admiral Osami Nagano to become Naval Minister in the succeeding government. See in Figure 4.4.1 the Naval Ministry staff that Admiral Nagano brought on board to accomplish the navy's mandates.

The revolutionaries were more than just a few fanatics – their numbers involved about 1600 troops of the army's Tokyo Division that had recently been ordered to Manchukuo. The attempted coup reportedly involved the complicity of high-ranking army officers including General Sadao Araki. During this era, Japan was close to becoming a "banana republic" with governments coming and going at the whim of colonels and generals. In reality, the chaos stimulated Emperor Hirohito to have a direct hand in the government and appointment of officials. The one unfortunate result was the establishment of martial law, which put the army in charge of maintaining order.

The following excerpt, taken directly from the translation of Koichi Kido's diary, gives his personal accounting of the incident as it unfolded (Ref. 4.4.2):

> *"The Lord Keeper of the Privy Seal is now being attacked in his private residence by a company of soldiers. He and his wife seem to have fallen victim. Ono added that the report had been given over the telephone by a house boy of the Saitos." I knew intuitively this was outbreak of an untoward incident of great magnitude. At once, I telephoned the Police Commissioner. Although I was able to contact him, I failed in making proper arrangements with the Metropolitan Police Board. Therefore, I sent for a car from the office and proceeded to the court at 6:00 am. While waiting for the car, I reported the incident to Prince Konoye and Baron Harada. Neither of them had known of it yet. ...I was told that the Grand Chamberlain Suzuki, Premier Okada and Finance Minister Takahashi had also been attacked.*
>
> *The car coming for me was stopped in front of the Metropolitan Police Board building by the rebels and had to make a detour. Knowing that the Metropolitan Police Board was in the hands of the rebels, I also made a detour around the Department of Overseas Affairs in order to get to the office.*

When the War Minister was received in audience by the Emperor, the Emperor said "Whatever their excuses are, I am displeased with this incident. It has brought disgrace on the fundamental character of our national policy."... Furthermore, because the Lord Keeper of the Privy Seal was killed, we decided to request that the President of the Privy Council, Ikki, come to the Imperial Palace.

...There are two different factions among the War Counselors. One asserted that the rebels should be disbanded with the Imperial Decree. The other insisted on the enforcement of the martial law.

...In the morning, the Chief of the Naval General Staff, his Imperial Highness Fushimi came to the Imperial Palace. The Prince gave his advice to the Throne. In his opinion it was better for the Emperor to have a new cabinet form quickly and not to enforce marshal law. Then the Prince sought the Emperor's opinion.

...It is understood that junior officers of the War Department and the Army general staff agreed to form a provisional cabinet and make such a proposal to their seniors. It seems that it would have a strong fascist tendency. This request had been shared by the insurgents. The War Minister demanded the enforcement of martial law. I hear that Colonel Ishiwara had insisted on this. The Naval Minister was of the opinion that there was no necessity for marshal law. ...

...At 8:30, Navy Minister, Mr. Osumi, told the Minister of the Imperial Household that some persons would like to have His Imperial Highness, Prince Fushimi or His Imperial Highness, Prince Higashikuni as the Premier ad interim and that some others recommended Masaki.

...At 9:00 pm, Home Minister, Goto, was installed as Premier ad interim. Then he tended the resignation of the cabinet members in block. The Emperor said, "Suppress the insurgents as soon as possible. Hold your post with sincerity until peace and order are restored."

...At 11:30 pm, the Privy Council in the Imperial presence passed the draft proclamation of the state of siege.

27 February 1936: At 3:00 pm, Prince Konoye came. We discussed current events for about an hour.

... Premier Okada was alive. He was rescued today. He was very excited and insisted on proceeding at once to the Imperial Palace. However, they managed to dissuade him from such an attempt.

...I received information from Parliamentary Vice Minister Okabe. In spite of being dissuaded by three generals, Masaki, Abe and Nishi, there were two junior officers refusing the terms. General Masaki stated that if they would not listen to reason, he, himself, would destroy the insurgents. Finally, the insurgents yielded to the general.

28 February 1926: At 7:00 am, I received information that despite last evening's sign of a favorable turn of events, two leaders of the insurgents were still insisting on their demands. Consequently, the authorities decided to bring pressure upon the insurgents.

...The Minister of the Imperial Household, Mr. Yuasa, consulted with me regarding the successor to the Lord Keeper. We could select no person other than Prince Konoye for the post. President of the Privy Counsel, Iki, agreed to this idea. At 8:30, I telephoned Prince Konoye asking him to come to the office to have an interview with Mr. Yuasa. At 11:30 I saw Prince Konoye, due to his poor health, he said he would be unable to accept the offer.

29 February 1936: At 8:30 am, actions were taken to destroy the insurgents. We were unanimous in the opinion that we should begin to select a succeeding cabinet in order to inspire confidence in the people. ...The Emperor added, "Forming a new cabinet will be difficult. The cabinet that would be welcome by Army circles would give rise to anxieties among economic circles. However, we cannot consider only the interests of the latter group."

2 March 1936: The following story was related after it being heard by Chichibu. "Officers forming the backbone of the Army assembled today and discussed Army reform. They came to the conclusion that all of the current generals should be retired and someone, such as Lt. Gen. Itagaki, appointed War Minister. They also decided that someone able to cooperate with Itagaki would be a desirable nominee as Premier. Neither Kawai nor Araki would be satisfactory, they said, and men who had no previous contact with the Army would be more preferable. It was their feeling that Hiranuma was also unsatisfactory. Some circles in the House of Peers seemed to be backing Gen. Masaki, but a Masaki cabinet would be out of the question, they said."

New Japanese Government, 1936

The Imperial Navy was a stabilizing force during the incident. Admiral Mitsumasa Yonai, Commanding Officer at Yokosuka Naval Base, sent in marines to secure the naval headquarters in downtown Tokyo and he moved battleships into Tokyo Bay. The intent was to quash the uprising by lobbing a few shells, as a last resort, at the insurgents' redoubt and the army headquarters in the city. Following mediation, the mutinied troops surrendered on 29 February 1936, avoiding further bloodshed.

The extent of the revolt shook the foundations of government and the next Premier would have to deal with army unrest. Social unrest persisted with the worldwide depression despite strenuous efforts of the U.S. and Britain, and the West in general, to alleviate economic stress. Unfortunately, some U.S. efforts – such as restricting imports from Japan – were exacerbating conditions in the home islands. Army Minister General Sadao Araki predicted that 1936 would be a "year of crisis," and he was right. With the expiration of the Naval Disarmament Treaties on 31 December 1936, there would be a naval arms race with the West. Diplomatically, Japan was isolated, having withdrawn from the League of Nations (Ref. 4.4.3).

In the *genro*, headed by Prince Kinmochi Saionji who was the last of the generals with links to Emperor Meiji, the group of elder statesmen recommended Prince Fumimaro Konoye to be Prime Minister. However, he declined claiming ill health as many politicians did to refuse high office in time of crisis. This was the second office he declined. An ideal choice for Premier was Koki Hirota who had served as Foreign Minister in the Okada cabinet. He had demonstrated his political acumen and expertise in foreign affairs in dealing with the Diet. He could stand up to the military and handle the politics of the ultra-rightist Seiyukai Party and the Minseito Party, which was favored by business community. The fact that he was a commoner, elicited his depiction as "a man in an ordinary suit."

Hirota, at 56, believed he was nearing the end of his government career having reached the pinnacle in the Foreign Ministry. Initially, he refused the appointment as Prime Minister because he was not part of the nobility or military elite. Forming a new government in a period of marshal law would be difficult. However, in this time of government crisis, his simple attributes made him suitable to the position. The army was an obstacle, rejecting many of Hirota's initial nominees. The military interpreted the constitution to mean that, if they disagreed with cabinet selections, they could refuse to appoint War or Navy ministers. This, in effect, would thwart establishment of a new government.

After the new Prime Minister's acceptance, the Emperor summoned Hirota to the Imperial Palace on 5 March 1936 and directed him to form a government. Hirohito instructed him: (Ref. 4.4.1)

1. To govern the country with respect for the provisions of the constitution
2. To exercise restraint in foreign affairs to avoid unnecessary friction
3. To avoid anything that would create any sudden upheaval in business world
4. *To see that the position of the nobility was not endangered*

The first three were standard directives, but Hirota wondered about Hirohito's charge to him about the nobility's standing – it was probably because these were tumultuous times and he was the "man in an ordinary suit."

Hirota set to work forming his cabinet. In accordance with the constitution, the navy nominated Admiral Osami Nagano for Navy Minister. He was *en route* from London after his walking out from the Second London Naval Conference had made him the "darling of the conservatives" and assured his approval by Naval Minister Mineo Osumi and Chief of the Naval Staff Prince Hiroyasu Fushimi. Amid the political turmoil of the time, Nagano is seen relaxing with a cigarette in Figure 4.4.2. His growing family, Makato and Misako are seen in Figures 4.4.3 and 4.4.4 playing with toys and enjoying a visit to a battleship.

General Hajime Sugiyama, Hirota's friend from his home prefecture, upon request nominated General Count Hisaichi Terauchi for Army Minister. He had been Governor General of Korea and was a political neophyte; however, Terauchi's detachment from army politics could possibly benefit his control of the disparate elements in the army. The Imperial Way (Kodoha) faction, lead by General Araki, promoted an ultra-national philosophy within the army with emphasis on Emperor Worship and loyalty to the Showa Restoration. Purist in outlook with regard to traditional Japanese values, their thrust was to overthrow the corrupt civilian government and install militarist rule. This was the mindset of junior officers in the February 26 revolt. Rising in contention to the Imperial Way was the Control Way (Toseiha) faction that represented the more conservative, cautious group of officers who opposed Araki. Led by General Hideki Tojo, they advocated cooperation with the civilian government and economic entities to prepare for a protracted total war. Both factions had Japan's military expansion and national strength at heart – the Imperial Way by preemptive strike, the Control Way by less aggressive tactics.

Working throughout the night of 6 March 1936, Hirota selected his Cabinet with assistance from his friend Shigeru Yoshida who was his choice for Foreign Minister. But the army held a long-term grudge against Yoshida, which went back to his 1931 stint as Counsel General in Mukden. The Military Affairs Bureau of the army complained that some candidates were too liberal and defiantly withheld their nomination for Army Minister. Hirota was horrified. He was working under Imperial Directive, but General Tomoyuki Yamashita and Major Akira Muto were not impressed.

Hirota compiled a new list of candidates and removed some of the more controversial picks, including his friend Yoshida. Still, Military Affairs was dissatisfied objecting to too many politicians in the Cabinet. This time, Hirota stood his ground insisting that if they did not accept this second group "we shall announce in tomorrow morning's papers that we have finally failed to form a government on account of obstructions by the military." The army backed down and accepted the cabinet. At their demand, Hirota issued the army's account: "The recent mutiny was not the sole responsibility of the military. Government is corrupt, the political parties must reconsider their behavior and domestic policy must be reformed." Although he felt this was innocuous, Hirota candidly remarked to his aides "The military are like an untamed horse left to run wild. If you try head-on to stop it, you'll get kicked to death. The only hope is to jump on from the side and try to get it under control while still allowing it to have its head to a certain extent. ...But somebody has to do it. That's why I've jumped on" (Ref. 4.4.1). Figure 4.4.5 shows Hirota's established Cabinet in March 1936 and a portrait of Prime Minister Koki Hirota is given in Figure 4.4.6.

At 2:30 am on 9 March 1936, Hirota trudged through the snow-covered streets of Tokyo from the Foreign Minister's residence to the Meiji shrine, accompanied only by an aide. Protocol dictated that he pay his respects and petition the gods for blessing on his administration. Koki Hirota was sworn in as Prime Minister at the Imperial Palace that evening. At 11:30 pm a crowd of well-wishers, including his 88-year old father, cheered upon his return home. It was a long day indeed.

Hirota's Administration

Prime Minister Hirota was the last commoner (up to 1945) to occupy the top administrative position in the Japanese government – all others were generals, admirals and nobility. From the start, he had his work cut out for him with military and civil unrest. The Army had immediately cleaned house and many generals were retired. The result was purging of the Imperial Way and ascendancy of the Control Way into position of power and influence with their China orientation. The Army and Navy were at odds on many matters and Admiral Nagano tried to change this culture. He suggested a southern orientation that would satisfy the Army – it also coincided with his concern for raw materials. Nagano's aim was to move away from a Soviet confrontation because he did not want to confront the Russian and American navies at the same time.

The administration's management tool to coordinate national policy took the form of conferences among five cabinet ministers. They were as follows:

- Prime Minister – Koki Hirota
- Foreign Minister – Hachiro Arita
- Army Minister – General Hisaichi Terauchi
- Navy Minister – Admiral Osami Nagano
- Finance Minister – Eiichi Baba

They came up with the following policy statements (Ref. 4.4.1):

> "The basic concern of Japan's policies on the continent shall be to ensure the healthy development of Manchukuo and to secure the defenses of Japan and Manchuria; to remove the threat from Russia in the north and, at the same time, to prepare for any threat from Britain and America and to promote economic development via close collaboration between the three countries of Japan, Manchukuo and China." This was a favorite Army theme.
>
> To satisfy the Navy, the following statement was added: "To promote the economic development of the Japanese people in southern waters and the outlying areas in particular and to extend Japanese power by gradual peaceful means, taking care not to offend other nations, thus contributing along with the completion of nation-building in Manchukuo to the amplification and reinforcement of national strength."

The army's incentive behind the policy statement was their desire to build up strength to oppose any possible Soviet deployment in the Far East. They wanted sufficient forces in Manchukuo to deal a decisive blow at the very outset of hostilities. The navy's aim was for funding to guarantee control of western Pacific waters against any possible incursion by the U.S. Navy. However, this was strictly precautionary, at least for Admiral Nagano, as he hosted an elaborate banquet for Admiral Orin G. Murfin, Commander-in-Chief for the U.S. Asiatic Fleet (see Figure 4.4.7).

Having just walked out of the London Naval Conference in January 1936 and demanding parity with American and British navies, Admiral Nagano was acutely mindful of his responsibility. The Washington Treaty would expire on 31 December 1936 removing any obstacles to fleet expansion. Actually, the size of the Japanese navy was nearing that of the American navy's. At the time, Nagano knew that America was in the process of pivoting from its isolationist posture and he was well aware of the shipbuilding capacity of the United States. One thing he did not want was to precipitate an outright naval race with the West. Hence, the Imperial Navy was reticent to telegraph its intentions with bellicose remarks. Nonetheless, the navy wanted to improve its shipbuilding infrastructure to achieve par with the Americans. Morison (Ref. 4.4.4) noted that American shipbuilding did not reach treaty size until 1944. Not to be outdone, the Imperial Army also had ambitious plans and wanted to develop an indigenous manufacturing capability. They had been purchasing much military hardware – artillery, machine guns, tanks and planes – from foreign vendors.

Prime Minister Hirota, son of a stonemason, asked his Cabinet how government would improve conditions for the common man. In certain areas of Japan – such as northern Honshu – unemployment was almost 90%. The Cabinet drew up seven major national policy initiatives as follows:

1. Step up national defense
2. Radical reform of education
3. Reorganize the tax system embracing both national and local taxes
4. Stabilize the people's livelihood entailing:
    a. Measures to forestall national disasters
    b. Expand health facilities
    c. Overhaul and encourage agriculture and fishing economies and encouragement of small and medium scale commerce and industry
5. Establish controls over industry, entailing:
    a. reinforce control over the electric power industry
    b. moves to make Japan self-sufficient in liquid fuels and iron ore
    c. secure stable sources of fibers
    d. promote and establish controls over trade
    e. promote aviation and shipping enterprises
    f. promote Japanese overseas development
6. Establish firm national policies on important matters affecting Manchukuo; steps to encourage emigration and encouragement of investment
7. Reorganize and improve administrative machinery

All of these initiatives meant that the proposed 1937 budget would swell to 33 billion yen (Ref 4.4.5). The military's portion of the proposed budget ballooned to 69% from 48% in 1936. The tug-of-war on the purse strings between civilian and military concerns ended when Emperor Hirohito called on Hirota and demanded, "I want you to see that the military appropriations for the Army and Navy are put before the Diet." Hirota was aghast that the Emperor had taken such a direct interest and had personally commanded him to carry out his order. Hirota delivered the budget to the Diet.

Anti-Comintern Pact

At this time, there were back-channel diplomatic efforts underway in Berlin between Hitler and Military Attaché General Hiroshi Oshima. They worked to form an alliance against Soviet Union, known as the Anti-Comintern Pact[1].

The Anti-Comintern Pact was an alliance uniting nations against Communist International subversion. Initially it was just between Japan and Germany, but later included other nations after Hitler twisted their arms. The Pact did not specifically mention Russia, which the diplomats liked. In Japan's favor, she reached an agreement with Germany that required German advisors to leave China and cease arms shipments. The protocol pledged the signatories to neutrality and mutual assistance if either was to be attacked by the Soviet Union, but the Pact was not a military alliance. Additionally, the Pact prohibited either party to form any political treaty with the Soviet Union and Germany

---

[1] The Anti-Comintern Pact was an international alliance to prevent infiltration by the Communist Party on a global scale.

agreed to recognize Manchukuo. Figure 4.4.8 shows the signing of the Anti-Comintern Pact in Berlin, 25 November 1936

The Foreign Ministry was initially against the alliance with Germany because it would further alienate the U.S., Britain and Russia from Japan. The strengthened Control Way was distrustful of Germany and Hitler. However, an alliance with Germany might be to the army's advantage, as it would eliminate Germany's support of the Chinese. Admiral Nagano's negotiating skills achieved the final solution that the Army, Navy and Foreign Ministries could live with. Hirohito showed his appreciation to the admiral for his help in obtaining the Anti-Comintern Pact approval. He presented a gift of silver sake cups to Nagano in 1938.

Budget battle in the Diet

In January 1937, there was political upheaval when Prime Minister Hirota presented his budget with military and civilian initiatives before the Diet. Budgetary discussions presented the rare chance for politicians to challenge the military. Mr. Kunimatsu Hamada of the Seiyukai Party launched a blistering attack, glaring directly at Army Minister General Count Hisaichi Terauchi. His charge was that the army interfered in the government and accused it of desiring a military dictatorship. Terauchi shot back accusing Hamada of insulting the military. Hamada demanded to know if Terauchi was convinced that his remarks were disrespectful. Terauchi was adamant, "That, at least, was the impression I had received." Hamada, thereupon, charged him with irresponsible statements. If the War Minister could prove that he had insulted the Army, he offered to disembowel himself and further suggested that Terauchi do the same if his own claim was not substantiated (Ref. 4.4.5). This ended the argument. Figure 4.4.9 shows Terauchi arguing in the Diet.

As a result, Terauchi resigned his post stating that no one but the Emperor could challenge the prerogatives of the army and that the Diet should disband because they did so. Dissolving the Diet would require new elections, but no one wanted that to happen. Nagano tried to negotiate a compromise between the Army and the politicians to no avail. The following day (5 February 1937) Hirota's Cabinet resigned (Ref. 4.4.6) one year after his being seated. General Senjuro Hayashi succeeded Hirota as Prime Minister and the newly formed Cabinet adopted the budget, which was passed a few months later.

Legacy of Nagano's Naval Ministry

Admiral Nagano was out, but, as Naval Minister, he presided over an ambitious program for modernizing the Imperial Navy. During his tenure, he believed that the Navy Ministry should be more attuned to strategic concerns such as access to raw materials. Therefore, he established a Naval Foreign Affairs Bureau to advise the Foreign Ministry on such matters to the extent they affected the navy.

He had confidence in the administrative and technical talents of Admiral Isoroku Yamamoto and selected him to be Vice Minister in November 1936. Yamamoto was believed to be of the Treaty faction while Nagano was a well-known Fleet faction man. It was typical of Nagano's personal philosophy to bring together opposing Fleet viewpoints. The two had worked together in Washington and Yamamoto attended the first London Naval Conference as well as the preliminary meeting for the Second London Naval Conference. Probably, more than any other Navy man in the 1930s, Yamamoto believed in the ascendancy of air power, of which Nagano was fully cognizant through his experience with General Billy Mitchell. Nagano brought him into the ministry to spearhead programs for aircraft carriers and naval air power. When Nagano left the Cabinet in 1937, Yamamoto stayed on as Vice Minister.

In retrospect, the Hirota Cabinet accomplished several milestones that stood out. They were as follows:

- The military prepared huge budgets. Most importantly, the Navy requested hardware, battleships and carriers to wage a naval war.
- The Army was supplied with the muscle in arms, tanks and aircraft to overwhelm Chinese armies under Chiang Kai-shek and the Russian Army on the Manchurian borders.
- The civilian population would benefit from better domestic conditions, especially education and utilities.

Nagano, ever the pragmatist and realist, favored some of these directions, but all indications were that he did not look upon the Japanese as a superior race. He believed that Japan could better provide for its populace and national interests by directly exploiting raw materials and strategic resources in the Far East. Japan wanted to break their dependence on western countries for finished goods, which by 1942 they did accomplish, but Japan proceeded more aggressively than the occidentals did. Nagano was pivotal in ensuring for the Imperial Navy that the necessary shipbuilding program was in place. By December 1941, Japan gained the means and confidence to challenge the west.

In June 1936, Admiral Nagano spoke to his countrymen in his radio address on morale and courage. To stimulate patriotism he affirmed that the Meiji Emperor, with the Japanese people, had made Japan the equal of any other country. With his Confucian philosophy, he equated courage with kindness and selflessness. He specifically advised against bluster and instructed that courage must be exercised through actions to do what is right. Courage "appears with the power to smash any obstacle and go forward." He told the Japanese people that they must "undertake a big job for self, for family and for the country." Nagano articulated his stance that "True courage is power." (Ref. 4.4.7)

CHAPTER 4, PART 4 REFERENCES

4.4.1   Shiroyama, Saburo, Translated by John Bester, *War Criminal: The Life and Death of Hirota Koki*, Kodansha International Ltd., Tokyo, 1977
4.4.2   Kido, Kochi, *The Diary of Marquis Kido, 1931-45*, University Publications of America, Inc., Frederick, MD, 1984
4.4.3   Bix, Herbert P., *Hirohito On the Making of Modern Japan*, Harper Collins Publishers, New York, NY, 2000
4.4.4   Morison, Samuel Eliot, *The Rising Sun in the Pacific 1931-April 1942*, Little, Brown and Company, Boston, 1988
4.4.5   Associated Press, "Japanese Diet Jeers Cabinet in Parliament," January 23, 1937
4.4.6   Byas, Hugh, "Navy Minister Intervenes," *New York Times*, January 23, 1937
4.4.7   Nagano, Misako, *Everlasting Ocean*, Minami-no-Kaze Publishing Company, Kochi City, 1995

Figure 4.4.1 Nagano, Yamamoto, Toyoda of the Naval Ministry staff

Figure 4.4.2 Nagano relaxing

Figure 4.4.3 Makoto and Misako

Figure 4.4.4 Misako and Makoto on naval ship

Figure 4.4.5 Hirota's Cabinet, March 1936. In uniform are Terauchi with Nagano to his left. Hirota stands forward in the center.

Figure 4.4.6 Prime Minister Koki Hirota, 1936-1937, "the man in the ordinary suit"

Figure 4.4.7 Welcoming Banquet in honor of Admiral Orin G. Murfin, The Commander-in-Chief, U.S. Asiatic Fleet, May 28, 1936 at the Official Residence of the Imperial Japanese Naval Minister Admiral Osami Nagano, Tokyo, Japan

1. *Naval Minister Osami Nagano (IJN)*
2. *Admiral Orin G. Murfin, (USN)*
3. *Ms. Joseph Grew*
4. *Admiral Mineo Osumi (IJN)*
5. *Vice Admiral Kiyoshi Hasegawa (IJN)*
6. *Vice Admiral Shigetaro Shimada (IJN)*
7. *US Ambassador Joseph Grew*
8. *Mrs. Osami Nagano*
9. *Mrs. O. G. Murfin*
10. *Vice Admiral Zengo Yoshida (IJN)*
11. *Rear Admiral Shiro Takasu (IJN)*
12. *Zenzaburo Nagata, Imperial Navy Counselor*
13. *Vice Admiral Soemu Toyoda (IJN)*
14. *Mrs. Zengo Yoshida*
15. *Mrs. K. Hasegawa*
16. *Mrs. Z. Nagata*
17. *Mrs. Stanley*
18. *Captain Woodson (USN)*
19. *Commander Sadayoshi Ishido (IJN)*
20. *Lieutenant Kuranosuke Yanagisawa (IJN)*
21. *Miss Murfin, daughter of Admiral Murfin*
22. *Lieutenant Harrison (USN)*
23. *Mrs. Charlton, wife of Commander Carlton*
24. *Mrs. Watts, wife of Lieutenant Watts*
25. *Captain Rogers (USN)*
26. *Mrs. S. Shimada*
27. *Mrs. Enomoto*
28. *Captain Yuzuru Tanuki (IJN)*
29. *Commander Kessing (USN)*
30. *Mrs. Rogers*
31. *Lieutenant Watts (USN)*
32. *Mrs. Tanuki*
33. *Commander C. Sigenaga (IJN)*
34. *Captain Guigacks (USN)*
35. *Lieutenant Commander Keisuke Matsunaga (IJN)*
36. *Captain Charlton (USN)*
37. *Mrs. Kessing*
38. *Captain Stanley (USN)*
39. *Counsel Nevil, US Embassy in Japan*
40. *Captaiin Kiyoshi Shiritani (IJN)*

Figure 4.4.8 Foreign Minister Joachim von Ribbentrop and Japanese Ambassador Kintomo Mushakoji at signing of Anti-Comintern Pact in Berlin, 25 November 1936

Figure 4.4.9 Hirota and Terauchi in the historic battle of the budget in the Diet that led to the fall of Hirota's government, 21 January 1937

Chapter 4

Diplomat, Sailor and Politician

1930 to 1941

PART 5:

COMMANDER-IN-CHIEF OF THE COMBINED FLEET, 2 FEBRUARY 1937 – 1 DECEMBER 1937

ADMIRAL Nagano ascended to Commander-in-Chief of the Combined Fleet on 2 February 1937. It was both the apex and culmination of his naval career. The Combined Fleet encompassed the First and Second Fleets, which comprised modern battleships and aircraft carriers of the Imperial Japanese Navy. It also included the Third Fleet, which was normally made up of auxiliary vessels such as cruisers, destroyers and river gunboats. In some instances these were obsolescent vessels not worthy of the frontline fleet. Figure 4.5.1 shows Commander Nagano aboard ship. His responsibilities were great in the strategic sense as Japan was facing off the Russian fleet at Vladivostok to his west. Added to that were the western fleets in China's waters where the England, America and France had concessions, granted under treaties over the centuries. Table 4.5.1 gives a chronology of events in 1937 when Admiral Nagano was Commander-in-Chief of the Combined Fleet.

Marco Polo Bridge Incident – 8 July 1937

Under Commander Nagano's watch the spark that ignited the China War resulted from an unintended clash at the Marco Polo Bridge, named after the Venetian explorer who ventured into China in the 13th century. A detachment of the Imperial Japanese Army (IJA) was deployed between Manchukuo and Nanking in a supposed demilitarized zone. General Chiang Kai-shek's nationalist troops were scattered throughout the area. Chiang had been forced under confinement, in Sian in December 1936, to reorient his position and take a more active role against the Japanese incursion in north China. There he met with local warlords, including Mao Tse-tung's representative, Chou En-lai. Chou had instructions from Stalin himself to the effect that if they united against Japan, Russia would provide armaments to all Chinese factions. This was General Chiang's conversion, which changed the dynamics of the confrontation with Japan. (Ref. 4.5.1)

Japanese troop maneuvers near the Marco Polo Bridge in the late evening of 7 July 1937, elicited gunfire from Chinese troops and the Japanese returned fire. When the shooting stopped, a Japanese soldier was reported missing and was assumed to have been abducted by the Chinese garrison. Japanese troops advanced into the town of Wanping in the Fengtai district of Peking, but were halted by Chinese troops. During the standoff, both sides reinforced their strength and shelling continued. Later, the missing soldier walked into camp unharmed to the embarrassment of the Japanese commander (Ref. 4.5.2).

Commanders on both sides in Peking wanted to keep the incident localized, but other attitudes prevailed. General Chiang wanted to get Japanese troops out of the area and, therefore, sent in his German-trained division to reduce the Japanese presence. In Tokyo on 19 July 1937, the Japanese Cabinet held a conference in the Imperial Palace on the new situation regarding additional Chinese forces in Peking district. They made the decision, in Emperor Hirohito's presence, to send in additional Japanese troops. General Hajime Sugiyama explained to Hirohito that it would take the troops two to three months to deploy and stabilize the situation. Both sides continued to reinforce their strength. (Ref. 4.5.1)

Prince Konoye belonged to the Fujiwara clan, which had ties to the Emperor that went back centuries. The Prince was in his first tenure as Prime Minister. His term lasted from 4 June 1937 to 4 January 1939 with the following Cabinet:

Koki Hirota	Foreign Minister
Okinori Kaya	Finance Minister
General Hajime Sugiyama	Army Minister
Admiral Mitsumasa Yonai	Navy Minister (Admiral Isoroku Yamamoto – Vice Minister)

The Cabinet had issued a press release: "11 July 1937 – Additional Japanese troops were ordered to North China because the Chinese had deliberately perpetrated an armed attack against Japan. As our Empire's constant concern is to maintain peace in East Asia, however, we have not abandoned our hope that peaceful negotiations may yet ensure our non-expansion of the conflict." The troop dispatch was confirmed with an imperial order "Chastise the Chinese army in Peking-Tientsin area and bring stability to the main strategic places in the region." (Ref. 4.5.3) The IJA was very successful and entered Peking on 8 August 1937. They held the territory until 8 August 1945 when Soviet troops descended from Siberia.

Atrocities

On 29-30 July 1937, in Tungchow the Japanese-trained Chinese garrison attacked and killed Japanese and Korean civilians while Japanese troops were deployed elsewhere in the Peking-Tientsin area. The total killed was 225 Japanese and Korean citizens and 18 Japanese soldiers who resided in the town. (Ref. 4.5.3)

Shanghai

The battle for Shanghai was a pivotal moment for General Chiang Kai-shek and Admiral Osami Nagano. On 13 August 1937, the Chinese air force bombed and strafed the Japanese naval aircraft base and the flagship Izumo of the Third Fleet offshore. Navy Minister Admiral Mitsumasa Yonai's bellicose response was "to teach the Chinese a lesson." Initially he was of the non-expansion camp, but he became an ardent supporter of the expansionist faction in the military as a result of this confrontation.

There were 12,000 Japanese sailors and marines stationed in Shanghai protecting the 25,000 Japanese civilian residents of the city. Within Shanghai, there were 60,000 Europeans and 4,000 Americans living in various international settlements. General Chiang Kai-shek hoped that some of these nations with treaty concessions would get involved and oppose Japanese troops entering the city.

Emperor Hirohito appointed General Iwane Matsui as Commander of the Shanghai Expeditionary Force on 15 August 1937. He no doubt was assisted by his old friend from Geneva, Admiral Nagano. The Force, composed of troops from Japanese home islands, Korea and Taiwan, was transported and protected by the Combined Fleet. An Imperial order was issued on 31 August to "destroy the enemy's will to resist." Among several landings there were two major landings, one west of Shanghai along the Yangtze River; the other on the north shore of Hangchow Bay. The forces made great headway inland with artillery support from the Third Fleet. But, beyond the 10 mile fire range they bogged down and were mired in the marshes and swamps surrounding Shanghai. Frustration was high on both sides and casualties piled up.

Chiang Kai-shek had deployed his best trained troops, but after three months of urban warfare and Third Fleet shelling, they fled demoralized on 8 November 1937 along the Yangtze River westward to Nanking. The Chinese suffered an estimated 250,000 fatalities, many of them women and children. The Japanese lost 9,115 dead and 31,257 wounded, but in the end they occupied Shanghai. (Ref. 4.5.3) A map of the War in Shanghai from Time Magazine, 30 August 1937, is given in Figure 4.5.2.

Nanking

Hirohito authorized the IJN to bomb Nanking and the battle for the city began on 20 November 1937. This was their chance to eliminate Chiang Kai-shek's regime from China. On 10 December, General Matsui ordered his ground forces to attack Nanking and three days later he entered the city. General Matsui and Admiral Kiyoshi Hasegawa raised the Japanese flag over the downtown Nationalist Government Building on 17 December. Emperor Hirohito issued an Imperial Rescript to Admiral Hasegawa applauding the officers and men of the Third Fleet for cooperating with the army, controlling China's coast and interdicting its lines of river transportation. He stated "We still have a long way to go before we achieve our goal. Increasingly strive to accomplish more victories." (Ref. 4.5.3)

Finally, Chiang Kai-shek fled by plane on 8 December to Hankhow, about 200 miles up the Yangtze River. Admiral Isoroku Yamamoto sent twenty long-range, type 96 bombers from Nagasaki to Nanking on 17 August 1937. This was a four hour, trans-ocean flight. On the same day, Prime Minister Prince Konoye's Cabinet warned "The Empire, having reached the limit of its patience, has been forced to take resolute measures. Hence forth, it will punish the outrages of Chinese army and thus spur the Nanking government to self-reflect." The Imperial Navy became one of the driving forces for Japan to occupy Nanking and eliminate General Chiang Kai-shek's influence in China.

What began as an incident, dragged on as an eight-year war. Urban warfare in a highly developed city with many foreign enclaves was not as easy as Chiang Kai-shek's troops originally assumed. Propaganda flew on both sides, not the least of which was the false reporting of Admiral Nagano's death in an attack on his flagship Nagato.

Atrocities

On 25 November 1937, the civilian population of Nanking started to flee. And thus ensued the "Rape of Nanking" that lasted for at least six weeks in the city and surrounding area. The casualties were estimated to be at least one quarter of a million Chinese soldiers and civilians from the original pre-attack population of one million. (Ref. 4.5.3) The American director of the Nanking Refugee Committee wrote "It is now Christmas Eve. In two short weeks we here in Nanking have been through a siege; the Chinese army left defeated and the Japanese army has come in. On that day, Nanking was still a beautiful city we were so proud of with law and order still prevailing; today it is a city laid waste, ravaged completely, looted, much of it burned. Complete anarchy has reigned for ten days. It has been hell on earth. ... many hundreds of innocent civilians are taken out before your eyes to be shot or used for bayonet practice and you have to listen to the sound of the guns that are killing them; and while a thousand women kneel before you crying hysterically, begging you to save them from the beasts who are preying on them; to stand by and do nothing while your flag is taken down and insulted, not once but a dozen times, and your own home is being looted; and then to watch the city you have come to love .... deliberately and systematically burned by fire – this is a hell I had never before envisaged." (Ref. 4.5.1)

USS Panay *Incident*

As the populace of Nanking fled, Japanese naval bombers and fighters bombed, strafed and sank the USS *Panay* on 12 December 1937. The gunship was transporting American civilian evacuees on the Yangtze River when three sailors were killed and 43 sailors and 5 civilians were wounded as a result of the attack.

HMS *Ladybird* and HMS *Bee* were also bombed and strafed injuring several people. Ambassador Joseph Grew believed that the attack and killing of American military men with such blatant disregard for a neutral power could provoke a war between Japan and America. It happened in Cuba in 1898 with the sinking of USS *Maine* which initiated the Spanish American war. The Americans moved a squadron of B-17 Flying Fortresses to Clark Field in the Philippines in response to the Panay Incident, but cooler heads prevailed. (Ref. 4.5.4)

Japan apologized and claimed that the boat was mistakenly bombed and paid $2.2 million in compensation. Eye witnesses refuted the excuse and testified that several American flags were clearly visible on the Panay. But neither side was ready for a confrontation in 1937. Despite President Franklin Delano Roosevelt's fireside chat on 18 October 1937 warning America of increasing tension in Asia, the American public was still mired in economic depression and isolationist in sentiment. The Panay Incident was one of the first incidents that drove home to the Americans an awareness of the China war. (Ref. 4.5.5)

Much to Ambassador Grew's surprise, the Embassy started to receive letters of apology for the Panay incident and donations from ordinary Japanese citizens. There were letters from school children which clearly showed that there were two Japans (Ref. 4.5.6) – one ruthless and the other much more caring and in line with Admiral Nagano's "True courage is power" address of a year earlier.

Report of Nagano's Death

During these cataclysmic days, the New York Times reported that 15 Chinese bombers sank the Japanese battleship Nagato on 24 November 1937 near Kiangyin and Admiral Osami Nagano later died of injuries (Ref. 4.5.7). The battleship Nagato is given in Figure 4.4.4. The Nagato was normally the capital ship of the Commander in Chief of the Combined Fleet, but the sinking and death were denied by Tokyo. The report was assumed to be Chinese propaganda for home and international consumption.

Retirement

In early November 1937, the command structure of the combined fleet was reshuffled. Admiral Zengo Yoshida was elevated to the command of the Combined Fleet. It was announced on 1 December 1937 that Admiral Nagano was retired and would sit on the Supreme War Counsel, which was made up of retired generals and admirals. Figure 4.5.3 shows Nagano with his family. The Third Fleet was separated from the Combined Fleet to be administered as an independent unit in the China Theater under the command of Admiral Hasegawa. He would serve directly under Chief of Naval Staff Prince Fushimi and Naval Minister Admiral Yonai.

Some members of the army general staff were against expansion of the China conflict. Major General Ishiwara resigned and was transferred to the Kwantung army. The non-expansionists believed that the real foe was Russia and Japan should not expand the war. General Araki stated it clearly "Do not get mired in the quagmire that China can be" (Ref. 4.5.3).

Early in 1937, General Chiang was sending Chinese troops to Shanghai's demilitarized zone and Emperor Hirohito was taking a cautious approach in China with Russia at his back. By the end of the year, Hirohito, backed up by Navy Minister Admiral Yonai, advocated the pursuit of Chiang westward back toward Chungking. The navy became a strong advocate of pursuing the China conflict in the interest of gaining access to resources in the southwest Pacific and Southeast Asia.

CHAPTER 4, PART 5 REFERENCES

4.5.1   Harries, Meirion and Susie, *Soldiers of the Sun*, Random House, New York, 1991
4.5.2   Calvocoressi, P., Wint, G. and Pritchard, J., *Total War*, Volume 2, Pantheon Books, New York, 1989
4.5.3   Bix, Herbert P., *Hirohito and the Making of Modern Japan*, Harper Collins, 2000
4.5.4   Power, T. S., "Oral History of General Thomas S. Power," Columbia University Library
4.5.5   Roosevelt, F. D., "Fireside Chat," October 12, 1937
4.5.6   Plante, Trevor K., *Two Japans: Japanese Expressions of Sympathy and Regret in the Wake of the* Panay *Incident*, Prologue, Summer 2001, Vol. 33, No. 2
4.5.7   *New York Times*, "Chinese Report Death of Nagano," December 15, 1937, pg. 19

TABLE 4.5.1

CHRONOLOGY OF EVENTS LEADING TO THE CHINA WAR

8 July 1937	Marco Polo Bridge incident
27 July 1937	Japanese North China army started campaign to drive Chinese from Peking area
29-30 July 1937	Tungchow Massacre – 243 Japanese and Koreans killed by Chinese troops in town
8 August 1937	Japanese troops entered Peking
8 November 1937	General Chiang Kai-shek fled Shanghai
20 November 1937	Emperor Hirohito approved bombing of Nanking
25 November 1937	Civilian and government officials evacuated Nanking
8 December 1937	General Chiang Kai-shek fled Nanking by plane to Hankow
10 December 1937	General Iwane Matsui ordered Japanese troops to attack Nanking
12 December 1937	USS Panay sunk and HMS Ladybird strafed in the Yangtze River by Japanese navy planes
13 December 1937	General Iwane Matsui entered Nanking
17 December 1937	General Iwane Matsui and Admiral Kiyoshi Hasegawa raised Japanese flag over the Nationalist Government headquarters

Figure 4.5.1 Commander in Chief Admiral Osami Nagano. Magazine cover "Dominant Over the Ocean," Spring 1937

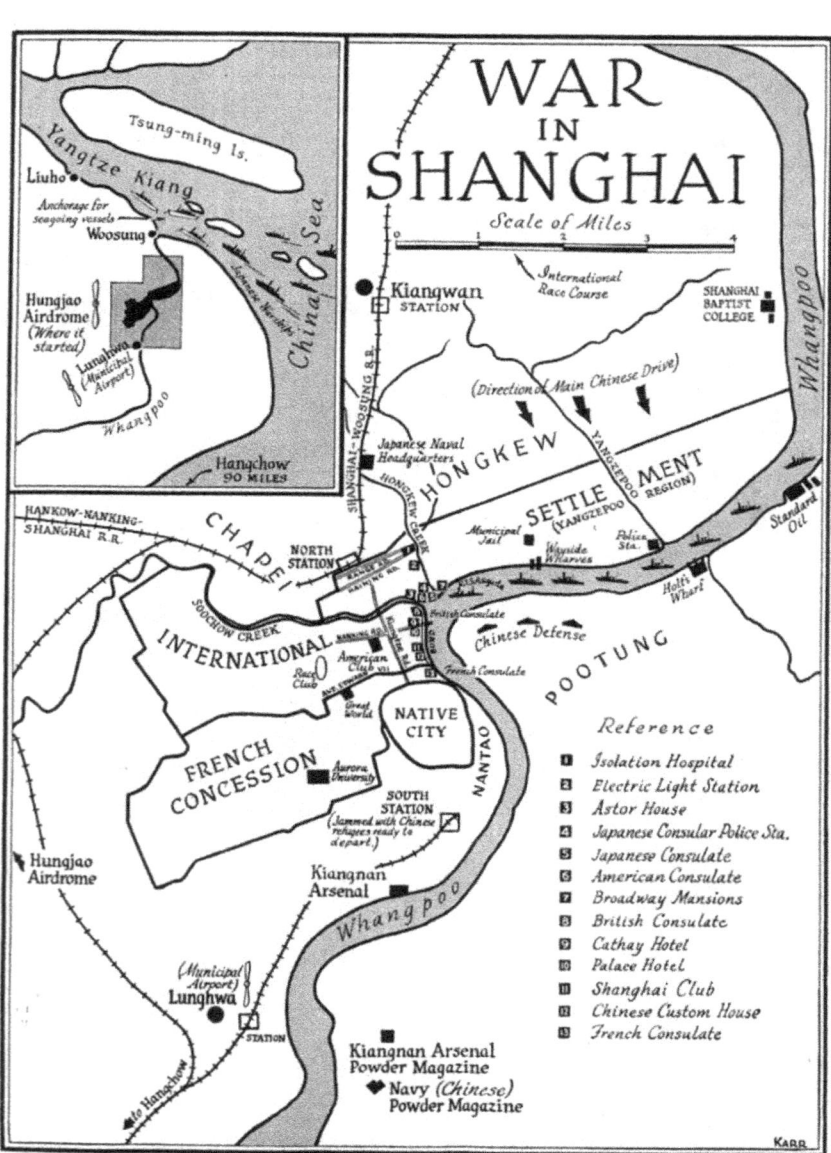

Figure 4.5.2 War in Shanghai from Time Magazine, 30 August 1937

Figure 4.5.3 Commander Nagano with family

Figure 4.5.4 Battleship Nagato, Flagship of the Commander-in-Chief of the Combined Fleet

Chapter 4

Diplomat, Sailor and Politician

1930 to 1941

PART 6:

THE RETIREE AND CELEBRITY: 2 DECEMBER 1937 – 8 APRIL 1941

Family life and Extraordinary Festival

IN retirement, Admiral Nagano had time to pursue his avocations and to develop skills as an amateur photographer. Figure 4.6.1 shows his artistic side with a Madonna-style photograph of his wife, Kyoko and baby Sakiko. He also enjoyed some manual labor as seen in Figures 4.6.2 and 4.6.3 where the admiral busied himself tending the garden at his home in Ishikawa. He enjoyed spending time with his family. Figure 4.6.4 shows Nagano with his wife Kyoko and their children Makoto, Misako and Takaaki in about 1938. His daughter, Hisako, and son, Hiroshi, from his third wife, Yu, are also included in the figure.

On 15 March 1941, Admiral Nagano was appointed Chief of the Extraordinary Festival of the Commemoration of the Yasukuni Shrine, see Figure 4.6.5. With the ongoing China War and the recent Nomonhan Incident, Japanese war dead had swollen to over 100,000. The Shrine is analogous to the Arlington National Cemetery in America, but it has become a point of contention with China and Korea when a Japanese government official visits the shrine. Among the dead are several Class A war criminals who were convicted at the Tokyo War Crimes Trial in 1947 (Ref. 4.6.1).

Sake cups and German-Russian Neutrality Pact, 1939

On 18 November 1938, Emperor Hirohito presented Nagano with silver sake cups engraved with the imperial symbol of the chrysanthemum in appreciation for his concluding the Anti-Comintern Pact with Nazi Germany while he was Navy Minister in 1936 (see Figure 4.6.6). Hitler wanted an alliance with Japan to keep Russia busy in the east, but many in the Japanese military and Foreign Service were against too close an alliance with Germany since it would complicate relations with Britain and America. Admiral Nagano's negotiating skills were put to good use because the Anti-Comintern Pact did not mention Russia explicitly. This satisfied all factions and only stated explicitly that the countries – Germany and Japan – were against communist subversion. These were terms every one could accept. However, there was a secret provision which stated that the Pact "committed the signatories not to assist Moscow in the event of war between one of them and the Soviet Union." On 23 August 1939, however, Stalin accepted a Neutrality Pact offered by Hitler. The Japanese were shell shocked since it was a direct violation of the Anti-Comintern Pact's secret provision. Thereafter, Japan directed her strategic interest to the Far East and did not try to coordinate war efforts with Hitler until she was reluctantly dragged into a Tripartite Pact by Yosuke Matsuoka (see Part 7, Chapter 4). Hitler disregarded treaties unless they were in his own self interest. In the end, this led to his demise.

Politics and Democracy

The various successive Japanese cabinets, from 1937 to 1941, tended to increase the political power of the military. Along the way they eventually eliminated political parties. Democracy, as practiced in the West, was fading and a Hitler-style, one-party rule was established. With the imperial system, young zealots in the military tended to respect the Emperor's divinity and ultimate authority, but they pursued their own militaristic agendas not necessarily in harmony with the Prime Minister and his cabinets. Cabinets came and went, mainly at the whim of the Army or Navy. The rotation of Prime Ministers during this era was as follows:

- General Senjuro Hayashi, 28 February 1937 – 31 May 1937
- Prince Fumimaro Konoye (first cabinet), 3 June 1937 – 4 January 1939
- Baron Kiichiro Hiranuma, 5 January 1939 – 27 August 1939
- General Nobuyuki Abe, 30 August 1939 – 12 January 1940
- Admiral Mitsumasa Yonai, 14 January 1940 – 16 July 1940
- Prince Fumimaro Konoye (second cabinet), 21 July 1940 – 19 July 1941
- Prince Fumimaro Konoye (third cabinet), 21 July 1941 – 18 October 1941

Many forces – economic, political, financial, military and social – were at work and tended to be compartmentalized and the Emperor became more involved to orient them in a unified whole (Ref. 4.6.2). The military realized that to be a world player they had to prepare for "total war." The army favored a Nazi-style, regimented society and incorporated fascist traits such as secret police and patriotic associations. Starting in 1937, industry was place on a war-footing and huge military budgets became the norm. With the expiration of the Washington Naval Treaty of 1922 (Part 4, Chapter 4), Naval Minister Nagano proposed an enormous escalation of the navy's 1937 budget.

Hirohito appointed General Nobuyuki Abe as Prime Minister to ensure that a militaristic economy would produce hardware for the army. Abe's Cabinet lasted only four and a half months as events swirled around in Europe and Asia. Poland was overrun and a "phony" war progressed on the western front with France. A converted naval "dove," Admiral Yonai, was installed as Prime Minister and lasted until France fell in July 1940 and the British Expeditionary Army fled France at Dunkirk with barely the shirts on their backs. Hitler was the master of Europe – except for the British Isles. The Far East resources were now "up for the asking" since the western powers were defeated. Japan saw her chance to control the Far East.

The one wild card was America. In 1940, President Franklin Roosevelt made an unprecedented successful bid for a third term – in his words "These are unprecedented times." The American people, having emerged from the war "to end all wars," were not eager to be drawn into another skirmish. The sentiment was: "Let the Europeans fight their own wars." There was more sympathy for China being trampled by a superior Japanese army.

Outer Mongolia Debacle – Nomonhan Incident

As the march to Armageddon proceeded in Europe from 1937 to 1941, the Japanese military saw their chance to spread outward from China. During Barron Hiranuma's premiership, however, the army stubbed its toes in a border incident with Russia at Nomonhan, an isolated town on the border between Outer Mongolia (a puppet state of Soviet Russia) and Manchukuo. The battle lasted from 11 May to 22 August 1939 and the Japanese were soundly defeated, losing 50,000 soldiers to the superior Russian army. The Russians were led by General Georgi Zhukov who went on to fame on the eastern front against German troops from 1941 – 1945 (Ref 4.6.3). A cease fire and armistice was arranged by Japanese Ambassador Togo in Moscow and both sides disengaged. Russia had other concerns to the west and accepted the Neutrality Pact offered by Hitler in August 1939. The Japanese army never again tried to take on the Russians until it was overwhelmed in the last days of World War II in August 1945. As a member of the Supreme War Council, Admiral Nagano was cognizant of these events and his role became pivotal as will be seen in Part 7, Chapter 4. Figure 4.6.7 shows the retired admiral aboard ship with his family.

Chapter 4, Part 6 References

4.6.1 International Military Tribunal for the Far East (Tokyo War Crimes Trial) 1946-1948, New York University Law Library
4.6.2 Bix, Herbert P., *Hirohito and the Making of Modern Japan*, Harper Collins Publishers, New York, 2000
4.6.3 Goldman, Stuart G., "A Long Shadow," *World War II*, May 2009

Figure 4.6.1 Nagano's photographic art of wife and child

Figure 4.6.2 The Admiral in his garden with paddle which reads "Long Life"

Figure 4.6.3 Retirement is hard work

Figure 4.6.4 The Admiral and family. Left to right: Hiroshi, Makoto, Takaaki, Kyoko, Misako, Hisako

Figure 4.6.5 Chairman of Extraordinary Festival

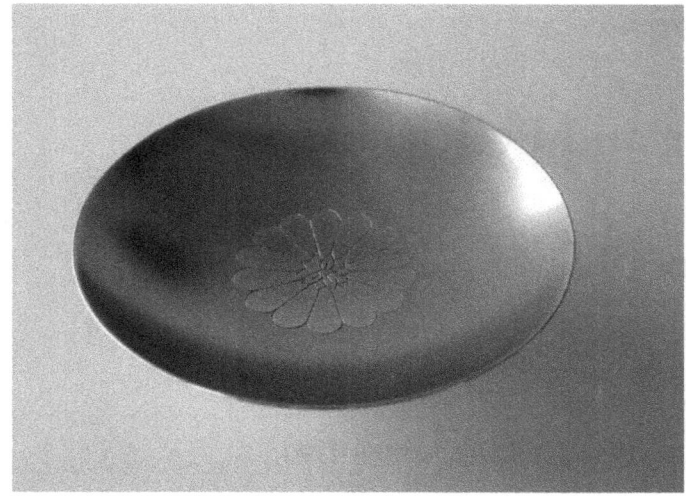

Figure 4.6.6 Sake cup presented to Admiral Nagano

Figure 4.6.7 Makato, Takaaki, Admiral Nagano, Sakiko, Kyoko, Misako. "On board Battleship Mikasa, front deck with my loving family" The Mikasa was the flagship of the Combined Fleet during the battle of Tsushima under the command of Admiral Togo.

Chapter 4

Diplomat, Sailor and Politician

1930 to 1941

Part 7:

Concerned Warrior, 9 April 1941 to 8 December 1941

Brief Summary of World Events

- 1940 was a tumultuous time on the world stage. On 9/10 May, "The Phony War" in Western Europe turned out to be not so phony when German troops spread across the Netherlands, Belgium and Luxembourg, outflanking the Maginot Line. They entered Paris on 14 June. In Versailles, Hitler mocked the peace treaty that was signed there in 1919.
- As England prepared for invasion, Winston Churchill replaced Neville Chamberlain as Prime Minister on 10 May 1940. As German troops advanced, the British Expeditionary Force in France barely escaped with the shirts on their backs. During the two weeks from 24 May to 6 June 1940, they were rescued at Dunkirk by an improvised armada of public and private vessels.
- Not to be excluded from this cauldron of events, Joseph Stalin incorporated Estonia, Latvia and Lithuania into the Union of Soviet Socialist Republic (USSR) on 25 August 1940. He had previously invaded Finland on 30 November 1939 where he signed a peace treaty on 12 March 1940.
- Benito Mussolini sent Italian troops into Greece on 25 October 1940 with disastrous consequence and had to be rescued by Hitler.
- On 21 July 1940, Emperor Hirohito selected Prince Fumimaro Konoye as Prime Minister of Japan. Konoye who was dubbed the "political hypochondriac." Figure 4.7.1 shows Konoye's cabinet which included:
  - Yosuke Matsuoka, Foreign Minister
  - General Hideki Tojo, Army Minister
  - Admiral Zengo Yoshida, Navy Minister
- Unmindful of world events, the New York World's Fair opened in 1939 in tranquil Flushing Meadow Park under the slogan "World of Tomorrow." Media commentary centered on the Soviet pavilion versus those of Ford and General Motors modernistic presentations. In its second year, the Fair reopened on a more somber note (14 May 1940). President Franklin D. Roosevelt decided in July to try for an unprecedented third term, citing unprecedented times.

Tripartite Pact and Neutrality Pact with Soviet Union

Germany, Italy and Japan established an alliance, which was solidified by their signing the Tripartite Pact on 27 September 1940. The Pact stipulated that if one of the three signatories were attacked by an outside power (i.e. America), the others would declare war on the aggressor. The Imperial Navy was particularly troubled by the terms of the Pact but Prince Hiroyasu Fushimi, Chief of Naval General Staff, reluctantly gave his approval. Navy Minister Admiral Zengo Yoshida resigned in protest.

The setting was that, in July of 1940, Foreign Minister Yosuke Matsuoka had big ideas for cooperating with Germany – the master of Europe from the Soviet border to the Spanish border. His predecessor, Hachiro Arita, had been working on a pact with Germany to gain access to strategic materials (oil, rubber, copper, tin), which were available in French Indochina and Netherlands East Indies. These colonies were currently rather rudderless since their mother countries were under Hitler's thumb. Japan had ideas of her own to establish the *"Greater East Asia Co-Prosperity Sphere."* Arita had discussed a tentative agreement with Germany whereby Japan would put pressure on Britain in East Asia and Germany would let Japan establish hegemony over the Dutch, French and British possessions. But Japan would not join the European war.

Matsuoka believed that Arita's arrangement was too tame because it did not take into account the potential U.S. interference. He formulated terms for the Tripartite Pact, aligning Japan with Germany, as an explicit deterrent to U.S. involvement in the European conflict. Matsuoka held the belief that the world was divided into spheres of influence, i.e. Japan in charge of Asia and Western Pacific, Germany had Europe and America commanded the Western Hemisphere. Of course, human destiny does not always turn out as planned. As events unfolded, rather than America attacking Germany, Japan attacked Pearl Harbor and Germany declared war on America. Toland recounted that Hitler was taken by surprise, but he was also elated exclaiming "Japan has not been defeated in the last 1000 years!" Nevertheless, upon reflection, he had grave doubts the morning after (Ref. 4.7.1).

Imperial Conference – 19 September 1940

The Imperial Conference of 19 September 1940 was convened to obtain the Emperor's approval for the Tripartite Pact. President of the Privy Counsel Yoshimichi Hara, spoke for the Emperor declaring that the Pact was "a treaty of alliance with the United States as its target." Germany and Italy intended to prevent American entry into the European war by making the pact public. Hara presented the position that "the United States has been acting as a watchdog in Eastern Asia in place of Great Britain. She has applied pressure to Japan but she has probably been restraining herself in order to prevent Japan from joining Germany and Italy." He went on "But when Japan's position becomes clear with the announcement of this Pact, she will greatly increase her pressure on us, she will greatly step up her aid to Chiang, and she will obstruct Japan's war effort." (Ref. 4.7.2)

Matsuoka opposed Hara's point. He contended that the pact would prevent America from joining Britain in the European war. America had already commandeered British positions in Asia and constrained the Netherlands East Indies and French Indochina from exporting oil and other strategic goods to Japan. Added economic pressure was exerted by refusing to import Japanese goods. Most importantly, Japan could not conduct war without oil in storage. Matsuoka maintained that the pact would neutralize America. He responded "We hope to get Germany to apply pressure on Netherlands East Indies and, if we abandon China, America might join hands with us, at least for the time being." Matsuoka was a newcomer to these inner sanctum discussions and he probably would not have made that comment later on.

Current American sentiment was strongly anti-Japanese, not to be reversed by a few conciliatory gestures. Matsuoka proclaimed "Only a firm stand on our part will prevent war. Hitler's idea is to avoid war with the U.S. if he can." Hara pondered what Japan's response would be if America encircled Japan by leasing bases in Australia and New Zealand. He mused "Would this be considered an act of war? America was a self-confident nation. Would a firm stand on our part have the opposite effect to what the Foreign Minister anticipates?" Matsuoka avowed "Japan is a great power with a great navy. America may stiffen and apply economic pressure, but I think she will take a responsible attitude – but the odds are fifty-fifty."

Prince Fushimi called for a decision to accept the Pact, presenting the following positions (Ref. 4.7.2):

"I foresee that as a result of this alliance our trade with Great Britain and the United States will undergo a change and that, if worse comes to worst, it will become increasingly difficult to import vital materials. Moreover, it is quite likely that a Japanese-American war will be a protracted one. What are the prospects for maintaining our national strength in view of the present situation, which finds our national resources deplete because of the 'China Incident' and what measures are contemplated?"

He added:

1. "...that even though the alliance is concluded, every conceivable measure will be taken to avoid war with the United States.
2. ...that the southward advance would be attempted as far as possible by peaceful means and that useless friction with third parties will be avoided.
3. ...that unrestrained discussion of the conclusion of this pact will not be permitted and that harmful, anti-British and anti-American statements and behavior will be restrained." (Ref. 4.7.2)

This close alliance with Germany disturbed many in the military and civilian bureaucracies, especially the older generation. But the younger generation, represented by mid-level military officers, believed that this was a golden opportunity. They saw what Hitler had accomplished in Europe and wanted to emulate him in Asia. In July 1940, with the American Regular Army legally limited to 365,000 men, they saw their chance for supremacy. Their elders saw this attitude as a stumbling block to relations with America. Regardless, the Emperor approved the Tripartite Pact.

Hara asserted "I give my approval on the ground that action to this end is essential to carry on the China Incident, and in the light of the changing international situation. We will encounter many difficulties in the future. We cannot be optimistic about the possibility of an American embargo. Even though a Japanese-American clash may be unavoidable in the end, I hope that sufficient care will be exercised to make sure that it will not come in the near future, and that there will be no miscalculations I give my approval on this basis."

Matsuoka, in his short, one-year term as Foreign Minister, concluded several important treaties in simple and straight-forward language. But these treaties had dire consequences for Japan, especially the alliance with Germany and Italy and the Neutrality Pact with Russia. Figure 4.7.2 shows Chancellor Hitler signing the pact on 27 September 1940. He is seen in Figure 4.7.3 shaking the hand of a confident Matsuoka during his triumphal tour of Europe (March to April 1941).

The Neutrality Pact with Soviet Russia

During March-April 1941, Matsuoka traveled to Rome and Berlin, stopping in Moscow both going to Europe and on his return to Tokyo. In fact he remained six days in Moscow, discussing treaty concessions that included access to the Northern Sakhalin oil and fishing rights. But, the proposal of a formal Neutrality Pact was a surprise – even for him. The treaty, known as the Japanese-Soviet Nonaggression Pact, provided terms for security of each nation in the event of attack by a third party. If any third party (America) attacked Japan, Russia would remain neutral and, conversely, if any country attacked Russia, Japan would stay neutral. The agreement also satisfied the Imperial Navy, which feared Russia at its back and, facing American forces in Asia. The Neutrality Pact would prevent a two-front battle in the Western Pacific. Russia wanted the accord with Japan in case of any strike from Germany. Since Hitler had already signed a Neutrality Pact with Stalin (August 1939), Japan felt free to do likewise.

The Japanese-Soviet Neutrality Pact (see Appendix F) was signed on 13 April 1941 by Vyacheslav M. Molotov, Yosuke Matsuoka and Ambassador Yoshitsugu Tatekawa. The irony was that only two years previously, Japan and Russia were embroiled in the 1939 Nomonhan border war – now Russia was looking west and Japan was setting her sights eastward. The former enemies were in agreement to leave each other alone.

Matsuoka reported to the 20th Liaison Conference on 22 April 1941:

"I met with Molotov three times, but because he stuck to his opinion and would make no concessions, I thought that the pact could not be agreed upon. I, therefore, expressed my ideas to him rather bluntly and gave him a letter in English for future reference. That evening, I received a phone call stating that Stalin could see me anytime the following day, so I made an appointment for 5:00 o'clock the following day. At 5:00 o'clock the following afternoon I greeted Stalin in his room. I took the opportunity to speak on *Hakko-ichi-u*[2]. Stalin had on his desk the protocol of the Neutrality Pact and the letter I had handed to Molotov and was impatient with my *Hakko-ichi-u*. Presently Stalin said 'I trust you and Konoye....' Stalin sent for a map and insisted that we sell Southern Sakhalin[3]. I stated Northern Sakhalin had belonged to Japan since the 16th century until it was divided by Russia and since then our nation had wanted to recover it... Our conversation became more and more interesting[4] and, at last, we agreed to conclude the pact." (Ref. 4.7.2) (See Figure 4.7.4 showing Matsuoka signing the pact with Stalin looking on.)

Conversations among Matsuoka, von Ribbentrop and Hitler, in April 1941 presented in the Tokyo War Crime Reports gave the impression that Germany was less interested in Japan going south and taking Singapore but that the enemy at the time was Russia—again. Matsuoka tended to ignore these hints.

Admiral Nagano Becomes Chief of Naval General Staff

In the midst of all this turmoil, Prince Fushimi (a relative of Emperor Hirohito) fell ill and asked to be relieved of his post (see Figures 4.7.5, 4.7.6 and 4.7.7). He had been Chief of Naval Staff for ten years and, if not physically ill, he was probably mentally fatigued. In this critical period of Japanese history, he recommended Admiral Osami Nagano to be his successor on 9 April 1941. The retired Admiral Nagano claimed to be chronically ill but he respected the Prince and, believing he had a duty to obey, stepped out of his retirement and into the office (see Figure 4.7.8). In his post-war writings, Nagano portrayed his personal involvement in his country's history (Ref. 4.7.3)

" ... In April of Showa 16 (1941), when Prince Fushimi, then Chief of Naval Staff, recommended me to the post he was to vacate due to his illness, I had great reservations; firstly due to my own chronic health matter, but also as I was not confident enough to properly handle the Army when our nation was facing the most difficult period of time.

This, however, was a special consideration for me on part of the Prince, Chief of Staff, which one does not and could not decline too lightly.

More importantly, I felt that if I do not accept, somebody who also lacks confidence may be forced to fill the position. After all, there were so many Army Elders involved where Navy definitely needed some old hand – like myself. I, therefore, ultimately decided to dedicate my life at the time of extreme difficulties of our nation... Even today, I have no regret about the decision I took at that time.

---

[2] Literally "eight corners of the world under one roof," a concept of universal brotherhood that came to mean Japanese domination of Asia.

[3] Northern Sakhalin was occupied by Russia.

[4] Dividing up Asia.

Well, in April of Showa 16, when I did become the Chief of Naval Staff, the China Incident was in its fourth year with no decisive progress as Army expected earlier and no apparent prospect to bring the enemy to a complete defeat.

Following the Tripartite Pact of the previous year (1940), war propaganda by the military clique increased; far-right wing was strengthened and became increasingly active; threat by the terrorist became rampant.

The relationship with the U.S./UK steadily deteriorated and any attempt to ease the tension was proving extremely difficult. Difficulties in the U.S./Japan negotiation were also added by the working-level of the U.S. State Department which kept hardening its position against Japan.

From Japan's view point, major obstacles were the issue of (demanded) withdrawal from China and the question of the Tripartite Treaty. The 'withdrawal' would cause serious 'loss of face' for the Army and the Tripartite Pact, born under the very leadership of the Army would be next to impossible to introduce any modification that could satisfy the U.S./UK. Army steadfastly maintained its strong trust and reliance on Germany.

Thus, Japan's negotiation with the U.S./UK based on Army's belief and 'guidelines' was difficult to improve. It was an unfortunate fact that no one could persuade Army to amend its fundamental belief and approach.

As for the Navy, Prince Chief of Staff at the time of concluding the Tripartite Pact expressed at the Imperial Council that "even if the Treaty is to be finally signed, we must not go to war against U.S./UK (owing to the Treaty)." And such view had not changed within the Navy.

As I stated earlier, the war against China continued with growing difficulties while the diplomatic negotiation was reaching a highly sensitive point and the domestic tension also continue to heighten.

Under those circumstances, any serious feud between Army and Navy could have touched off domestic unrest even some limited riot which would only please China and help strengthen their resolve against Japan. No doubt, the U.S./UK observing such development would harden their attitude further.

Considering this situation, any confrontation between Army and Navy had to be avoided at all cost, simply to prevent ultimate domestic catastrophe. Such catastrophe at that time would have destroyed our nation right there.

It is most regrettable that no one could change the course of the current which stemmed from the Army's conviction but, then, the war itself was not entirely Japan's fault either.

There were apparently many of those who were simply against Japan or set to humiliate this country among the U.S. national leadership at the State Department, even among the ranks of U.S. military – they were very active indeed.

The (unilateral) breach of the Treaty of Commerce and the evident manipulation of Holland to cut her oil supply to Japan were in fact the U.S. attempt to destroy Japan further to annihilate Japanese people without engaging actual military power.

The U.S. military assistance to China already far exceeded the norm of open military alliance. The U.S./UK rapidly increased their military facilities (targeting Japan) especially the airfields apparently designed to attack our nation.

This is what finally forced Japan to commence its 'War of Self-Defense.'

At this time, I will not go any further as others may debate separately.

> We endeavored without unruly political intrigues to prevent the War against the U.S./UK but admittedly could not cope with the formidable current of power as initiated and defended by the Army (to this end).
> This is my deep-felt regret and sincerest repentance."

In the Imperial and Liaison Conferences during summer and fall of 1941, Admiral Nagano (shown in Figure 4.7.9) was forthright in his comments on the Navy's search for oil and, at the same time, indicating a glimmer of hope in the quest for peace with America. He repeatedly stated "I feel confident in a short war with America (one to two years) as happened with the Russo-Japanese war of 1904-1905, but not in a prolonged war (greater than two years)." On 31 July 1941, in an audience with Emperor Hirohito, Nagano expressed the Navy's concern for oil supply following an embargo by America. He also confided his worry over Japan's odds in a U.S.-Japan war.

Kido recorded in his diary (Ref. 4.7.4):

1. "Nagano's opinion regarding war is the same as Prince Fushimi's. He said that we should focus our efforts on trying to avoid war as much as possible.
2. He entertains a strong opposition to the Tripartite Pact, which is, according to his opinion, a great hindrance to the restoration of friendship between America and Japan.
3. If the restoration of diplomatic relations between the U.S.A. and Japan is impossible, we will be cut off from supplies of oil, our store of which will run out in two years if we leave the matter as it now is. And if we open a war with the U.S.A., the supply of oil will fail in one and a half years. Under these circumstances, he was of the opinion that the bolder course would be better.
4. According to the report of the Navy, the future prospects for a war are not so discouraging, and he is of the opinion that we would gain a victory, even if it was not the sweeping victory we secured in the Russo-Japanese War. But Admiral Nagano's overall outlook on a war is quite pessimistic."

Kido expressed "trepidation by the imperial anxiety that our war against the U.S.A. would be a hopeless one. My answer to the imperial words was as follows:

1. Admiral Nagano's opinion was too simple.
2. The U.S.A. had recognized the existence of the Tripartite Pact in our previous parley with America, and I was very doubtful whether we could deepen the confidence of the U.S.A. in us by annulling the treaty, for the U.S.A. was a nation which showed respect for an international treaty. We would only be held in contempt by the U.S.A. We are not quite out of means for the restoration of friendship between America and Japan. We must deliberate on the matter in a constructive manner. I would demand the premier's careful consideration to this point.

I met with Navy Minister Oikawa at noon to talk over Admiral Nagano's report to the Throne. The chief aide-de-camp to the Emperor visited me at one o'clock to talk with me on the same subject. Prince Konoye visited me in my office. I talked with him after he left the imperial presence, from 3:40 to 4:05 pm."

The Emperor's anxiety was relieved somewhat by Prince Konoye's "quest for peace."

FRENCH INDOCHINA

Move into North French Indochina

French Indochina, the gateway to Southeast Asia (see map in Figure 4.7.10), was essential to air and naval bases for a strike at Singapore and, hence, on to the Netherlands East Indies (NEI). Foreign Minister Hachiro Arita (in Prime Minister Yonai's cabinet 14 January to 16 July 1940) asserted Japan's great interest in continuing the flow of oil from NEI. He set the diplomatic groundwork for takeover of the Dutch colony when he declared: "Especially in the Netherlands Indies, Japan is economically bound by an intimate relationship of mutuality in ministering to one another's needs ...and cannot but be deeply concerned over any development ... that may affect the status of Netherlands Indies." In other words "don't meddle with us, this is our turf" (Ref. 4.7.5).

Economically, the NEI was the top rubber producer and third largest oil producer in the world in 1940. Japan's imported goods from the NEI included 25% of their oil requirements (in normal times). They also imported sugar, coffee, quinine, tobacco, copra, spices, cattle, lumber, coal, tin, gold, silver, textiles and cheap manufactured goods. America also depended upon NEI for supplies of rubber and tin and rivaled Japan's interest in these commodities.

For decades, the Imperial Army had been marching aggressively all over East Asia, but was repeatedly pulled back by the leadership in Tokyo. In July 1940, the Imperial Japanese South China Army sent Major General I. Nishihara, a French-speaking Japanese officer with experience at the League of Nations, to Hanoi to negotiate with the French Consul General to station troops in Haiphong and Gulf of Tonkin area. The army's presence would cut off supplies to Generalissimo Chiang Kai-shek in Chunking by closing Haiphong Harbor and eventually the Burma Road all the way to its terminus at Kunming. The intent was to settle the China Incident once and for all. Apparently, the Army General Staff in Tokyo was not aware of the impenetrable topography and difficulty in going directly to Kunming as they had initially intended.

However, in June 1940, General Kyoji Tominaga and a cabal of junior officers from the Imperial South China Army flew to Hanoi and stormed into the office of the Consul General with swords drawn. The demand was entry of Japanese troops into French Indochina and, if opposed, there would be bloodshed. Their goal was to create a "Mukden-style" incident and take over all of French Indochina. Later when these details were reported to Matsuoka, he complained bitterly to General Tojo who at this point was not willing to stage a coup. Tojo ordered Tominaga and company back to their barracks. Later some of these officers were court marshaled and Tominaga was sent to Manchukuo (Ref. 4.7.6). Moreover, there had been no formal approval from the Emperor for this incursion.

Matsuoka wanted to peacefully gain access to northern French Indochina and started negotiations with Vichy France. He also demanded that Britain close the Burma Road, which she did. This was July 1940 and Britain, having just fled continental Europe, was in no condition to oppose Japan. France had already surrendered to Hitler on June 18th, Netherlands and Belgium had also capitulated. Matsuoka sent a negotiator to the NEI to purchase oil. But, he was rebuffed by British and American firms in control of the oil fields and refineries, which were stiffened by American resolve. Japan was almost totally dependent on imported oil and the militarists felt vulnerable.

The Imperial Navy was not pleased at the army's attempt to provoke an incident and immediately withdrew after having deposited the soldiers on the beach at Haiphong Harbor (Ref. 4.7.6). The troops could have been annihilated had Matsuoka's negotiations not succeeded at the last moment on 22 September 1940, which authorized the army's peaceful entrance into the northern sector. The resulting division of Indochina had more lasting consequences than anyone might have predicted at the time. It eventually led to the separate entities of North Vietnam and South Vietnam, which lasted until 1975.

Japan's naked power grab was little noticed by the world at large. America was preoccupied by Roosevelt's third presidential campaign, but was waking up to Japan's southward push which would endanger the viability and survival of an independent Philippines. They feared its becoming a Japanese protectorate analogous to Manchukuo. The geopolitical maneuvering was obvious and America was taking steps to counterbalance Japan's advance. But there was an isolationist sentiment in America that Roosevelt's administration had to deal with. While the Imperial Navy opposed occupation of northern French Indochina lest Japan antagonize the Americans, so far advances by the Army were bringing nothing but economic misery to the Japanese people. According to Ambassador Joseph Grew (Ref. 4.7.7), the economic and political conditions in Japan were dire and anything could happen. Extremists on the right or left might cause a *coup de etat*. Japan, with an ongoing "China Incident," was hurting. On 14 August 1941 a right-wing activist made an assassination attempt on Home Minister Hiranuma (Ref. 4.7.8). On 18 September 1941, four men attacked Prince Konoye with daggers and short swords, but were overwhelmed by plain clothes men at his residence. Ambassador Grew carried a gun to protect himself if he was attacked in the embassy compound. As he stated, he was determined to prevent a group of roughnecks from cutting him up without a struggle.

Lend Lease

America was doing business with Japan, who was importing scrap metal from demolition of the Second Avenue El in New York City and other places. Many Americans stated that this resource would 'come back at us in bullets' (which it did). But, on the whole, there was a strong isolationist sentiment in America. Having gotten into World War I in 1917 to "make the world safe for democracy," America was not eager to get involved in European or any other overseas conflicts. 'Let them fight their own conflicts, which they have been doing for the last thousand years' was the general attitude. Politically, President Roosevelt had to tread carefully because he did not have a free hand. Help to Britain and China, the only remaining allies, had to be approved by Congress. Actually, President Roosevelt, who was on a Caribbean cruise in December 1940 following his re-election, hit upon the Lend Lease concept. He explained the concept in a news conference with the following metaphor: "Who would not lend his neighbor his hose when his house was on fire." In March 1941, Congress approved seven billion dollars in Lend Lease funds and President Roosevelt, in reviewing the first shipments to England under Lend Lease, was glad to find $900,000 for fire hoses. This brought a round of laughter at the press conference. Prime Minister Churchill called the Act a "New Magna Carta... an inspiring act of faith."

Why was Lend Lease important? Up to March 1941, pursuant to the Neutrality Pact, all armaments shipped to belligerents had to be paid for with money up front. By 1941, France, Belgium and the Netherlands had succumbed and Britain was broke. President Roosevelt had been involved with disarmament in the 1920s and 1930s, which had aroused much animosity among the Allies. Therefore, rather than grant loans, materiel support was granted in exchange for territories leased for American bases. There would be no post war repayment.

Thai-French Indochina Border Clash

Japanese agents in Thailand were hard at work to incite a border clash with French Indochina for the purpose of establishing air and naval bases in southern French Indochina. Beginning in October 1940, intermittent border clashes were breaking out between Thailand and French Indochina. Using Thailand as their agent, the Imperial South China Army hoped to take over French Indochina by emulating Hitler-style "diplomacy." The long history of the border dispute dated back to 1867 when France seized part of Thailand's border area. In 1940, Japan believed that Vichy France would acquiesce to Thailand's land grab, but Vichy did not acquiesce. In fact, the French Navy shelled Bangkok.

The Imperial Army flexed its muscles and, in this adventure, the Imperial Navy acquiesced. The Army insisted that, as "the most stabilizing power in the Far East," Japan alone had the right to settle Oriental differences. Under pressure, Vichy France and Thailand, accepted the Japanese mediation. On the Japanese cruiser, Natori, in Saigon harbor, the Thai and French delegates signed an armistice under the watchful eyes of Major General Raishiro Sumita. Japan's prize for brokering the deal was monetary payment as well as air and naval bases at Cam Ranh Bay. An observer described the scene by remarking "The bows were deeper and the smiles toothier as Japan's mediators sent French and Thai delegates ashore" (Ref. 4.7.9). Formal peace terms were settled in Tokyo by the Thai and Vichy France diplomats overseen by Matsuoka. The Thai Ambassador in Washington, when asked whether accepting Japanese mediation was not like letting a fox mediate between rabbits in a cabbage patch, he replied: "What would you do if you were a rabbit?" (Ref. 4.7.10)

Konoye and Matsuoka Address the Diet, January 1941

Unrest in Asia with Japanese troop movements made the Americans and British very nervous. The British reinforced Singapore and sent troops to the Thai-Malayan border. A southward strike by the Imperial Army was rumored in Tokyo. Konoye and Matsuoka addressed the Diet to at least clarify where Japan hoped to go. Prime Minister Prince Fumimara Konoye was called the "Political Hypochondriac" presumably because every time he had to make an important and difficult decision, he took sick and went to bed. As an example, on 13 June 1941 he visited the Heian and Shinmei Shrines in Kyoto to quiet his nerves because President Wang Ching-wei, Japan's puppet in Nanking, was due in Tokyo for a week. (Ref. 4.7.8)

Generalissimo Chiang Kai-shek was America's ally in Chunking and this strained Japan's relations with the United States. But, Konoye's principal goal in his administration was to avoid war with America. He wrote in his memoir that the Meiji Constitution worked against him and, while he was responsible for civil government operations, the armed forces had supreme authority on military matters, answering only to the Emperor. That was fine in the horse and buggy days of prior centuries, but not with the demands of mechanized warfare. He tried valiantly to alter the path to war with America. The underlying reason for avoiding war was the relative lack of physical assets of Japan as a poor nation, which imported most of its physical needs. One answer to this physical dilemma was the touted "Greater East Asia Co-Prosperity Sphere" that would elevate Japan to the status of a world power.

Prime Minister Konoye's aversion to war with America was affected by Japan's experience in the China War, which began during his first term as prime minister (June 1937 to January 1939). The conflict was euphemistically known as the "China Incident" because American laws forbade trading with any nation at war. In his State of the Empire address to the Japanese Diet (27 January 1941), Prince Konoye acknowledged (Ref. 4.7.11):

> "It is five years since the start of the China conflict, billions of yen spent and 100,000 Japanese lives sacrificed. I must apologize to the Emperor and public at large. ... The fact that the 'China Incident' is still unsettled is neither the fault of the military nor of anyone else. I am alone responsible. I am determined, as my last public service, to settle this incident."

With the China War on his conscience, Konoye did not want another one.

Foreign Minister Yosuke Matsuoka was volatile in his oratory and dealings. He was Japan born but educated in America, which included a law degree from the University of Oregon. His character was, in one word, mercurial. He had certain underlying principles that were sometimes submerged in his rhetoric, what he pronounced on one day might be reversed the next day. Nonetheless, Matsuoka touted moral diplomacy, but moral diplomacy went out the window with Hitler's attack on Russia. Ambassador Joseph Grew, in his first encounter with Matsuoka, was favorably impressed with his forthrightness, but further dealings with him left Ambassador Grew disillusioned. Like Konoye, Matsuoka wanted to avoid war with America and his actions were oriented in that direction, or so he thought. He negotiated the Tripartite Pact to keep America out of the European war.

Matsuoka had a vision of the world as he related in his Diplomacy Address to the Diet on 11 January 1941 (Ref. 4.7.12) as follows:

> "Japan, Germany and Italy certainly would accomplish their goal of a new world order, if only given time and express the hope that the U.S. will bend her utmost efforts to allay impending crisis of civilization.
>
> Should both the U.S. and Japan become involved in a new world war because of the triple military alliance, no one could guarantee that it would not develop into a war spelling the downfall of modern civilization.
>
> He continued, "U.S. trade embargoes against Japan left this country no alternative save to build up a self-sufficient trade sphere in the Greater East Asia.
>
> Establishment of a new world order, the goal of the powerful triple Pact, if only given time will surely be accomplished.
>
> The U.S. apparently entertains the idea that her first line of national defense lies along the mid Atlantic in the east and not only westward along the entire Pacific but even as far as China and South Seas.
>
> It is my earnest hope that great nation, exerting the influence that the U.S. legitimately does, will realize her responsibility for the maintenance of peace, will reflect deeply on her attitude with a truly God-fearing duty, will courageously liquidate part of the circumstances and will bend her utmost efforts to allay the impending crisis of civilization.
>
> Should the U.S., unfortunately, become involve in the European war and should Japan, too, be compelled to participate in war, another great world war, both in name and reality, would ensue and precipitate a situation which would defy all attempts at saving it.
>
> Should the war take its furious course, unleashing formidable new weapons, which have not hitherto been used, no one could guarantee that it would not develop into a war spelling the downfall of modern civilization."

The formidable new weapons to which Matsuoka was referring were probably chemical, biological weapons and even rockets that were being developed by the army in Manchuria. He may also been aware of the fission research at Tokyo University cyclotron. Most likely he was aware of some of this research since he was president of the South Manchurian Railroad Co. from 1935 to 1939.

Debates on the Empire's Strategy and Admiral Nagano's Quest for Oil

June of 1941 was an important month for the Japanese hierarchy and their next step in the southern or northern strategy. Hitler's legions were poised for Germany's next adventure and the British were bracing for an invasion. America was rearming and, at the same time, helping the Allies by providing the tools for their defense. Basically, the Allies included Britain, Canada, Australia, New Zeeland, Netherlands East Indies, China and, after Hitler's invasion, Russia but as we will note the Allies will differ by theater of operation.

Around 1 June 1941, General Hiroshi Oshima, Japanese Ambassador in Berlin, was invited to Berchtesgaden by Hitler and told about "Operation Barbarossa" – the attack on Russia that was planned for 21/22 June 1941. Oshima alerted Tokyo – America was also alerted having broken the Japanese diplomatic code. Hitler realized the gravity of his adventure and invoked God's blessing to get the German people behind him – ignoring his previous immoral acts (Ref. 4.7.1). German troops attacked on the 8000 mile front from the Arctic Circle to the Caspian Sea.

Hitler's attack on Russia threw the Japanese into confusion and dismay – not the least of them was Matsuoka. Japan was debating her next step with an eye toward the resources of the south in French Indochina and the Netherlands East Indies. It required nine liaison conferences, which was partly due to complications resulting from Hitler's invasion. A southern strategy had already been worked out between the Imperial Army and Navy and within the Supreme Command there was a united front. Now they had to get the Prime Minister and Foreign Minister on board to present the southern strategy to the Emperor for approval. This turned out to be more difficult in light of the German-Soviet war.

The Liaison Conferences were held at the Imperial Palace for the most important actors to debate of a pros and cons of a decision to be presented for the Emperor's approval at the Imperial Conference. Conference attendees included the Prime Minister, Foreign Minister, Army and Navy Ministers and Chiefs of Army and Navy General Staffs. Each of these principals stated their opinions as follows:

Liaison Conference, 11 June 1941

Admiral Nagano affirmed "We must build bases in French Indochina and Thailand in order to launch military operations. We must resolutely attack anyone who tries to stop us. We must resort to force if we have to." During the following conferences the proposal of going into Thailand was deleted and military operations only included sending troops into southern French Indochina as the first step (Ref. 4.7.2).

Liaison Conference, 12 June 1941

Matsuoka declared "Sending in troops should be regarded as military occupation. What effect would this have on French Indochina? Japan declared she would respect the integrity of Indochina when she recently acted as a mediator in the conflict between Indochina and Thailand. Sending in troops will antagonize Britain and the United States and hasten a clash with them. We should initially state that we are going to build air and naval bases."

The principals discussed "Acceleration of the Policy Concerning the South," the document presenting the following points:

1. A military union would be established with French Indochina and troops would be sent into southern Indochina.
2. Diplomatic negotiations for this purpose would be begun and at the same time preparations would be made to send in troops. If Indochina refused to accede to Japanese demands, force would be used.
3. If Britain, United States and the Netherlands tried to obstruct Japan, and if it was necessary for her survival, she would not refuse to risk a war with Britain and the United States.

Nagano gave a briefing on this policy statement and strongly recommended using force if Great Britain, United States and the Netherlands hindered Japanese efforts. But in the end the Draft was agreed to with the following clauses added:

a. We will carry out the present Draft in the end.
b. It is permissible to negotiate on matters in two separate stages since it will take considerable time to prepare troop movements.
c. When negotiations at the first stage are completed, second stage negotiations will be started without delay.

Liaison Conference, 16 June 1941

Matsuoka continued to express his concern regarding sending troops to southern French Indochina. "The agreement of 31 August 1940 will become null and void and troops in northern French Indochina will be illegal. The recently signed mediation agreement will become null and void and it will have an effect on Netherlands East Indies and Thailand and we may not get the rubber and tin that was agreed on." He added that "If Vichy does not agree to the occupation – occupation by force is an act of bad faith. Japan is internationally stated to lack integrity. I will fight for our international reputation even if I have to fight all by myself. How can we say a forceful occupation is not an occupation? Frankly as Foreign Minister I must tell the Emperor that this is an act of bad faith..."

Sugiyama rebutted "No. We must go to southern French Indochina."

But, Admiral Oikawa argued "An alliance between Britain and Soviet Russia I have heard for the first time. If this is so, I might reconsider. However, it is not good to alter what was decided the other day." This would indicate that some sections of Supreme Command – primarily the Navy – were not well briefed on the strained relations between Germany and Russia over the last couple of months.

Tojo barked "If we don't finish the job before the end of the year, we will have to abandon our policy of establishing the 'Greater East Asia Co-Prosperity Sphere.' After the preparations are completed, what we need is a decision."

Nagano suggested "How about making all preparations and then obtaining His Majesty's approval?" But Matsuoka warned that this was not an appropriate procedure because of previous experience where, after the troops were in place, too much time was spent getting His Majesty's approval. He was adamant that it was necessary to get overall approval for the southern operation before troops could be moved into place. The military plan was to send the troops to Hainan Island which would take about 20 days and then to move them into southern French Indochina by end of July. It would take August, September and October to build the bases.

Sujiyama snapped that once approval was obtained, Matsuoka could indulge in his "blitzkrieg diplomacy."

Liaison Conference, 25 June 1941

The rumors were over – war between Russia and Germany was a fact. Matusoka tried to explain his diplomacy over the last few months which did not anticipate this event. He maintained that the Tripartite Pact was not affected by the signing of the Neutrality Pact. Furthermore, the incursion of Germany into Russia would not affect the Tripartite Pact and, therefore, the Tripartite Alliance did not come into action. Article Two of the Neutrality Pact certainly was operative mandating that Japan would "observe neutrality throughout the duration of the conflict." Matsuoka lamented "I would not have concluded the Neutrality Pact if I thought Hitler would attack Russia."

Matsuoka told the German Ambassador Eugen Ott that he would adhere to the Alliance. "If there is any change I will inform him." He told essentially the same words to the Soviet ambassador who replied "Japan is calm but nothing seems to be clear."

Matsuoka urged an aggressive policy against Russia but the Imperial Army and Navy protested:

- preparations for war are not complete
- we are still engaged in a war in China
- we are concerned about an outbreak of an incident along the border with Siberia
- we are watching very carefully both the movement of Soviet troops to the west and if the Soviet Union collapses

The military wanted to wait until the outcome of the Russian-German war was clearer before deciding on a north or south strategy.

Matsuoka chimed in: "When Germany wins and disposes of the Soviet Union, we cannot take the fruits of victory without having done something. We have to either shed blood or engage in diplomacy. It's best to shed blood. The question is what Japan would want when the Soviet Union is disposed of. Germany is probably wondering what Japan is going to do. Aren't we going to war when the enemy forces in Siberia have gone westward? Shouldn't we at least make a diversionary move?" The military replied that there were a variety of diversionary moves. "The fact that our Empire stands firm is in itself a diversionary move."

Tojo stated "The dispatch of far eastern troops to the West no doubt affects the Germans greatly but, it is natural that Japan should not feel strongly about it. We shouldn't put our complete faith in Germany."

Admiral Oikawa emphasized "The Navy is confident about a war against the United States and Britain, but not confident about a war against the United States, Britain and the Soviet Union. Suppose the Soviet Union and the Americans get together and the United States builds naval bases, air bases, radar stations, etc. on Soviet soil. Suppose the submarines stationed at Vladivostok are transferred to the United States. This would make it very difficult for naval operations. In order to avoid a situation of this kind, don't tell us to strike at Soviet Russia and also tell us to go south. The Navy does not want the Soviet Union stirred up."

Army Chief of General Staff General Sugiyama offered "We should go south to settle the China Incident by increasing pressure on Chunking regime by severing her links with Britain and the United States. This policy should not be altered by a change in the world situation. With reference to the German-Soviet war, it seems appropriate for us *not* to participate for the time being. Nevertheless, if developments of the German-Soviet war should turn out to be favorable to our Empire, I believe we would have to decide on using force to settle the northern problem. We will, in secret, make necessary preparations for military operations and be in a position to act independently."

At the end of the conference on 25 June 1941 and following the format of the Meiji Constitution, Prince Konoye, Admiral Nagano and General Sugiyama requested and the Emperor approved the movement of troops into southern French Indochina (See Meiji Constitution articles in Appendix F). Matsuoka immediately set out to reach an agreement with Vichy France, which was signed on 25 July 1941. Since America was listening in to their diplomatic code, they were aware of Japan's preparations to move troops into southern French Indochina. Japanese troops entered French Indochina peacefully, but this was the 'last straw' for the United States.

Summary of Discussions on the Document
"Outline of National Policy in View of the Changing Situation"

Liaison Conferences, 26, 27, 28, 30 June, 1 July 1941

On 25 June 1941, the document 'Acceleration of the Policy Concerning the South' was discussed and agreed to by everyone including Prince Konoye and Matsuoka as well as the military representatives; Admiral Nagano and General Sugiyama. They had obtained the Imperial sanction for troop movement into southern French Indochina. The conferees then debated a broader document entitled 'Outline of National Policy.' Vice Chief of Army General Staff General Tsukada presented the main points of the document which included:

1. "Our Empire is determined to follow a policy that will result in establishment of the Greater East Asia Co-Prosperity Sphere and will, thereby, contribute to world peace no matter what changes may occur in the world situation."
2. "Our Empire will continue its efforts to affect a settlement of the china incident and will seek to establish a solid basis for the security and preservation of the nation. This will involve taking steps to advance south and, depending on changes in the situation, will involve a settlement of the northern question as well."
3. "Our Empire is determined to remove all obstacles in order to achieve the above mentioned objectives."

Since the proposal involved a potential war with Britain and the United States, the matter was given considerable study. Matsuoka wanted to know whether taking steps to go south indicated that only preparations were to be taken into account, but Admiral Nagano was not able to explicitly state what the term meant. Admiral Nobutake Kondo, Vice Chief of Staff, stated it meant going south, not just making preparation to go south.

At the Imperial Conference on 2 July, the Emperor withheld approval to go either south or north. But Matsuoka continued to press the issue – "Which is more important? Going north or south?" In addition, he wanted to know whether Japan was going to consult Hitler on their next move. This brought a barrage of pronouncements:

General Sujiyama: "There is no difference between north and south in importance. It depends on circumstances when we are ready."

General Tsukada: "On matters pertaining purely to Supreme Command, we will not consult Germany. We are going to make decisions independently in order to avoid delays. Has not Germany done what she wanted to do without consulting anyone?"

General Tojo "To date Germany has not consulted us."

But Admiral Nagano, ever the compromiser, remarked: "I think that when we are about to go to war it will be necessary to consult Germany because of the friendship involved in the Alliance. Unless the declaration of war can be tied in with instantaneous military action, I don't think we will make a declaration." In fact, this is what happened on 7 December 1941 (Hawaii time).

Matsuoka tried to explain that his past actions were to settle the China Incident by surrounding Chunking. He sought and obtained a Neutrality Pact with Russia and an alliance with Germany. Finally, he wanted some type of agreement with the United States, but no agreement had been made to date. He summarized his belief in moral diplomacy, but did not bring up the Neutrality Pact when he advised to strike northward. The military indicated that fifty days would be required to ready the troops for a northern advance. By then the situation between Russia and Germany would be clarified.

Imperial Conference, 2 July 1941

At this Conference, the southern strategy and establishment of Greater East Asia Co-Prosperity sphere was considered. The conclusion was to continue preparations for the southward push but to closely follow the German-Russian conflict. Japan would enter the clash if it seemed opportune. As Matsuoka dogmatically pronounced "The conflict will be over within two to three months – the German war machine was invincible." (Ref. 4.7.2)

Admiral Nagano gave the Imperial Navy's view:

"Let me explain the principal items. On the solution of the Southern Question: I believe that under present circumstances our Empire, in order to secure our defenses in the South and attain a position of self-sufficiency with Greater East Asia Co-Prosperity Sphere, must take immediate steps to push steadily southward by coordinating political and military action with reference to key areas in the South, in accordance with developments in the situation.

However, Great Britain, the United States, and the Netherlands are currently stepping up their pressure against Japan. If they obstinately continue to obstruct us, and if our Empire finds itself unable to cope with this, we may, it must be anticipated, finally have to go to war with Great Britain and the United States. So we must get ready, resolved that we will not be deterred by that possibility. As the first step, it will be necessary for us to carry out our policy with respect to French Indochina and Thailand in accordance with 'Outline of Policy Concerning the South' and thereby increase our ability to move southward.

On the attitude of our Empire regarding American participation in the war: It goes without saying that if the United States should enter the war in Europe, our Empire will act in accordance with the Tripartite Pact. This action should not be limited to fulfilling our obligations to assist Germany and Italy. I believe that we should also endeavor to carry out our policy to establish the Greater East Asia Co-Prosperity Sphere, even if this ultimately involves the use of force.

However, it cannot be predicted when and under what circumstances the United States may enter the war in Europe. Therefore, I believe it will be necessary for us to decide independently when and in what manner we should use armed force against Great Britain and the United States, taking into consideration the situation at the time."

Yoshimichi Hara, President of the Privy Council,[5] declared "I give my approval on the ground that action to this end is essential to carry on the 'China Incident' and in the light of the changing international situation; we will encounter many difficulties in the future. We cannot be optimistic about the possibility of an American embargo. Even though a Japanese-American clash may be unavoidable in the end, I hope that sufficient care will be exercised to make sure that it will not come in the near future, and that there will be no miscalculations. I give my approval on this basis."

General Tsukada, who took the notes at the Conferences, observed that the Navy representatives Nagano and Oikawa did not make a comment after their opening remarks. With Emperor Hirohito seemingly in favor of a northern strike, the Navy kept a low profile.

The Soviet-German war had become a factor in Japanese military planning since its inception on 22 June 1941. Hitler had continually urged Japan to strike at Russia and, as a result, the Imperial Army began to waiver on the southern strategy. Nagano, in opposition, rebutted: "To secure our defenses in the south and attain a position of self sufficiency within the *'Greater East Asia Co-Prosperity Sphere,'* we must take steps to push steadily south by coordinated political and military action.... If they (UK and U.S.) obstinately continue to obstruct us and, if our Empire finds itself unable to cope with this, we may, it must be anticipated, finally have to go to war with Great Britain and the United States..." Nagano believed that if the U.S. went to war in Europe, Japan would act in accord with the Tripartite Pact, but continue pursuit of its objectives in the south – even if it required the use of force. General Tojo, who did not fully trust the Germans despite Matsuoka's ranting, stated: "We were supposed to be partners in the Tripartite Pact, but they did not consult us in their attack on Russia." Hitler lost a buddy.

---

[5] As was the custom, the President of the Privy Council is speaking for the Emperor and, in most instances, this is the Emperor asking the questions.

Japan's Move into Southern French Indochina and American Response

In accordance with the Imperial decision, Matsuoka initiated diplomatic talks with Vichy France and the Imperial Army and Navy completed plans to enter southern French Indochina. On 24 July 1941, Vichy France signed a pact with Japan permitting peaceful access to southern French Indochina for Japanese troops and the establishment of air and naval bases. The advance of Japanese troops into southern French Indochina left no doubt as to where they were eventually headed. President Roosevelt took the situation into his own hands and, on the following day, he met with Ambassador Admiral Nomura, and made these three demands:

- evacuate troops from French Indochina
- joint guarantee of French Indochina neutrality
- guarantee access to economic resources

Events moved rapidly. America froze Japanese credits and embargoed critical supplies to Japan making it more difficult for her to purchase and obtain needed provisions from U.S., British and Dutch firms. President Roosevelt intended that the embargo would not be absolute, but controlled by issuing export permits. However, the bureaucracy instituted an absolute embargo against Japan. This settled matters for Admiral Nagano and the Imperial Navy—war preparations went into high gear.

Nationalist Regime in Nanking

Submerged in these events was Prime Minister Konoye and Foreign Minister Matsuoka's idea for stabilizing events in China. Japanese industry and the Imperial Army were involved in multiple enterprises, including mining, manufacturing and production of narcotics. One solution was to install Wang Ching-wei as President of the nationalist government in Nanking. It was believed that this might serve to unify the centrifugal forces made up of Chiang Kai-shek in Chungking, Mao Tse-tung in Yenan Province and the Manchu Emperor in Peking and, added to that, the numerous warlords scattered around the country. President Wang was an illustrious nationalist who helped establish the Nationalist regime in Nanking with Sun Yat-sin in 1911, but he had a falling out with Chiang Kai-shek and left. He was re-established in Nanking and the Japanese government was to recognize his regime when he visited Tokyo during the period 17 to 25 June 1941. Some Japanese opposed this, since Japan was asking the U.S. to get Chiang Kai-shek to negotiate with Japan. Wang died in 1944 in Nagoya Imperial University Hospital. He is now regarded as a collaborator and traitor by regimes in Peking and Taipei.

The one lasting effect of Japan's occupation of China was that it unified the Chinese – they all hated the Japanese for the harsh treatment by the Imperial Japanese Army but a few admired the Japanese for their initial encouragement of Sun Yat-sin's republic.

KONOYE'S GRASP FOR PEACE IN THE PACIFIC

Prime Minister Konoye desired peace with America, but he was up against deadlines established at the Imperial Conference of 6 September 1941. The question of war or peace was contingent on several issues – Japanese troops in China, the Tripartite Pact and embargoes by *U.S. and Britain* on oil and other exports. He grasped for peace through formal diplomacy with Washington as well as outside messengers who came through the back door with a Draft Understanding that supposedly would satisfy both east and west interests.

John Doe Associates

The "backdoor" diplomacy was formulated by an unlikely group of Roman Catholic priests and concerned Japanese citizens who drafted a memo to initiate a dialogue toward peace in the Far East. They became known as the John Doe Associates comprised of the following individuals:

- Bishop James Edward Walsh, Maryknoll Order
- Father John Drought, Maryknoll Order
- Colonel Hideo Iwakuro, Imperial Army Attaché in Washington DC
- Mr. Tadao Ikawa, Farmers Cooperative Bank of Japan

The Maryknoll Order had missions in China since 1911, therefore, had great interest in maintaining peace in the region. In April 1941, the John Doe Associates developed a "Draft Understanding" entitled *Proposal Presented to the Department of State Through the Medium of Private American and Japanese Individuals on April 9, 1941*. The document suggested a basis for discussions between America and Japan citing the following salient points:

1. The concepts of the United States and of Japan respecting international relations and the character of nations.
2. The attitude of both governments toward the European War.
3. China Affairs.
4. Naval, aerial, and mercantile marine relations in the Pacific.
5. Commerce between both nations, and their financial cooperation.
6. Economic activity of both nations in the Southwestern Pacific area.
7. The policies of both nations affecting political stabilization in the Pacific.

The John Doe draft proposed a conference between delegates to be held in Honolulu and presided over by President Franklin D. Roosevelt and Prime Minister Prince Konoye. The meeting's purpose was to draw up details governing each item.

On 12 April 1941, Secretary of State Cordell Hull accepted the draft but added four underlying principles that the agreement must follow (Ref. 4.7.13):

1. Respect for the territorial integrity and the sovereignty of each and all nations
2. Support of the principle of non-interference in the internal affairs of other countries
3. Support of the principle of equality, including equality of commercial opportunity
4. Non-disturbance of the status quo in the Pacific except as the status quo may be altered by peaceful means.

Ambassador Kichisaburo Nomura, who was friend of FDR from his days in Washington, submitted the Draft to Tokyo, but he did not include Hull's four principles. When Admiral Nagano read the initial Draft, he remarked of his old naval academy buddy "It was only men of Nomura's stature who could affect such a splendid, diplomatic triumph." In addition, General Tojo told Prime Minister Konoye "The Draft is the best chance to end the China conflict." (Ref. 4.7.14)

At the time, Foreign Minister Matsuoka was in Siberia on the Trans-Siberian Railroad returning from his grand tour of Hitler's Europe, He visited Rome and Berlin with stopovers in Moscow on each leg of the journey. Prince Konoye wanted him to read the Draft and reply immediately, but the Foreign Minister stalled. At first, Matsuoka was under the impression that the Draft was the result of his discussions with Laurence A. Steinhardt, American ambassador in Moscow. But, upon careful reading he realized that it was not for it did not include the strong language of the Tripartite Pact.

While Nomura urged a response, Matsuoka came up with his own version of the document in which he required concurrence of the Ministers of Army and the Navy – as well as from Germany.

When Hull received Tokyo's response of 12 May 1941, (See Table 4.7.1) he composed another Draft which was sent on 21 June 1941. Whether deliberate or not, this was the date that Hitler broke his word – for the umpteenth time – with an invasion of Russia on an 8,000 mile front from the Arctic Circle to the Black Sea – obviously long in preparation. This diverted attention from negotiations between Washington and Tokyo and they dragged on until September without agreement. It was not until July that the Japanese response was drafted and sent to Washington on 21 July 1941. However, it was not delivered to Hull until sometime later because of upheaval in Tokyo. Prince Konoye's second cabinet resigned and Matsuoka was ousted.

Matsuoka "Canned"

Prince Konoye instructed his Foreign Minister to respond to Washington's revision of the "Draft" that was received 21 June 1941. Matsuoka sent no official response, but he rejected Hull's oral statement which was directed against Matsuoka (Ref. 4.7.15). Hull charged:

> "Some Japanese leaders in influential official positions are definitely committed to a course which calls for support of Nazi Germany and its policies of conquest, and that the only kind of understanding with the United States which they would endorse is one that would envisage Japan 'fighting on the side of Hitler should the United States become involved in the European hostilities through carrying out its present policy of self defense ...' So long as such Japanese leaders maintain this attitude in their official positions and apparently seek to influence public opinion in Japan in the direction indicated, it is not illusory to expect that the adoption of a proposal such as the one under consideration offers a basis for achieving substantial results along the desired lines."

Matsuoka had three criteria for a Draft Understanding – the United States must:

1. Contribute to end the China Incident by getting Chiang Kai-shek to agree to armistice
2. Avoid interference in the provisions of the Tripartite Pact
3. Do not destroy Japan's international credibility

Matsuoka was relatively stable in his performance as Foreign Minister and concluded many important treaties, but he was thrown into a dilemma with Hitler's invasion of Russia. It made no sense to him in his concept of world order and it showed in his performance at the Liaison Conferences in May and June 1941. At one point one commentator asked rhetorically "Is Matsuoka sane?" At the Foreign Ministry, some claimed that Matsuoka's tenure was a breath of fresh air because the Matsuoka's cyclone got rid of some dead wood.

Matsuoka, in good character, worked to help Jews in Europe and expressed that "It would not be Japanese policy to emulate Hitler's policy on Jews." Despite urging by Joseph Goebbels and his disciples to institute anti-Semitic policies, Matsuoka addressed Jewish businessmen on 21 December 1940 stating "I am the man responsible for the alliance with Hitler, but nowhere have I promised that we would carry out his anti-Semitic policies in Japan. This is not simply my personal opinion; it is the opinion of Japan. I have no compunction with announcing it to the world." Later, however, the Imperial Japanese Army in conquered territories, interned a few Jews (10,000) in Shanghai and NEI, but their treatment was innocuous compared to the military's treatment of the local Asian populations. (Ref. 4.7.16) A few commentators noted that Japan's aid to Jews was more than America had done during the holocaust.

At the Imperial Conference on 2 July 1941, the next strategic move was considered – should Japan strike north at Russia or south to Singapore. Both options were discussed but no firm decision was made. They adopted a wait-and-see attitude regarding the German-Russian war. After Hitler invaded Russia – obviously neglecting previous attempts to conquer Russia – Matsuoka conferred with Hirohito and told him "We will have to invade Russia." He insisted on the northern strike "Unless we shed blood, we may not reap the rewards when Russia is overrun." This disturbed the Emperor greatly. He called Prince Konoye to clarify the Foreign Minister's comments. Konoye explained that Matsuoka was speaking as an individual and not giving the opinion of the Cabinet since there was no joint approval by the government to strike Russia at the present time. Prince Konoye sent a letter to Matsuoka to calm him down.

Matsuoka fully understood the enormity of such a decision for war with Russia and would abide by the majority opinion of the Cabinet. But, he continued to press the issue vigorously following Hitler's line. It appeared that he looked up to Hitler for direction rather than to Hirohito. What finally led to Matsuoka's dismissal were three complaints by the Cabinet:

- Procrastination in responding to American Drafts of 17 April and 21 June 1941
- Ignoring army and navy urgings to continue American negotiations – "We are not prepared to go to war with America and Britain just yet."
- Urging an immediate strike against Russia

At the 39th Liaison Conference of 12 July 1941, Matsuoka recommended rejecting outright the 21 June 1941 American Draft Understanding which was at variance with the approach that had been worked out by the navy staff. Admiral Takasumi Oka, Chief of Naval Affairs Bureau, warned that a rejection of the Draft would cause unease among the lower ranks. He proposed that Japan should continue to string the Americans along until the army and navy were ready for war. At first Nagano backed Matsuoka but later withdrew his support. This was Matsuoka's last official conference as Foreign Minister.

Konoye met secretly on 16 July 1941 with Army Minister Tojo, Navy Minister Oikawa and Home Minister Hiranuma to discuss Matsuoka's status. It was felt that they could not fire him outright due to his popularity in certain rightist quarters. So they took a backdoor approach. The Cabinet resigned *en masse*, which forced Matsuoka's hand to resign as well. The third Konoye Cabinet was formed on 19 July 1941 with Admiral Teijiro Toyoda as Foreign Minister. With this stroke, Konoye hoped that normalization of relations with America might be arranged. In fact, the opposite occurred.

It was shocking to Matsuoka when the Cabinet Secretary appeared at his residence for his signature on resignation papers and to collect the official government seal. Only reluctantly did he sign and relinquish the seal. Merely two months earlier he had celebrity status when he returned from his grand European tour. He even dreamed of becoming Prime Minister, but his chance would be slim with Emperor Hirohito in charge.

Konoye's Quest for Peace

Foreign Minister Teijiro Toyoda took a few days to get up to speed and coordinate Japan's response to a *fait-accompli* – the movement of Imperial Army into southern French Indochina. He had to study the details of America's response to the southern strike into French Indochina. He learned soon enough when Roosevelt updated his demands and presented them to Nomura on 31 July 1941. Toyoda coordinated the Japanese response and sent it to Ambassador Nomura on 5 August 1941. The main provisions were as follows:

1. Japan has no intention of sending troops further than French Indochina and will withdraw them after settlement of the "China Incident"
2. Japan will guarantee neutrality of the Philippines
3. America will remove her armaments from southwest Pacific
4. America will cooperate with Japan's gaining access to resources in the Netherlands East Indies
5. America will preside over direct negotiations between Japan and China and will recognize Japan's special position in French Indochina after the settlement

However, Toyoda's response was not formally presented to Secretary Hull and President Roosevelt because Nomura did not believe that it had the full approval of the Emperor.

With the southern push to Singapore set to go, Prime Minister Konoye believed that time was running out for diplomacy. He spoke to Emperor Hirohito about a visit with Roosevelt for a last-gasp effort to divert the drift toward war. On Sunday, 3 August 1941, communication was sent to Ambassador Nomura regarding a Roosevelt meeting. Konoye met at his residence with Army, Navy and Foreign Ministers to get their approval for this venture. He asked them about a possible meeting of heads of state between Konoye and Roosevelt postulating "I do not believe that Japanese-American talks are impossible if they are carried out with broadmindedness."

Ever present in these negotiations was the German-Russian war. Japanese-American relations had to be resolved now because, as Konoye submitted, "The German-Russian war will peak in September and if the Germans are losing, America won't negotiate." He added "If the Germans are winning, it still won't be bad for Japan and there is no way Germany will rule the world and conquer Britain and America."

Navy Minister Oikawa expressed his approval and expected that Konoye's meeting with Roosevelt would be successful. The Imperial Army, in the person of General Tojo, was cautious and penned the army's opinion as follows:

> "If the Prime Minister were to personally meet with the president of the United States, the existing diplomatic relations of the Empire, which are based on the Tripartite Pact, would be unavoidably weakened. At the same time, a considerable domestic stir would undoubtedly be created. For these reasons, the meeting is not considered a suitable move. The attempt to surmount the present critical situation by the Prime Minister's offering his personal services is viewed with sincere respect and admiration. If, therefore, it is the Prime Minister's intention to attend such a meeting with determination to firmly support the basic principles embodied in the Empire's Revised Plan to the "N" Plan and to carry out a war against America if the President of the United States still fails to comprehend the true intentions of the Empire even after this final effort is made, the army is not necessarily in disagreement. However, it is not in favor of the meeting if, after making preliminary investigations, it is learned that the meeting will be with someone other than the president, such as Secretary Hull or one in a lesser capacity. You shall not resign your post as a result of the meeting on the grounds that it was a failure, rather, you shall be prepared to assume leadership in the war against America." (Ref. 4.7.8)

Immediately upon his return to Washington from the Atlantic Conference with Winston Churchill, Roosevelt met with Nomura on Sunday, 17 August 1941. The President assumed a cautious attitude regarding a meeting between heads of state in Honolulu. But, ever the optimist in personal diplomacy, Roosevelt recommended Juneau, Alaska as a better meeting place rather than Hawaii. In Tokyo, Foreign Minister Toyoda met with Ambassador Grew regarding a Roosevelt-Konoye meeting.

One American Cabinet officer, Postmaster General Frank Walker, was optimistic. He had also been involved in behind-the-scenes diplomatic efforts of the John Doe Associates. The talks continued.

In order to address the immediate impasse in Japanese-American relations, the Konoye's Cabinet held a meeting on 26 August 1941 and settled on two replies to Roosevelt's proposals. In effect, the Japanese stepped back from their previous proposal – or so it seemed. Prince Konoye sent a personal note to Roosevelt, apparently accepting his Presidential invitation. But the reply to Secretary Hull was in "diplomatese," which did not satisfy the Americans. Ambassador Nomuro personally met Roosevelt again on 28 August 1941 and handed him both replies.

In his direct message to Roosevelt, Konoye wrote "...freeing myself from past business-like negotiations, I would like to discuss Japanese-American problems from a broader point of view. I frankly state a sincere intention of proposing an interview which would aim at tiding over the present crisis. I also express my hope that the interview would take place as early as possible."

Compared with FDR's optimism, Secretary Hull's attitude was more cautious and he proposed that the meeting should take the form of ratifying already agreed-to proposals. Hull also stressed two areas of American concern:

- evacuation of Japanese troops from China—this involved the China Incident
- the right of America to self defense and its impact on the Tripartite Pact

These two issues would cloud the negotiations over the next several months. Although FDR remained optimistic, Hull remained the pessimist. The right of self defense, at least presently, did not seem to be the big hang-up – it was the China Incident. Within the Japanese government, two schools of thought arose – one optimistic, the other pessimistic. The Foreign Office, relying on FDR's optimism, was hopeful for a successful resolution of their differences. The military remained pessimistic.

On 3 September 1941, FDR met with Ambassador Nomura and handed him the formal American reply which followed the State Department's position based on Hull's principles of noninterference with regard to internal national affairs. Japan had to agree to basic principles of national sovereignty before a meeting of the heads of state could take place. This threw cold water on personal diplomacy of a face-to-face meeting. But Marks put a different spin on the responses and contended that there was more coordination between FDR and Hull (Ref. 4.7.17).

Many of the participants in that fateful spring, summer and fall of 1941 knew each other – some on a first-name basis – but each had his own perspective on the situation. Fumimaro Konoye wanted to avoid war with America. Roosevelt did not want a two-front war, one in the Pacific, one in the Atlantic. Secretary Cordell Hull was frustrated by the Japanese Imperial Army marching all over China despite assurances to the contrary. Admiral Nagano dreaded Japan's two-front war, with Russia at his back and America and Britain at his front door. He correctly opined that, currently, America was totally unprepared for a two-ocean war and now was Japan's opportunity to get the upper hand. Matsuoka wanted to keep America out of the European war and neutralize Russia.

American response stiffened following the Japanese troop movement into southern French Indochina. Japan's military stated that a decision had to be made soon or the navy would be dead in the water. If Japan were to retain its dignity, there were several factors working against American *rapprochement*:

- the military wanted to emulate Hitler's style in Asia
- the populace was being stirred up by reports of encirclement by ABCD powers (American, Britain, China, Dutch).

With such a background, Konoye believed that, unless a drastic step was taken, war between America and Japan was likely. The military and civil government gathered to set an agenda for Japan's direction in face of American pressure. At the 50th Liaison Conference held on 3 September 1941 (Ref. 4.7 9) Nagano presented the basis for *The Essentials for Carrying out the Empire's Policy*. This document had undergone the scrutiny of bureaus and agencies of the Ministries and General Staffs of Imperial Army and Navy. It was well vetted in all aspects of war-making with America and Britain.

Nagano put forth that timing was critical. As the monsoon season would come in the spring, the southern strategy should be executed quickly – the northern thrust into Siberia could wait until springtime. General Hajime Sugiyama, Chief of Army General Staff, advocated that diplomacy be completed by 15 October so that war could begin by 30 October 1941. War Minister Tojo was concerned with the moving of military supplies into French Indochina lest it tip their hand and alerts the Allies. Takasuni Oka, Chief of Naval Affairs, asked "Can't you pretend you are going to Kunming?" Kunming was the terminus of the Burma Road and the Chinese road to Chunking. Sugiyama replied "We can't hide everything."

There were also discussions on the consequence of Japanese actions in regard to the Tripartite Pact. To avert any misinterpretation, two sentences were added to the Empire's Policy document: "Japan's interpretation of the Tripartite Pact and her actions therein, in the event that the U.S. should enter the European war, would be made by herself acting independently." And an added note: "The above does not alter our obligations under the Tripartite Pact." These two ambiguous statements were sufficient to satisfy the military and allay the fears of diplomats – primarily Konoye and Toyoda.

Imperial Conference, 6 September 1941

On 5 September, Hirohito confronted Admiral Nagano and General Sugiyama regarding the southern strategy and broad implications of taking Singapore. Prince Konoye's memoir tells the story (Ref. 4.7.8):

> "The Emperor asked the Army Chief of Staff, General Sugiyama, what was the Army's belief as to the probable length of hostilities in case of a Japanese-American war. The Chief of Staff replied that he believed operations in the South Pacific could be disposed of in about three months. Turning to the Chief of Staff, the Emperor recalled that the General had been Minister of War at the time of the outbreak of the China Incident, and that he had then informed the Throne that the incident would be disposed of in about one month. He pointed out that despite the General's assurance, the incident was not yet concluded after four long years of fighting. In trepidation, the Chief of Staff went to great lengths to explain that the extensive hinterland of China prevented the consummation of operations according to the scheduled plan. At this the emperor raised his voice and said that if the Chinese hinterland was extensive, the Pacific was boundless. He asked if the General could be certain of his three month calculation. The Chief of Staff hung his head, unable to answer. At this point the Navy Chief of Staff lent a helping hand to Sugiyama by saying that, to his mind, Japan was like a patient suffering from a serious illness. He said the patient's case was so critical that the question of whether or not to operate had to be determined without delay. Should he be let alone without an operation there was danger of a gradual decline. An operation, while it might be extremely dangerous, would still offer some hope of saving his life. The stage was now reached, he said, where a quick decision had to be made one way or the other. He felt that the Army General Staff was in favor of putting hope in diplomatic negotiations to the finish, but that in case of failure a decisive operation would have to be performed. To this extent, then, he was in favor of the negotiation proposals. The Emperor,

pursuing the point, asked the Chiefs of the Supreme Command if it was not true that both of them were for giving precedence to diplomacy and both answered in the affirmative."

At the Imperial Conference of 6 September 1941, the Emperor formally approved a southern strategy to advance toward NEI. Nagano's recommendation for the southern thrust can be summarized in his statement found in Ike's writings (Ref. 4.7.2):

> "In various respects, the Empire is losing materials: that is, we are getting weaker. By contrast the enemy is getting stronger. With the passage of time, we will get increasingly weaker and we won't be able to survive. Moreover, we will endure what can be endured in carrying our diplomacy, but at the opportune moment we must make some estimates ultimately when there is no hope for diplomacy and when war cannot be avoided, it is critical that we make up our minds quickly. Although I am confident that at the present time we have a chance to win a war, I fear that this opportunity will disappear with the passage of time. Regarding war, the navy thinks in terms of both a short war and a long one. I think it will probably be a long war. Hence, we must be prepared for a long war. We hope that the enemy will come out for a quick showdown; in that event there will be a decisive battle in waters near us, and I anticipate that our chances of victory will be quite good. But I do not believe that the war would end with that. It would be a long war. In this connection, I think it would be good to take advantage of the fruits of an initial victory in order to cope with a long war. If, on the contrary, we get into a long war without a decisive battle we will be in difficulty especially since our supply of resources will become depleted. If we cannot obtain these resources, it will not be possible to carry on a long war. It is important to make preparations so that we will not be defeated by getting essential resources and making the best of our strategy. There is no set series of steps that will guarantee our checkmating the enemy. But even so, there will probably be measures we can adopt depending on changes in the international situation.
>
> In short, our armed forces have no alternative but to try to avoid being pushed into a corner, to keep in our hand the power to decide when to begin hostilities and thus to seize the initiative. There is no alternative but to push forward in this way."

Emperor Hirohito closed the conference with a Meiji poem[6] – Two different translations give the poem as: "Since all are brothers in this world, why is there such constant turmoil?" (Ref. 4.7.8) "All the seas in every quarter are as brothers to one another. Why then do the winds and waves of strife rage so turbulently throughout the world?" (Ref. 4.7.2) Nagano replied to the Meiji poem but the meeting adjourned in an atmosphere of unprecedented tension. (Ref. 4.7.8) The conferences resulted in an agreement for Japan to advance the southern strategy but diplomacy would continue until 15 October 1941.

The Draft Understanding dialogue continued back and forth between Tokyo and Washington. On 2 October 1941, Hull submitted the final response to Japan's proposal of 3 September 1941 reiterating "Whereas we had understood that Japan would, at once, withdraw all of its troops from China, sign a new treaty and, through its terms, station armed forces in fixed areas according to the terms that were unofficially submitted, it would have a portion of its expeditionary forces then abroad remain just as they were and would withdraw the rest, if this is so, the stories differ." Though the effect was the

---

[6] As noted, translations from Japanese to English can sometimes take different paths.

same, America's attitude was that the forms differed in reality. Japan refused to remove troops from China.

Foreign Minister Toyoda visited Counselor Eugene Dooman at the American embassy and explained that the reason for continuing Japanese troops in China was to thwart communist takeover. America had no objection but, the problem arose as to the form of Japanese occupation to be followed. On this point the Americans did not yield. In the 2 October 1941 memo, the Americans complained that "Japan agrees with the four principles and gives wide guarantees for peace, but, on concrete matters it contracts those or insists on delineating them unreasonably." With this memo, Japan-American negotiations took on a darker color all at once. A feeling existed among some Japanese that America believed she had found the innermost mind of Japan. It was felt that there was no sincerity on the part of America negotiators and that negotiations would fall victim to delaying techniques.

On 13 October 1941, Minister Reijiro Wakatsuki from the Japanese embassy in Washington spoke with Under Secretary Sumner Welles who maintained that "There is no change at all in the point that the President and Hull desire a meeting with Premier Prince Konoye, just as soon as the three problems that are outstanding are resolved." The problems were:

- Establishment of the principle of equal economic opportunity
- Stationing troops in China
- Problem of Tripartite Pact

Konoye called a liaison conference on 4 October 1941 to discuss the American memo of 2 October. Konoye invited Tojo to his home in Ogikubo on the evening of 5 October to inform him that negotiations would continue to the end. Tojo again visited Konoye late on the night of 7 October and told him "As to the problem of withdrawing troops from China, such a formality as to once withdraw, in principle, all troops and after that to station them there, as insisted upon by the United States, is something that is difficult for the army to submit to."

On 14 October 1941, Prince Konoye met with Bishop Walsh of the John Doe Associates and asked him to relay this message to President Roosevelt: (Ref. 4.7.8)

> "From the beginning of these negotiations, I and my Government have had nothing but a sincere and wholehearted desire to conclude an agreement that would result in the peace of the pacific, and we have worked very hard to bring this about.
>
> I regret very much the delays and misunderstandings, some of them due, I believe, to the maneuvers of Third Powers that have operated to retard the negotiations and render difficult the attainment of their important aim.
>
> I still entertain hope of a successful issue, and I will continue to work for the attainment of the object sought, namely an agreement that will establish friendly relations between our two countries, restrict the scope of the war, pacify and stabilize the pacific region, and contribute to world peace. And now that the terms have been discussed as completely as is practicable under present conditions, it is my confident belief that a meeting between the heads of the respective governments would readily bring about a completely satisfactory understanding that would insure the great objectives we mutually seek."

Unfortunately, Bishop Walsh did not return to Washington until 16 November 1941. His trip was delayed, as one can imagine, with Japan set to strike south to Singapore. He had, however, several interventions, both by Japanese and American officials and he was able to board very scarce flights that took him from occupied Canton to Macao, on to Hong Kong, Manila and finally Washington. (Ref. 4.7.13)

Konoye understood that with the Emperor's approval for diplomacy to be completed by 15 October and war to begin with America and Britain by 30 October 1941. He made great efforts to ensure that no stone was left unturned to avoid war. The meetings and remarks of the officials were as follows:

- In view of the stiff army attitude, Konoye invited the Army, Navy and Foreign Ministers to his home to avoid a crisis.
- Konoye, on his 50th birthday, 12 October 1941, held one of the last meetings of his Cabinet.
- Before the Liaison Conference, Admiral Oka stated "The Navy does not desire a rupture of negotiations. The Navy wants to avoid war with America but will not bring this out in the open – it will state that the decision for peace or war rests solely with the Premier."
- At the Conference, the Navy Minister Oikawa stated "If we are to have peace we have to go all the way. If we are to have war, we need a decision now." Tojo stated "The problem of stationing troops in itself means the life of the Army and we shall not be able to make any concession at all." Konoye replied "Isn't it all right to forget the glory, but to take the fruits, perform the formality the Americans want and achieve a result that will, in actuality, be the same as stationing troops." To this Tojo did not yield. The conference lasted from 2:00 pm to 6:00 pm.
- Konoye asked Tojo to come to this official residence and stated "I have a great responsibility for the China Incident and today, when the Incident has lasted four years and still sees no end, I find it difficult to agree no matter what is said to enter upon a great war, the future of which I can not at all see." Tojo expressed the thought that since they were not following through on the decision of the Imperial Conference of 6 September 1941, the Cabinet should resign *en masse*.

As noted, American and Japanese notes regarding *rapprochement* had gone back and forth since 17 April 1941 and are summarized in Table 4.7.1. At the end, there were two sticking points: (1) Japanese troops in China, (2) Japanese interpretation of the American self-defense and America escorting British convoys to the 25° west longitude and whether America was entering the European war and the Tripartite Pact might be effective.

In the end, the second point was not the major stumbling block but the stationing of Japanese troops in China. Tojo stated that to maintain harmony at all levels of the Japanese Army the troops had to remain in China.

Prince Konoye and his third Cabinet resigned on 16 October 1941. He recorded in his memoirs that prevention of the American-Japanese war floundered around three individuals; Tojo, Matsuoka and Hull. (Ref. 4.7.8)

- Tojo would not remove troops from China
- Matsuoka's formulating the Tripartite Pact
- Hull would not agree to at least a superficial stationing of Japanese troops in China even though for the past 150 years many nations had been stationing troops under treaties with the existing Chinese government

Konoye tried hard but could not secure the peace.

TABLE 4.7.1

MEMORANDA OF UNDERSTANDING IN PEACE NEGOTIATIONS BETWEEN JAPAN AND UNITED STATES

SOURCE	TITLE	DATE
America to Japan	Draft Understanding	17 April 1941
Japan to America	Draft Understanding	12 May 1941
America to Japan	Oral statement Draft Understanding	21 June 1941
Japan to America	Oral statement Counterproposal	25 July 1941
FDR to Nomura	I. Evacuate Japanese troops from French Indochina II. Joint guarantee by America, England, Holland and China of the neutralization of French Indochina III. Guarantee access to French Indochina goods (rubber)	24 July 1941 (Washington time)
Sumner Welles to Nomura	Elaborated proposals of FDR	31 July 1941
Nomura to Hull	Prince Konoye would like to meet FDR and resolve differences broadmindedly	5 August 1941
Nomura to Hull	I. Japan has no intention to send troops further and will withdraw troops at settlement of "China Incident" II. Japan guarantees neutralization of Philippines III. America removes armaments in Southwest Pacific IV. America cooperates with Japan for access to Netherlands East Indies resources V. America will act as intermediary in direct negotiations between Japan and China	7 August 1941
America to Japan	Hull states that Japan's reply of 5 August made no reference to FDR's proposals of 24 July 1941	8 August 1941
FDR to Nomura	I. Japanese troops will move no further II. Reply to Prince Konoye's suggestion for a Konoye-FDR meeting	17 August 1941
Japan to America Nomura to FDR	I. Konoye to FDR II. Answer to American proposal Hull's comment to Nomura: Sticking points are: • Japan's troops out of China • Japan's attitude toward self defense (America in European war)	28 August 1941
America to Japan FDR to Nomura	I. Personal memo: FDR to Konoye II. American response and Hull's four basic principals enumerated on 21 June 1941	3 September 1941
Japan to America	Proposal generated by Japanese Foreign Office but did not directly address Hull's four points	4 September 1941
Japan to America	Final Proposal for Understanding	24 September 1941
America to Japan	Response to Japanese proposal of 4 September The "hang up" was stationing Japanese troops in China	2 October 1941

TOJO AND THE MARCH TO PEARL HARBOR

Upon his resignation, Prince Konoye recommended Prince Naruhiko Higashikuni as his successor but he was rejected by Marquis Koichi Kido, Lord Keeper of the Privy Seal. Subsequently, General

Hideki Tojo was recommended as the next Prime Minister. Tojo was approved by Emperor Hirohito to succeed Konoye on 19 October 1941. He directed Tojo that his first priority was to resolve the differences between America and Japan. Figure 4.7.11 shows Tojo's cabinet, which was comprised of the following officials: (Ref. 4.7.9)

    Shigenori Togo, Foreign Minister
    Okinori Kaya, Finance Minister
    Hideki Tojo, War Minister
    Sugiyama, General Army Chief of Staff
    Shigetoro Shimada, Admiral Navy Minister
    Osami Nagano, Admiral Navy Chief of Staff

Foreign Minister Shigenori Togo was a Foreign Service diplomat who had served in Berlin and Moscow, but he was dumped from his post by Matsuoka's "Foreign Service Cyclone." Marquis Koichi Kido who was a close advisor to Emperor Hirohito advised the Cabinet that they were not bound by the 6 September 1941 Imperial Conference deadline to go forward into war in October. However, Admiral Nagano indicated that the Navy was consuming 400 tons of oil per hour and he cautioned that, unless they got oil resources from the Netherlands East Indies, the Navy would be grounded. He forewarned "If we have to go to war against Britain and America, now is the best time."

With the emperor's directive for "diplomacy before war," Tojo realized that Togo, Shimada and Kaya would need briefing on recent conference discussions. Kaya was an interesting character who asked some probing questions. He was Finance Minister in Konoye's first cabinet (1937-1939) at the start of the "China Incident." He had heard the same brazen statements by military officials, which turned out to be untrue. The army was still trying to correct the China situation.

Tojo also demonstrated his hard-working character in getting the job done – in this case the job was war or peace with America and Britain. His test of endurance was in conferences that lasted up to 17 hours. He was warned by the Emperor, through spokesman Yoshimichi Hara, to not engage in a racial war of white versus yellow race. Tojo was known to complain about the righteous Americans who accepted only 1000 Japanese immigrants annually, the lowest quota in the U.S. Immigration Law.

As Foreign Minister Togo got to work to formulate a new approach to avoid war with the West, America warmed up to his ideas. In fact, Nagano told Admiral Ugaki – Chief of Staff of Admiral Yamamoto's Combined Fleet – that peace may be obtained with America. But, Ugaki felt that "Nagano does not know what he's talking about" as he revealed in his memoir (Ref. 4.7.18).

59th Liaison Conference, 23 October 1941

This Liaison Conference was the first one with Tojo as Prime Minister. The agenda item was to reconsider *"Essentials for Carrying out the Empire's Policies."* This had been discussed in some depth previously but, because of the Emperor's caution to put diplomacy before war, it was reconsidered.

Based on intelligence from military attachés in Berlin, London and Washington, Naval Intelligence Section Chief Rear Admiral Minoru Maeda, observed that England and U.S. were getting stronger and the European war would be a long one. By the end of 1942, the U.S. would be able to fight a two ocean war. England was strengthening its defenses of Singapore and Suez Canal. Foreign Minister Togo complained about the lack of information regarding operational plans and statistical data on soldiers, sailors, ships and planes. He was frustrated with the traditional secrecy of the Imperial Army and Navy. Even Tojo was unaware of the navy's plan to start war until about a week prior to the attack on Pearl Harbor. But, the overall objectives of war to gain vital resources and establish the Greater East Asia Co-Prosperity Sphere were accepted by military and the Cabinet.

Liaison Conferences 60 through 66, 24 October to 1 November 1941

Several questions were raised at the conferences: (Ref. 4.7.2)

Question: "What are the prospects of operations in the beginning, and after a few years, in a war against the United States, Great Britain and the Netherlands?" This question plagued Tojo's administration right up to 8 December 1941. The army estimated it would need four to five months to gain a strong foothold in the south, but the navy estimated six to eight months. The army balked at the navy's request to liquidate the China front but agreed that, if the north were attacked, they would be forced to liquidate it.

Question: "If we begin hostilities in the South this autumn, what will we face in the North?" The army, navy and foreign ministry were in agreement that they would not take any action in the North, but they could not rule out U.S. and Russia cooperating in the Far East. If war were prolonged in Asia, a Japanese-Soviet war could not be ruled out.

Question: "What is the extent to which we can get cooperation from Germany and Italy?" Foreign Minister Togo offered that they should not expect much cooperation from Germany. Admiral Nagano suggested specifying the spheres of influence on Ceylon with Japan in charge east of Colombo and Germany in charge west of Colombo. Japan should also get Germany to agree to the following:

- Declaration of war on the U.S.
- No separate peace
- Act in concert with Japan through stepped up operations in the near east
- Cooperate in warfare against communism

It was decided not to make too many demands on Germany, such as invasion of the British Isles since they may request explicitly to attack Russia.

Question: "Can't the oil problem be solved by producing synthetic oil?" Suzuki, Director of Planning, stated it would take a great expenditure in steel and coal and would take three years to complete. Yamada, Chief of Navy Bureau of Supplies and Equipment, stated it was unacceptable to rely on a future source of supply when the need was urgently in the present.

Question: "What were the prospects for diplomacy?"

- No hope of success over the short term
- What are the limits to Japan's concessions

The results of the discussion were as follows:

- Tripartite Pact – no change
- Application of Hull's four principles
- Equal opportunity for commerce in China
- Withdrawal of troops from French Indochina – no change
- Withdrawal of troops from China – no change but applied a period of about 25 years for withdrawal

On the last point there was much discussion by Sugiyama and Tsukada, Vice Chief of Army General Staff. Foreign Minister Togo, forgetting reality, stated "If we withdraw, it would be better in the long run." The navy was not enthusiastic about stationing troops in China. The army strongly advocated this point and the discussion was heated. Prime Minister Tojo proposed a certain number of years for stationing the troops, but Tsukada objected to showing any weakness by specifying a certain number of years.

Question: "What would happen to Japan if American proposals were accepted in their entireties?" All except the Foreign Minister believed that Japan would become a third-rate power. Kaya, Finance Minister, and Togo wanted a day to consider this question. Prime Minister Tojo stated that every minute counted and a decision must be reached by 1 November 1941. Three proposals on the agenda were:

- Proposal 1 – avoid war with U.S. and Britain
- Proposal 2 – decide on war and set a date
- Proposal 3 – decide on war but continue preparations and continue diplomatic exchanges

Two questions dogged the Liaison Conferences; one was diplomacy before war and the other was prospects in a war against America.

Prime Minister Tojo drove his cabinet to arrive at a consensus. This was not an easy task and there was no agreement in the beginning. The military view enunciated by General Tsukada, Vice Chief of Staff for the Army, eventually prevailed. They had to reach a decision or the present cabinet would fall. There was a high probability that the new administration would be anti-war. This was a surprise conclusion, but may be based on Hitler's juggernaut bogged down in mud and ice before Moscow in October 1941 and an underlying anti-war sentiment after four years of the China war.

In a 17-hour session on 1 November 1941, a consensus was reached and sent to Ambassador Nomura in Washington. Foreign Minister Togo sent Saburo Kurusu to Washington to prop him up. The consensus had two parts: (1) war with Great Britain and the United States would start on 1 December 1941, (2) negotiations with the United States and Great Britain would continue to 30 November 1941.

Imperial Conference, 5 November 1941

The Emperor Hirohito approved the pivotal decision entitled "Essentials for Carrying Out the Empire's Policies" at the Imperial Conference:

I. Our Empire, in order to resolve the present critical situation, assure its self-preservation and self-defense, and establish a New Order in Greater East Asia, decides on this occasion to go to war against the United States and Great Britain and takes the following measures:
   1. The time for resorting to force is set at the beginning of December and the Army and Navy will complete preparations for operations.
   2. Negotiations with the United States will be carried out in accordance with the attached document.
   3. Cooperation with Germany and Italy will be strengthened.
   4. Close military relations with Thailand will be established just prior to the use of force.
II. If negotiations with the United States are successful by midnight of 1 December, the use of force will be suspended.

Diplomacy

Foreign Minister Togo was pessimistic about the diplomatic effort. He would try his best but with the deadline of 30 November it may have been fruitless. He wanted a diplomatic attack in a systematic manner. This meant that he wanted Ambassador Nomura to present to the U.S. State Department in sequence, initially Proposal A, which was a rehash of the Draft Understandings that had gone back and forth between Washington and Tokyo since April 1941. Proposal B was an attempt at an interim solution to tide over the present condition for Japan.

Proposal B was the brainchild of Admiral Nomura, who Admiral Nagano described as "... a remarkable man. The Japanese-American negotiations seemed hopeless, but things might turn around. If it were not for Nomura, this would not have been possible." (Ref. 4.7.14)

It was agreed that the two proposals would be presented to the U.S. State Department as follows:

Proposal A – A rephrasing of previous Draft Understandings with the U.S.
Proposal B – A simplified Pact involving just the southern thrust:
1. Both Japan and the United States will pledge not to make an armed advance into Southeast Asia and the South Pacific area, except French Indochina.
2. The Japanese and American Governments will cooperate with each other so that the procurement of necessary materials from the Netherlands East Indies will be assured.
3. The Japanese and American governments will restore trade relations to what they were prior to the freezing of assets. The United States will promise to supply Japan with the petroleum Japan needs.
4. The Government of the United States will not take such actions as may hinder efforts for peace by both Japan and China.

Notes: (1) As occasion demands, it is permissible to promise that with the conclusion of the present agreement, Japanese troops stationed in southern Indochina are prepared to move to northern Indochina with the consent of the French government; and that the Japanese troops will withdraw from Indochina with the settlement of the China Incident or upon the establishment of a just peace in the Pacific area.

(2) As occasion demands, we may make insertions in the provisions on non-discriminatory trade and on the interpretation and execution of the Tripartite Pact in the above mentioned proposal (Proposal B).

The basic aim was to restore the relationship between the United States and Japan to the status it was before 25 July 1941. Prime Minister Tojo told his subordinates "Proposal B is not an excuse for war. I am praying to the Gods that somehow we will be able to get an agreement with the United States with this proposal." (Ref. 4.7.2)

Togo sent Saburo Kurusu to Washington to compliment Nomura in peace negotiations with Cordell Hull. Kurusu was a seasoned diplomat who Nomura had originally requested. Figure 4.7.2 shows Kurusu co-signing the Tripartite Pact in 1940 after which he resigned his diplomatic position in protest of the Pact. In November 1941, he was described by Grace Tully, FDR's secretary, as "a sly-looking little man who was obviously deemed the real front for his government's two-faced pretense of carrying on talks toward maintenance of peace with this country." (Ref. 4.7.19)

The clock was ticking. Kurusu arrived in Washington on 15 November and on the 17th and 18th he and Nomura presented Proposals A and B to Cordell Hull. After reading the Proposal B, Undersecretary of State Welles caustically remarked "It is like reading Hamlet – without Hamlet." The obvious Hamlet was China, which appeared to be but an afterthought at the end of the Proposal. But, surprisingly, with this brush-off by the State Department, Postmaster General Frank Walker visited Nomura and Kurusu with a message from FDR that the President would like to discuss Proposal B to arrive at a *modus vivendi*. This was 19 November 1941. The information was wired to Tokyo and there was an inkling that a breakthrough in relations might occur. However, in preparation for the attack South, the Japanese army moved additional troops into southern French Indochina. Nomura and Kurusu received another visit on 25 November 1941 from Frank Walker who warned that advancing Japanese troops made a breakthrough impossible. (Ref. 4.7.14)

Togo informed Nomura that negotiations must be completed by 29 November 1941. One additional suggestion entered the equation to break the deadlock – an exchange of telegrams between FDR and the Emperor. FDR's telegram arrived on the Emperor's desk the day after the Pearl Harbor attack. This started Phase 2 of World War II.

Preparing for the Strike

Nagano told his defense counselor, John G. Brannon (Ref. 4.7.20), that he was against the attack on Pearl Harbor for two reasons: (a) It was too risky – two thirds of Japan's carrier force was assigned to the mission, but they had to be accompanied by a large fleet of oil barges to Hawaii and returned. There was a high probability that they would be detected. (b) The effect on the American psyche would be like striking a hornet's nest. Nagano expressed that he was wrong about the risk of detection, but right about the hornet's nest. It was a brilliant tactical strike, but a strategic blunder. Nagano confided "I knew America and I understood American People and I knew they would fight if properly aroused. I was afraid a sudden blow at your Pearl Harbor would be the kick of the hornet's nest."

Nagano had argued with Yamamoto about the mission but Yamamoto insisted "If we have to go to war against America – which I am against – we must attack Pearl Harbor or our flank will be attacked as we are striking south to get the oil and resources we need for a long war." He contended "If there must be a war with the United States, and I hope against hope it shall never occur, we cannot succeed without this initial thrust. Our oil is in the south, and if we are to move south to get it, we cannot risk a flank attack by the American navy now at Pearl Harbor. We must cripple their fleet so that we will have time to strengthen ourselves."

In his argument to attack Hawaii first, Yamamoto asserted that there was an extremely important strategic reason to attack the American fleet in Hawaii, lest the American fleet were to attack Japan from the east with aircraft carriers and burn down Tokyo and Osaka. He argued "The fact that the other side has brought a great fleet to Hawaii to show us that it's within striking distance of Japan means, conversely, that *we're* within striking distance too. In trying to intimidate us, America has put itself in a vulnerable position. If you ask me, they're just that bit too confident."

During map maneuvers at the Navy Staff College, Ryunosuke Kusaka, Chief of Staff of the Eleventh Air Fleet, remarked that he was "strongly opposed to the Pearl Harbor plan. It was like putting one's head in the lion's mouth. It was a mistake to engage in such a gamble in the first battle of a major war on which the nation's future depended." After hearing the others, Yamamoto broke his silence with "But what would you do if, while we were engaged in the South Pacific, the U.S. fleet launched air raids on Japan from the east? Are you suggesting that it's all right for Tokyo and Osaka to be burned to the ground so long as we get hold of oil? Still, the fact is I'm determined that so long as I'm Commander in Chief we shall go ahead with the Hawaiian raid." He then retorted "I may be fond of bridge and poker but I wish to hell you'd stop calling it a gamble!" (Ref. 4.5.21)

Quoting Brannon, "The actual attack plans were more than ultra secret. They were confined to a very few. Vice-Admiral Chuichi Nagumo, commanding the carrier fleet, relied greatly on Commander Minoru Genda, his deputy chief of staff, for the actual paper work. Young Commander Mitsuo Fuchida, was called in during October, 1941, and told it was just a paper plan but that he was assigned to working it out as a practical matter. Later Fuchida led the pilots in their foray over the actual targets at Pearl Harbor.

As the pilots trained they did not know the purpose of the maneuver. They were not told until the task force put out on the mission. Two great physical difficulties arose: (1) How to use aerial torpedoes since the Pearl Harbor waters were shallow and the drop had to be reduced from the regulation 100 meters to 10 or 20 meters. (2) How to effectively strike a ship with the usual nine plane formation reduced to five. In the event torpedo netting was used by the Americans, the Japanese decided to resort to direct bombing at 3000 meters, using 16-inch cannon shells modified by taking off the iron nose and putting on a steel point."

Agawa pointed out that the crews were being trained with ships at anchor in Kagoshima Bay (topography similar to Pearl Harbor). The pilots complained bitterly of "being treated like kids." They knew precisely where they were going. (Ref. 4.7.21)

Declaration of War

Admiral Nagano told Foreign Minister Togo that the attack would be an ambush and he wanted no declaration of war. Togo objected "There must be a declaration of war." Nagano relented and a long diplomatic message was transmitted to Ambassador Admiral Nomura reiterating Japan's position. The end result was a break off in diplomatic relations. An ultimatum was to be delivered to Hull at 1:00 pm Washington time on 7 December 1941. But, it was delivered actually at 2:00 pm due to a delay in getting the message translated. Secretary of State Hull, however, knew the message content through MAGIC, the deciphering system. But, he was still appalled and described them as "scoundrels and pissants." (Ref. 4.7.22) Figure 4.7.12 shows Japanese planes attacking Pearl Harbor.

CHAPTER 4, PART 7 REFERENCES

4.7.1 Toland, John, *Adolf Hitler*, Volume II, Doubleday & Company, Inc., Garden City, New York, 1976

4.7.2 Ike, Nobutaka, *Japan's Decision for War, Record of the 1941 Policy Conferences*, Stanford University Press, Stanford, CA 1967

4.7.3 Nagano, Admiral Osami, Prison diary, 1946

4.7.4 Kido, Koichi, *The Diary of Marquis Kido, 1931-1945*, University Publications of America Inc., Frederick, MD, 1984

4.7.5 Time Magazine, *Japan: Dutch in Dutch?*, April 29, 1940

4.7.6 Harries, Merion and Susie, *Soldiers of the Sun, The Rise and Fall of the Imperial Japanese Army*, Random House, New York, 1991

4.7.7 Grew, Joseph Clark, *Ten Years in Japan, 1932-1942*, Simon & Schuster, New York, 1944

4.7.8 Konoye, Prince Fumimaro, *Memoirs of Prince Konoye*, translation prepared by the Language Section G2, United States Strategic Bombing Survey, 1946

4.7.9 *Time Magazine*, Bows were deeper

4.7.10 Thai Delegate

4.7.11 *New York Times, Others Are Absolved*, January 27, 1941 (United Press)

4.7.12 *New York Times*, January 21, 1941 *Matsuoka's Address to the Diet*

4.7.13 Butow, R.J.C., *The John Doe Associates, Backdoor Diplomacy for Peace 1941*, Stanford University Press, Stanford, California, 1971

4.7.14 Mauch, Peter, *Sailor Diplomat, Nomura Kichisaburo and the Japanese-American War*, Harvard East Asian Monographs 333, Cambridge, Massachusetts and London, 2011

4.7.15 Lu, David J., *Agony of Choice, Matsuoka Yosuke and the Rise and Fall of the Japanese Empire, 1880-1946*, Lexington Books, New York, 2002

4.7.16 Kapner, D. A., Levine, S. *Jews of Japan*, Jerusalem Center for Public Affairs, Jerusalem Letter, No. 425, 24 Adair I 5760, 1 March 2000

4.7.17 Marks, Frederick W., *The Presidency and National Security Policy*, Center for the Study of the Presidency and Congress, Presidential Studies Quarterly, 1985

4.7.18 Ugaki, Admiral Matome, *Fading Glory, The Diary of Admiral Matome Ugaki 1941-1945*, University of Pittsburgh Press, Pittsburgh, Pennsylvania, 1991

4.7.19 Tully, Grace, *F.D.R.: My Boss*, Charles Scribner's Sons, New York, 1949

4.7.20 Brannon, John G. private papers, Special Collections, Georgetown Law Library, obtained 2012
4.7.21 Agawa, Hiroyuki, *The Reluctant Admiral, Yamamoto and the Imperial Navy*, translated by John Bester, Kodansha International Ltd. Tokyo, 1979
4.7.22 Togo, Shigenori, *The Cause of Japan*, Greenwood Press, 1977

Table 4.7.2

Background — World Scene

1940

9/10 May	Germany invades Belgium, Luxembourg and Netherlands
10 May	Winston Churchill replaces Neville Chamberlain as British Prime Minister
15 May	Netherlands army surrenders
28 May	Belgian army surrenders
4 June	British Expeditionary Army evacuates from Dunkirk
14 June	Soviet troops enter Lithuania
14 June	German troops enter Paris
22 June	Franco-German armistice signed
18 July	Churchill announces temporary agreement for stoppage of war supplies to China through Burma and Hong Kong
25 August	Estonia, Latvia and Lithuania incorporated into Soviet Union
22 September	Japan and France signed an accord permitting entry of Japanese troops into northern French Indochina
27 September	Tripartite Pact signed in Berlin by Japan, Germany and Italy
28 October	Italy attacks Greece
30 November	Japanese peace treaty signed with Wang Ching-wei regime in Nanking, China

1941

18 January	President Franklin Delano Roosevelt (FDR) inaugurated as 32nd president of the United States
30 January	French Indochina - Thai armistice signed at Saigon
11 March	Lend Lease Act signed by FDR
6 April	Germany attacks Yugoslavia and Greece
13 April	Japanese-Soviet Five Year Neutrality Pact signed in Moscow
17 April	Yugoslav army surrenders
27 April	German troops occupy Athens
9 May	French Indochina - Thai Peace Treaty signed in Tokyo with Japanese guarantee of new borders
27 May	FDR proclamation of Unlimited National Emergency
22 June	Germany invades Soviet Union
12 July	British-Soviet Mutual Assistant Agreement signed in Moscow
25 July	Britain renounces commercial agreement with Japan
2 August	US-Soviet exchange of notes on economic assistance
14 August	Atlantic Charter jointly declared by Churchill and FDR
11 September	FDR announces "shoot-on-sight" order to US Navy in American defensive waters
16 October	Successful conclusion of Manchukuo-Outer Mongolian border talks in Harbin, Manchukuo
25 November	Renewal for five years of Anti-Comintern Pact of 25 November 1936 at Berlin by German, Japan and Italy and others
6 December	FDR message to Japanese Emperor, Hirohito, regarding Pacific conversation
7 December	Japan attacks Pearl Harbor, Hong Kong and international settlement at Shanghai. Japan declares State-of-War with US, Great Britain, Canada and Netherlands East Indies

Figure 4.7.1 Prince Fumimaro Konoye and cabinet, 22 July 1940. War Minister General Hideki Tojo, Navy Minister Admiral Zengo Yoshida and Foreign Minister Yosuke Matsuoka, second, third and fifth from left in second row.

Figure 4.7.2 Signing the Tripartite pact, Suburo Kurusu, Galleazzo Ciano and Adolf Hitler, 27 September 1940

Figure 4.7.3 Matsuoka shakes hands with Hitler on his grand tour of Europe, 28 March 1941. Schmidt and Goering in attendance.

Figure 4.7.4 Matsuoka signing Neutrality Pact. Molotov and Stalin standing behind 13 April 1941

Fig. 4.7.5 Admiral Nagano soon after being named as Chief of the Naval General Staff with former Chief, Prince Fushimi (with wife and children in front row)

Fig. 4.7.6 Emperor Hirohito second from left (1940) with Army Chief of Staff Prince Kanin (third fromn left in front row) and Navy Chief of Staff Prince Fushimi (far right).

Fig. 4.7.7 Nagano attending reception in Prince Hiroyasu Fushimi's garden (1940)

HE GAVE THE ORDER

Fig. 4.7.8 Imperial Headquarters staff. Admiral Nagano (center)

Fig. 4.7.9 Admiral Nagano and friends

HE GAVE THE ORDER

Fig. 4.7.10 Map of Southeast Asia including French Indochina

Fig. 4.7.11 Prime Minister Tojo's cabinet. Front row left to right: Takasumi Oka, Tei-ichi Suzuki, Osami Nagano, Hideki Tojo, Shigetaro Shimada and Hajime Sugiyama. Second row second from right: Kenryo Sato. 19 October 1941

Fig. 4.7.12 Japanese planes attacking Pearl Harbor 7 December 1941

Chapter 5

Post Script

Overview June 1942

- In June 1942, Matsuoka's World Order played out as he envisaged. Hitler dominated Europe, Japan controlled Asia and America had the Western Hemisphere.
- Hitler honored the Tripartite Pact and declared war on the United States. He boasted "We cannot lose the war now. We have a partner who has not been defeated in 3000 years." He waged total war on the "two major "enemies of human survival – International Marxism (Russia) and International Capitalism (America), both creatures of International Jewry." The war became the exact opposite to what Emperor Hirohito warned Prime Minister Tojo against. In one stroke, Americans were united in the war against the aggressors. (Ref. 5.1)
- Stalin honored the Neutrality Pact and stayed neutral in the Pacific
- In essence, World War II had two theaters: (1) European war with Germany and satellites versus the United States, Britain Russia and allies, (2) Pacific war with Japan and puppet states versus United States, Britain, China and allies.
- While General Sugiyama had predicted that it would take the Imperial Army from four to six months to take Singapore, they were in Singapore in three months.
- General Tojo's Greater East Asia Co-Prosperity Sphere was within his grasp.
- Admiral I. Yamamoto's armada was on its way to capture Midway Island.
- Admiral O. Nagano and the Imperial Navy had deposited a landing party on Guadalcanal to build an airstrip in order to isolate Australia. In response, Admiral Chester Nimitz diverted the 1st Marine Division, which was on its way to New Zealand, to Guadalcanal and they successfully captured the airfield. The Japanese retaliated and sent a crack regiment headed by the notorious firebrand, Colonel Ichiki Kiyonao, to Guadalcanal. He scoffed that it would only require swords and sabers to defeat the Americans. Another remarked "Westerners – being haughty, effeminate and cowardly – intensely dislike fighting in the rain or mist or in the dark." A U.S. Army Air Force officer returning from Guadalcanal reported to General Hap Arnold "there's another Bataan coming and so you'd better get ready for it." (Ref. 5.2)
- Hitler's hoards were at the gates of Stalingrad.
- The Japanese were riding high in June 1942, but the World Order did not turn out as predicted.

Battle of Midway, 4-7 June 1942

After defeat at the Battle of Midway, a despondent Admiral Yamamoto wrote to Admiral Nagano lamnenting, "We lost many ships at the battle. I will atone for it with my life." Nagano burned the letter stating, "This is not good for Yamamoto." In his distress, Yamamoto showed prescience since his life was lost in a plane shot down by U.S. forces over Bougainville. The decision to target Yamamoto was not taken lightly given that it was carried all the way up to President Franklin Roosevelt.

Sendai Air Raid, 9/10 July 1945

In November 1944, the 20th Air Force commenced its bombing campaign against the Japanese home islands. As Admiral Isoroku Yamamoto predicted, Japanese wooden and cardboard houses in the cities were going up in flames. The B-29s were taking off from fields in China after flying "The Hump" from their home bases in India. Later, they flew from air fields in Saipan, Tinian and Guam in the Marianas. Most of these raids were initially to major metropolitan and industrial areas in central Honshu, Kyushu and Shikoku (Ref. 5.7). In June, July and August 1945, minor Japanese cities were hit and one was Sendai in northern Honshu. This raid hit Osami Nagano personally. His wife Kyoko had family in Sendai and he had his second son, Takaaki, sent there with his mother-in-law. In addition, a POW camp was located in Sendai so Nagano assumed his family would be relatively safe. But, in Mission No. 257 on 9/10 July 1945, the 58th Bomb Wing out of Tinian sent about 100 planes and dropped 911 tons of incendiary and explosive bombs on a town of approximately 200,000 inhabitants. The strike devastated 1.26 square miles of the populated area (Ref. 5.7).

In the raid, the nine-year-old Takaaki Nagano was killed as well as several members of Kyoko's family, including her mother (Ref. 5.6). America was involved in psychological warfare and leaflets and newspapers were dropped specifying a number of targets to be hit and warned the populace to evacuate.

In Sendai, when the raid started, Americans in the POW camp fled with most of Sendai's population. Later, the prisoners were recaptured and were court-martialed by the Japanese. At the trial, the judge asked prisoner John Cowalski who was going to win the war. He defiantly stated "the United States." He was given a two-year sentence. POW Oklahoma Atkinson reminisced that America might be winning since in their early days of captivity he would have been beheaded (Ref. 5.8).

Misako Nagano in her memoir (Ref. 5.6) stated that her mother and father had an argument over the death of their son and how it affected Osami. She wrote "I heard a rare argument between my mother and father about the death of their son, Takaaki. My mother made an abrupt and rather strong question to my father. Just tell, you must, which saddened you more – the loss of our son or the loss of the war. My father shouted back that the loss of the war hurts more. My mother broke down in tears in her kitchen. ...on the day of Takaaki's funeral, I saw my father in uncontrollable tears for the first time. Then I saw his true answer to my mother." (Ref. 5.6)

INTERNATIONAL MILITARY TRIBUNAL FOR THE FAR EAST: 1946 TO 1948

Three Escaped Judgment

Following four years of bloody conflict, Hitler's Germany and Hirohito's Japan were defeated. General Douglas MacArthur was in charge in Tokyo where the Allies convened the International Military Tribunal for the Far East (IMTFE).

Originally, 28 Japanese citizens were arrested in 1946 and indicted by military tribunal. The tribunal consisted of 11 nations that participated in the Pacific War from 1941 to 1945. Several ideas were floated on the best approach for a war crimes trial. One was to have the charges announced and shoot them all (Soviet Union). The other approach was that the 28 were all innocent and should be freed immediately (Justice Radhabinod Pal, India). General MacArthur, Supreme Commander of Allied Forces in the Far East, took over and followed the standard U.S. military practice of holding a tribunal. All defendants would be charged and given an opportunity to defend themselves. They were all provided legal counsel, both western and Japanese. The Chief Prosecuting Attorney was the American, Joseph Keenan, a lawyer from Pawtucket, RI. He was assisted by attorneys from the other allied nations. Figure 5.1 shows a photograph of Nagano at his arraignment and Figure 5.2 shows Nagano with fellow defendants in transit to court.

Appendix G tables the 28 defendants with their verdicts and sentences. There were three, however, who escaped judgment – Okawa, Matsuoka and Nagano.

Shumei Okawa

In 1946, Dr. Shumei Okawa, author and philosopher, was arrested and charged as a Class A war criminal and was tried before the International Military Tribunal. He was accused of "crimes against peace by planning and initiating a war of aggression" for his complicity in plotting the Mukden Incident of 18 September 1931 that led the Japanese army to invade Manchuria and subsequently the Japanese government set up the puppet state of Manchukuo.

On the first day of trial – 3 May 1946 – sitting in the defendants' section of the courtroom in an agitated state, Okawa was clasping his hands and repeatedly unbuttoning and buttoning his shirt. The clerk read the formal charges to the court and when Count Number 22, "on or about 7 December 1941, initiating a war of aggression..." was read it prompted Okawa to slap the back of Tojo's head (see Figure 5.3). Tojo was stunned but Okawa slapped him again. But Tojo, knowing the source, remained calm (Ref. 5.9). Military Police immediately removed Okawa from the courtroom and in the corridor the prisoner uttered "I must kill Tojo – it will be good for my country if I do." He was true to his character as he was implicated several times for assassinations and assassination attempts in 1931 and 1932. In this instance he was ahead of the court in his own indictment of Tojo. Okawa was sent for psychiatric examination.

Okawa was an interesting character. A scholar of Indian philosophy and ancient Sanskrit literature, he was fluent in German, English, French and Pali (the language of early Buddhist scriptures). He worked for the Imperial Japanese Army as a translator and held a position in the South Manchurian Railway Company. He was an ultra-nationalist with staunch anti-western philosophy and was one of the founders of Pan-Asianism, which eschewed western capitalism and strove to rid Asia of western influence. His philosophical scapegoats for Japanese and Asian poverty were the westerners, particularly British and American. In his own words he defined Pan-Asianism as the "freeing of Asia of white domination; the expelling by force under the leadership of Japan of all white interests, governmental and commercial, in Asia; and the eventual domination of the world by Japan." This quote was taken from A Brief Outline of Acts in the career of Dr. Shumei Okawa from the Tokyo War Crimes Trial. (Ref. 5.10) Okawa published many works, the most prominent of which was "Japan and the Way of the Japanese." He was called the Japanese equivalent of Joseph Goebbels, the Nazi propagandist.

Upon his removal from the IMTFE courtroom proceedings, Okawa was declared *non compos mentis* and committed to the Matsuzawa mental hospital in Tokyo. During his confinement from 1946 to 1948 he translated the entire Quran into Japanese. An observer of Okawa at Matsuzawa hospital recorded that "He no longer babbles German like an insane person. He has improved greatly, and when one speaks to him alone, aside for a few instances, it is difficult to believe that this is the insane person who surprised the world." Okawa lived out his life in Tokyo where he died 24 December 1957 at the age of 71. Okawa was crazy like a fox. He was the only one of the 28 Class A defendants to escape a prison sentence or execution.

Yosuke Matsuoka

After his dismissal by Prime Minister Konoye in July 1941, Matsuoka retired to his country home and isolated himself in a second-floor room without radio or newspapers. On 25 October 1941, after General Tojo became the Prime Minister, Tojo sent a letter to Matsuoka, which after he read it, had his assistant burn the letter. With wartime rationing and dire shortages, a friend of Matsuoka loaned him the use of his house in Koni near a hot spring, which was a great relief for Matsuoka. He had tuberculosis which was life-treatening disease at that time. As Japanese wartime fortunes deteriorated, some military officers contemplated sending Matsuoka to Moscow to salvage the Japanese from defeat, but Stalin and Molotov refused to receive him. Matsuoka urged a last-ditch, desperate stand on Honshu Island. A day or so after the atomic bomb were dropped on Hiroshima, Matsuoka dismissed its importance, obviously oblivious to the true extent of the devastation it caused.

On 19 April 1946, Matsuoka was arrested and placed in Sugamo Prison for war crimes defendants. Friends offered him cyanide pills, but he stated that he had no need for them. Dr. Inoue, a convert to Catholicism and long time friend, kept Matsuoka well informed of his health with regard to his tubercular condition. In June 1946, he took sick and was placed in the 325 Station Hospital. His condition deteriorated and he was transferred to Tokyo University Hospital where he expired on 26 June 1946. Dr. Inoue baptized him again in the Catholic sacrament although he had been baptized in the Methodist faith in America. His wife also converted to Catholicism. To what effect his visit with Pope Pius XII during his European trip in March-April 1941 is not known, but he was much impressed with the Pope.

Mrs. Matsuoka had him buried in a Catholic service at Kanda Catholic Church in Tokyo. The priest in his homily stated "The judgment of heaven will be fuller in love and warmth than the earthly judgment" (Ref. 5.4). In is own poem, Matsuoka left the words "With no regret nor grudge shall I proceed to the other world."

Brackman wrote (Ref. 5.9) that Matsuoka made the following futuristic statement to A. E. Werner, a Reuters correspondent in 1910: "I foresee that, in 30, 40, perhaps it will be 50 years, Japan will make a war against the West and after a desperate struggle will be completely destroyed by a combination of powers."

Osami Nagano

After his arrest for the International Military Tribunal for the Far East, Class A prisoner Osami Nagano, took full responsibility for having ordered Japan's attack on the U.S. fleet at Pearl Harbor in December 1941. While incarcerated at Sugamo Prison he wrote a memoir and cooperated with his American defense attorney, John G. Brannon, who is portrayed in Figure 5.4. Nagano's health was deteriorating and conditions at Sugamo led to his death from natural causes, specifically pneumonia and heart failure. He died on January 5, 1947 prior to judgment on his Class A charges of crimes against peace. Following his funeral he was cremated and his ashes were interred at a Buddhist tomb near his home in Ishikawa and in a tomb near his birthplace, Kochi, on Shikoku Island. Admiral Nagano's memory is enshrined at Yasukuni Shrine in Tokyo.

John Brannon had developed a relationship with Admiral Nagano while developing his defense strategy and wrote of his conflicts over defending the enemy and his American patriotism. He penned a telling manuscript on the story of Osami Nagano.

Story of Osami Nagano – John Brannon Collection (Ref. 5.3)

The Pearl Harbor holocaust at Japanese hands December 7, 1941, was carried out against the personal wishes of the man who ordered it. Five-star Admiral Osami Nagano, Chief of Navy General Staff, and highest ranking active naval officer in those days of Japanese belligerency, authorized the issuance of Ultra-secret Operational Order Number 1, but he maintained he didn't approve of the attack.

Throughout nearly nine months in 1946, after Nagano had been placed on trial along with Premier Tojo and other Japanese war leaders before the International Military Tribunal for the Far East in Tokyo, I carried on friendly and intimate conversations with him. Sometimes we conversed in the old Japanese War Ministry where the trial was being held, but usually our hours were spent at Sugamo Prison. As his lawyer it was my duty to do so, but actually it was a period of fascinating study at the hands of a keen, brilliant teacher.

He seemed to sense that he would not last out the long legal procedure and often spoke to me of his impending death. Although he had once been a plump, robust man, the war years had carved him down to a frail, aging individual, gaunt of frame and with an almost skeleton-like face. His frequent plaintive smile seemed unreal, like an echo from the past, but his mind was sharp and clear; his courage was great. His only complaint in those days was his treatment at Sugamo Prison when greater security measures were taken with the prisoners to insure against suicide.

Almost on the fifth anniversary of the Japanese attack on Pearl Harbor, in December 1946, he confided that the prison routine requiring him and the other defendants to dress and undress in difference rooms before and after the trial day, a requirement that forced them to walk naked down a long, cold corridor, was not only embarrassing to men of the advanced age but had caused him to contract a cold. Shortly afterward, on January 4, 1947, he died of pneumonia. Although he was absent from the trial for a few days, I was never told of his critical condition. Perhaps I failed in my duty when I neglected to call his gently protestations to the attention of proper officials; but then, so did the Admiral fail in his duty to Japan and the world when he unleashed the infamous attack on Pearl Harbor a decade ago – and his sin was greater than mine.

Basically, the Admiral had told me, the attack on Pearl Harbor had been a naval academy problem for many years. It was a tactical question often thrust at the cadets. He point to the American naval academy and suggested it was not unlike their problems relative to naval maneuvers against Japan. American war games in the Pacific in 1940 added certain information to the observing Japanese, and especially Admiral Isoroku Yamamoto, Commander-in-Chief of the Combined Fleet.

Throughout 1940 and 1941, the Japanese Army and Navy fought to get more than their meager allotment of oil. They were rivals for this precious fluid, often misrepresenting to each other in their efforts to obtain replenishment for the rapidly dwindling reserve supply. Nagano told me, "America had the oil. We were helpless as long as a hostile country could ultimately sail our ships or move our armies. We had a two year reserve supply of oil; after that we were helpless. If we remained idle our oil would soon be gone, and the United States would have crushed us without a shot."

As we sat there in that small room in the prison, he would often repeat, "It was a black war – it was an oil war!" And this, he said, was why he finally agreed to the Pearl Harbor operation.

Nagano opposed the attack on Pearl Harbor for two reasons: (1) It was too risky. (2) It was psychologically bad. He told me he had been in America on many occasions, and that he once was a special student at Yale University (sic). "I know America and I understood American people," he said, "and I knew they would fight if properly aroused. I was afraid a sudden blow at your Pearl Harbor would be the kick of the hornet's nest."

On the operational side, Nagano feared the heavy odds against him. "Our aircraft carriers were not equipped to cross the Pacific to Pearl Harbor and return under their own supply of fuel oil. It meant oil barges would have to be taken along in the task force. This increased our chances of being discovered and destroyed before the mission even reached its destination," he pointed out. "Also," he said, "two-thirds of our carrier fleet were required in the plans. If we were discovered, attacked and destroyed, our navy would have been almost hopelessly crippled at the very outset of the war. It was a fearful risk."

So Admiral Nagano discussed, debated and argued with Admiral Yamamoto, the author of the new version of the Pearl Harbor attack plans. But Yamamoto was adamant. "If there must be a war with the United States, and I hope against hope it shall never occur, we cannot succeed without this initial thrust," he pounded at Nagano.

"Our oil is in the south," he reasoned, "and if we are to move south to get it, we cannot risk a flank attack by the American Navy now at Pearl Harbor. We must cripple their fleet so that we will have time to strengthen ourself."

And it was not until the extremely popular Yamamoto, an admitted naval genius who was likened by the Japanese people to the worshipful Admiral Togo of the Russo-Japanese days, threatened to resign, that Nagano finally yielded to the attack plan. Later, after the attack was successfully achieved, Nagano admitted he was elated, and that he considered it a "glorious victory." For this, Nagano cannot be criticized. American naval experts have never discounted it as a remarkable naval feat.

The actual attack plans were more than ultra secret. They were confined to a very few. Vice-Admiral Chuichi Nagumo, commanding the carrier fleet, relied greatly on Commander Minoru Genda, his deputy chief of staff, for the actual paper work. Young Commander Mitsuo Fuchida, was called in during October, 1941, and told it was just a paper plan but that he was assigned to working it out as a practical matter. Later Fuchida led the pilots in their foray over the actual targets at Pearl Harbor.

As the pilots trained they did not know the purpose of the maneuver. They were not told until the task force put out on the mission. Two great physical difficulties arose: (1) How to use aerial torpedoes since the Pearl Harbor waters were shallow and the drop had to be reduced from the regulations 100 meters to 10 or 20 meters. (2) How to effectively strike a ship with the usual nine plane formation reduced to five. In the even torpedo netting was used by the Americans, the Japanese decided to resort to direct bombing at 3000 meters, using 16 inch cannon shells modified by taking off the iron nose and putting on a steel point.

Nagano would usually sum up by saying he was right and wrong about the whole thing – wrong about the success of the attack, but right about the hornet's nest.

Brannon wrote to his brother that Nagano was the most interesting of the Tribunal defendants and that he could write a book on him. Nagano is shown in the courtroom defendants' box in Figure 5.5. In his letter to Sonny Brannon, dated 13 January 1947, he wrote "Nagano had no personal contact with any Americans. He personally ordered no atrocities and through my contact with him in the nature of letters and personal interviews, I am convinced that he was one of the gentlest men I have ever known to hold or occupy a high military position." Figures 5.6 and 5.7 shows Brannon with Nagano family members.

Concluding Remarks

Until 8 December 1941, Admiral Osami Nagano led a charmed life. He traveled widely, entertained and was entertained by world leaders and was highly decorated for his standing in the Imperial Japanese Navy. He was bedecked with medals, orders and decorations, which included some of the highest bestowed by the government of Japan and other nations (see Appendix E). Nagano's naval career was unique in which he served his country from the Russia-Japanese war, disarmament conferences to World War II as a sailor, diplomat and politician. As loyal as he was to his country and its navy, Nagano was a devoted family man. His family life, as with many military men, had many interruptions and the life span of individuals was relatively short by today's standards. He married four times. His first three wives died in childbirth or from tuberculosis. His fourth wife, Kyoko, died two years after Nagano died on 5 January 1947. Admiral Nagano fathered seven children – his daughter, Tazuko, died at age 16 from tuberculosis. His son, Takaaki, was sent away to avoid the fire raids in Tokyo but he was killed at age 9 in a B-29 raid on Sendai in 1945. Three of his children are alive today and Misako Nagano has published a memoir of her father "Everlasting Ocean." (Ref. 5.6). Photos of the man clearly show how greatly he enjoyed his family and career.

As a military man, Nagano did not accomplish what one of his predecessors, Admiral Heihachiro Togo accomplished in defeating the Russian navy in the Russo-Japanese war (1904-1905). He did, however, sting and wake up the Americans by ordering Admiral Isoruku Yamamoto to attack Pearl Harbor on 8 December 1941 (Tokyo time). This event followed arguments between Yamamoto and Nagano on appropriate way to initiate a war for oil with America. This did not, however, bring victory, but as many in the Imperial Navy predicted, prolonged the war which ended as forecast by Yosuke Matsuoka with the unleashing of a terrible new weapon – the atomic bomb – which could spell the end of modern civilization.

Chapter 5 References

5.1 Toland, John, *Adolph Hitler*, Volume II, Doubleday & Co, Inc. Garden City, NY, 1970
5.2 Bartlett, Lt. Col. Merrill L., "Guadalcanal: A Red Hot Potato," *Proceedings* U.S. Naval Institute, Vol. 133/11/1257, November 2007
5.3 Brannon, John G., Private papers, Special Collection, Georgetown Law Library
5.4 Lu, David J., *Agony of Choice*, Lexington Books, Lanham, MD, 2002
5.5 *New York Times*, Obituary Shumei Okawa, December 27, 1971
5.6 Nagano, Misako, *Everlasting Ocean*, Minami-No-Kaze Publishing Company, Kochi City, 1995
5.7 Bradley, F. J., *No Strategic Targets Left*, Turner Publishing Company, Paducah, Kentucky, 1999
5.8 Daws, Gavan, *Prisoners of the Japanese: POWs of World War II in the Pacific*, Wm. Morro & Company, Inc., New York, NY, 1994
5.9 Brackman, Arnold C., *The Other Nuremberg: the Untold Story of the Tokyo War Crimes Trials*, Quill – William Morrow, New York, 1987
5.10 Brief Outline of Acts in the Career of Dr. Shumei Okawa, 15 March 1946, accessed on 29 October 2012 at http://lib.law.virginia.edu/imtfe

Figure 5.1 Osami Nagano at his arraignment, 1946. Photo by Alfred Eisenstaedt

Figure 5.2 Japanese war crime prisoners on way to be arraigned at the War Ministry Building in Tokyo

Figure 5.3 Okawa in court behind Tojo

Figure 5.4 John G. Brannon, Osami Nagano's defense attorney (Georgetown Law Library)

Figure 5.5 IMTFE defendants 14 May 1946. Osami Nagano in back row, third from left.

Figure 5.6 Attorney John Brannon with Nagano's family and friends (Georgetown Law Library)

Figure 5.7 Brannon with Kyoko and children

Glossary

20th Air Force:	US Army Air Corps was divided into Air Forces and the 20th Air Force was located first in India then in the Marianna Islands of Guam, Saipan and Tinian.
58th Bomb Wing:	The various Air Forces were divided into Bomb Wings. The 58th BW was part of the 20th Air Force and was initially located in India.
America:	One of the descriptions of the United States of America.
Anti-Comintern Pact:	Treaty between Germany and Japan against communist subversion.
Army General Staff:	Unit of Japanese Imperial Army that gave instructions to the army in the field.
Axis Powers:	Alliance of Germany, Italy and Japan in World War II
B-29	Superfortress high altitude, pressurized bomber manufactured by Boeing for the Army Air Corps.
Bangkok	Capital of Thailand (Siam)
Britain	Great Britain, sometimes United Kingdom
Burma Road	Access road from Lashio in Burma to Kumning in southwest China
Cam Ranh Bay	Deep-water bay on southeastern coast of French Indochina (Viet Nam)
Central Powers	Alliance of warring powers in World War I consisting of Austria-Hungary Empire, German Empire, Ottoman Empire and Kingdom of Bulgaria
China Incident	China War 1937-1945
Chungking	Capital of China from 1937 to 1945 under Chiang Kai-shek
Control Way	Political faction in Japan right of political center 1937-1945 mainly in the Army
Diplomatic Cyclone	Diplomatic change in the Foreign Service by Foreign Secretary Matsuoka during his administration, July 1940- July 1941
Draft Understanding	Initial proposal by John Doe Associates for agreement between Japan and United States to prevent conflict
Eta Jima	Island location of Japanese Imperial Naval Academy in Hiroshima Bay
FIC, SIC and NIC	French Indochina, Southern Indochina and Northern Indochina
French Indochina	Southeast Asian peninsula located on the southeast coast of Asian mainland composed of present-day Viet Nam, Cambodia and Laos
Geneva Disarmament Conferences 1927 and 1932 -1933	Disarmament conference under the League of Nations
German-Russian Neutrality Pact 1939	Neutrality treaty between Germany and Russia signed in August 1939 to assure non-aggression if either were to be attacked by third power
Great Britain	Britain, United Kingdom
Greater East Asia Co-Prosperity Sphere	Economic region composed of Netherlands East Indies (present day Indonesia), Burma, Malay sia, Singapore and Borneo
Haiphong Harbor	Major harbor on east coast of French Indochina
Humning	Terminus of the Burma Road in south China
Imperial Conference	Conference in the presence of the Emperor with the Prime Minister, Army and Navy Ministers, Chief of Army Staff, Chief of Navy Staff to make important decisions
Imperial Japanese Army (IJA)	Japanese army under the Emperor
Imperial Japanese Navy (IJN)	Japanese navy under the Emperor
Imperial Japanese South China Army	Part of the Japanese army located in southern China under the Emperor
Imperial Way	Political faction specifying divinity of the Emperor (1900-1945)
Indonesia	Present day name for Netherlands (Dutch) East Indies

International Military Tribunal – Far East (IMTFE)	Tokyo war crime trial under General Douglas MacArthur
Ishikawa	A Tokyo suburb where Admiral Osami Nagano built his home
Japanese Diet	Parliament composed of two houses, the upper house consists of peers and lower house is elected by the people
John Doe Associates	Group of two Maryknoll priests and two concerned Japanese citizens who formulated a Draft Understanding to achieve peace between US and Japan in China 1940 – 1941
Lend Lease	Act of Congress passed in March 1941 permitting US government to loan materiel to the Allies in exchange for military bases
Liaison Conference	Meetings of important Japanese government, military and political figures to discuss and make decisions on military and civil issues
London Naval Disarmament Conferences	Two conferences were held in London to decide on important naval matters in 1930 and 1936
Lord Keeper of the Privy Seal	Important advisor to the Emperor (a carry-over from British Royal tradition)
Manchukuo	Puppet state established by Japanese government in the former China province of Manchuria
Manchuria	Northern province of China
Marco Polo Bridge Incident	Skirmish between Japanese and Chinese troops that occurred on 18 July 1937, which initiated the China War
Meiji Constitution	Constitution enacted under Emperor Meiji in 1875 and was amended in 1885
Mukden	Town in Manchuria where the Mukden Incident occurred on 18 September 1931 which initiated the takeover of Manchuria
Nanking	Capital of the Nationalist government of China from approximately 1910 to 1937 and reinstated by Japan from approximately 1941 to 1944
Nationalist regime	Government set up in China by Sun Yat-sen which lasted under various leaders from 1900 until 1949
Navy General Staff	Military body responsible for planning naval operations for Japanese naval fleets
Netherlands East Indies	A series of islands in southwest Pacific composed of the major islands Java and Sumatra (present day Indonesia)
Neutrality Acts	Acts of US Congress passed in 1930s prohibiting US trade in military hardware with any warring nation, which were initiated by isolationist policy. Ended in 1941 with US Lend Lease policy and declaration of war after Pearl Harbor.
Neutrality Pact between Soviet Union and Japan	Treaty between Japan and Soviet Union in which they agreed to remain neutral if either were to be attacked by a third nation
Nomonhan Incident	Border battle between Soviet and Japanese troops at the village of Nomonhan in Outer Mongolia from May to September 1939
North Sakhalin	Soviet-controlled northern region of Sakhalin Island off the coast of Siberia. The southern region was controlled by Japan from 1855 to 1945.
Pearl Harbor	US Naval Base on Oahu Island in the Hawaiian Islands, attacked by Japanese Navy 7 Dec 1941 (8 Dec Tokyo time)
Phony War	Britain and France declared war on Hitler's Germany on 3 September 1939 but little military action occurred until 10 May 1940
POW	Prisoner of War
Prime Minister	Political leader primarily of a parliamentary government
Russia	Also called Russian Empire located in East Europe and North and West Asia allied with US and Great Britain in the European theater of World War II
Samurai	Japanese warrior class in feudal Japan up to approximately 1870
Sendai	Capital city of Miyagi Prefecture in northeastern coast of Honshu Island.

Shanghai Incidents	There were two battles between China and Japan, January to May 1932 and August to November 1937
Shogun	Japanese leadership in the Edo Era from 1640 to 1867
Showa Restoration	Term used to describe return of political power to the Emperor starting 1867
Singapore	Major port in southeast Asia at the southern end of Malaysian peninsula
South Manchurian Railroad Company	Private company controlling operation of the rail system and other business enterprises in Manchuria during Japanese occupation, 1932 to 1945
South Sakhalin	Japanese-controlled southern region of Sakhalin Island off the coast of Siberia up to 1945
Soviet Union	Union of Soviet Socialist Republics (USSR) Group of republics that lasted from 1922 to 1991
Sugamo Prison	US Army XI Corps stockade No. 1 housing 700 cells where 28 Class A defendants were imprisoned during Tokyo War Crime Trial
Supreme Command – Imperial Command	Military command consisting of Chief of Army Staff and Chief of Navy Staff and their deputies who coordinated the operational plans of the army and navy in field operations. Relocated to Imperial Palace in July 1941.
Thai-French Indochina Border Clash	Incident initiated by Thailand in January 1941 involving a disputed border
Thailand	Country of southeast Asia formerly known as Siam
Tonkin Gulf	Gulf of Tonkin forms the coast of northern French Indochina (Vietnam). It is an arm of the South China Sea.
Tosa Clan	Feudal clan located on Shikoku Island with the principal city of Kochi
Treaty of Commerce	Commercial treaty between United States and Japan signed in 1911 and abrogated 1940
Tripartite Pact	Treaty between Japan, Germany and Italy signed on 24 September 1940, which specified that, if a third party entered the European war, the signatories would declare war on the third party
United Kingdom	Sovereign state of United Kingdom of Great Britain and Northern Ireland located off the northwest coast of continental Europe
United States	The United States of America is a constitutional republic consisting of 50 states located in North America and Hawaiian Islands
USS Panay Incident	The sinking of the US warship, Panay, by Japanese planes on 18 December 1937 on the Yangtze River near Peking
Vichy France	France and her territories from July 1940 to September 1944 following surrender to Hitler's army. She was ruled by Marshal Philippe Petain from the capital in Vichy.
Washington Naval Treaty 1922	Treaty between Britain, US, Japan, France and Italy specifying number of capital ships allotted to each signatory
World War I	Sometimes called the "Great War" centered in Europe, which lasted from August 1914 to 18 November 1918 between the Central Powers and the Allies
World War II	War between Axis Powers and Allied Powers. The European phase 3 September 1939 to 9 May 1945. Pacific phase was from 7 December 1941 to 2 September 1945.
Yasukuni Shrine	Shinto memorial shrine located in Tokyo honoring Japanese war dead
Yokosuka Naval Base	Japanese naval base located on Tokyo Bay

Significant Individuals

Abe, General Nobuyuki	Japanese Prime Minister 1 September 1939 – 14 May 1940
Araki, General Sadao	Imperial Japanese Army Minister 193-1934
Brannon, James G.	American defense attorney for Osami Nagano at the IMTFE, 1946-1947
Chiang Kai-shek	Chief military and political leader of the Nationalist government in Nanking 1927 – 1937 and later in Chungking December 1937 - 1945
Churchill, Winston	British Prime Minister 1940-1945
Coolidge, Calvin	30th President of the United States 1923-1929
Drought, Father John	Maryknoll priest and member of the John Doe Associates
Fushimi, Prince Hiroyasu	Uncle of Emperor Hirohito, Chief of Naval Staff 1933 – 9 April 1941
Grew, Joseph C.	American ambassador to Japan 1933-1941
Hara, Yoshimichi	President of Japanese Privy Council who often asked questions at Imperial Conferences for Emperor Hirohito
Harding, Warren G.	29th President of United States 1921 – August 1923
Hayashi, General Senjuro	Imperial Japanese Army Minister in Okada cabinet 1934-1936, Prime Minister of Japan February to June 1937
Henderson, Arthur	British Foreign Minister 1929-1931, President of Geneva Disarmament Conference 1931-1935
Hiranuma, Baron Kiichiro	Japanese Prime Minister January 1939 – August 1939, Minister of Home Affairs in Prime Minister Konoye's cabinet 1940 - 1941
Hirohito, Emperor	Emperor of Japan 1925-1989
Hirota, Koki	Japanese Prime Minister March 1936 to February 1937, Japanese Foreign Minister 1934–1936 and 1937-1938
Hitler, Adolf	German Chancellor 1933 - 1945
Hoover, Herbert	31st President of the United States 1929-1932
Hughes, Charles Evans	US Secretary of State 1921 - 1925, Chairman of Washington Naval Conference 1921 - 1922
Hull, Cordell	American Secretary of State 1933-1945
Inukai, Tsuyoshi	Japanese Prime Minister November 1931 – 5 May 1932 (assassinated)
Kato, Admiral Kanji	Imperial Japanese Navy Minister
Kato, Baron Tomosaburo	Japanese Prime Minister 12 June 1922 – 23 August 1923, Chief Japanese Delegate to Washington Naval Conference 1921 – 1922
Kaya, Okinon	Finance Minister in Prime Minister Konoye's cabinet 1937– 1939 and in Prime Minister Tojo's cabinet 1941– 1944
Kido, Baron Koichi	Lord Keeper of the Privy Seal 1939 – 1945
Konoye, Prince Fumimaro	Japanese Prime Minister 1937 – 1939 and 1940 – 1941
Lytton, Victor Bulwer	Second Earl of Lytton, Chairman of commission investigating Japanese invasion and takeover of Manchuria 1931 - 1932
MacArthur, General Douglas	Commander of Allied Forces in southwest Pacific 1942 – 1944, Supreme Commander Allied Forces in Japan 1945 - 1951
Matsudaira, Tsuneo	Japanese ambassador to Great Britain 1930 – 1935, Japanese delegate to London Naval Conference 1930
Matsui, General Iwane	Commander of Shanghai Expeditionary Force, 1937 Japanese delegate to Geneva Disarmament Conference 1931 – 1933
Matsuoka, Yosuke	Japanese delegate to League of Nations Conference investigating Japanese invasion of Manchuria 1932 – 1933, Japanese Foreign Minister in Prime Minister Konoye's second cabinet July 1940 – July 1941
Meiji Emperor	Japanese Emperor 1867 – 1912
Molotov, Vyachislav	Foreign Minister of Russia 1939 – 1949, Chairman of the Council of the

	People's Commissars 1930 – 1941
Muto, General Akira	Chief of Military Affairs Bureau, Army Ministry 1940-1941
Nagano, Admiral Osami	Navy Minister 1936, Commander of Combined Fleet 1937, Chief of Naval Staff 1941-1944
Nagumo, Vice Admiral Chiuchi	Commander of First Air Fleet under Admiral Isoroku Yamamoto 1940-1945
Nimitz, Admiral Chester	US Commander of Allied Forces in Central Pacific 1942 – 1945
Nomura, Admiral Kichisaburo	Japanese ambassador in Washington DC December 1940 – December 1941
Oikawa, Admiral Koshiro	Japanese Navy Minister 1940 - 1941
Okawa, Shumei	Professor, translator and ultra-right activist IMTFE Class A defendant
Oshima, General Hiroshi	Japanese Ambassador and Military Attaché in Berlin 1937 – 1945
Osumi, Admiral Mineo	Japanese Navy Minister in Prime Minister Tsuyoshi Inukai's cabinet, 1931-1932
Osumi, Admiral Mineo	Japanese Navy Minister 1931 – 1936
Ott, Eugene	German Ambassador in Tokyo 1940 – 1945
Perry, Commodore Matthew	US Naval Commander of Pacific Squadron that visited Japan in 1853 and 1854
Roosevelt, Franklin Delano	32nd President of United States 1933 – 1945
Saionji, Prince Kinmochi	Advisor to Emperor Hirohito 1930 – 1940, Japanese Prime Minister 1906 – 1908 and 1911 – 1912
Shimada, Admiral Shigetaro	Japanese Navy Minister in Prime Minister Tojo's cabinet 1941 – 1944
Simon, Sir John	British Foreign Secretary in Prime Minister Ramsey MacDonald's cabinet 1931 – 1935
Stalin, Joseph	General Secretary of the Communist Part of Soviet Union 1922 – 1952
Stimson, Henry L.	US Secretary of State 1929 – 1932, US Secretary of War under President Franklin Delano Roosevelt 1940 – 1945
Sugiyama, General Hajime	Chief of Japanese Army General Staff 1937 – 1944
Taisho Emperor	Japanese Emperor 1912 – 1925
Teraushi, General Hisachi	Commander of Southern Expeditionary Army Group
Togo, Admiral Heihachiro	Commander-in-Chief of Combined Fleet that defeated the Russian Navy in the Russo-Japanese War 1904-1905.
Togo, Shigenori	Japanese Foreign Minister 1941 – 1942, Japanese Ambassador in Moscow 1938 – 1939
Tojo, Hideki	Japanese Prime Minister 1941 – 1944
Tokugawa, Yoshinobu	Last Shogun of Tokugawa Shogunate of Japan 1866 – 1867
Toyoda, Teijiro	Japanese Foreign Minister 1941
Von Ribbentrop, Joachim	German Foreign Minister 1935 – 1945
Walker, Frank	US Postmaster General 1940 – 1945
Walsh, Bishop James Edward	Maryknoll priest and member of John Doe Associates, later interned in Communist China 1950 – 1970
Wang, Ching-wei	Nationalist political and government leader in Nanking during Japanese occupation 1940 – 1944
Wilson, Woodrow	28th US President 1913 – 1920
Yamamoto, Admiral Isoroku	Japanese Vice Navy Minister December 1936 – 1939, Commander in Chief of the Combined Fleet July 1939 – 18 April 1943 (killed in action)
Yonai, Admiral Mitsumasa	Japanese Prime Minister May – July 1940, Japanese Navy Minister 1944 – 1945
Yoshida, Admiral Zengo	Japanese Navy Minister January – September 1940

Appendix A1

Christmas Recess – Geneva Disarmament Conference

1932-1933

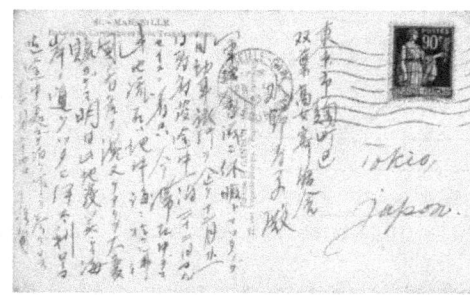

25 December 1932 To Hisako: I could have a vacation planned to travel around Europe. I left Geneva on 22 December, I visited Marseille, will enjoy warm weather at Mediterranean Sea. Tomorrow after sunset will take a walk on the beautiful boardwalk. Before going to Italy, will stop by some places on the coast.

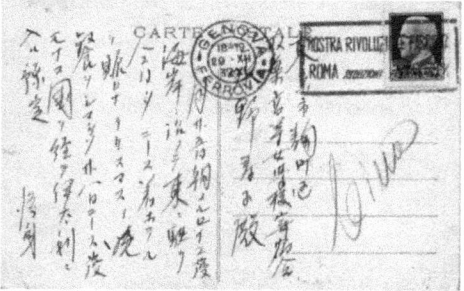

29 December 1932 To Hisako: I visited Marseille and went to east, now I am in Nice. The hotel is very crowded and lively for Christmas. We had a nice Christmas dinner in this hotel. On 28 December, we will leave Nice and go to Monaco – after that will go to Italy.

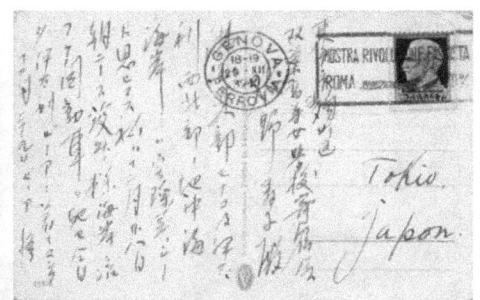

To Hisako: I left Monaco, southeast of France, came to northeast coast in Italy - very beautiful, very peaceful. On 28 December, I left Nice and traveled by car, the coast was beautiful. Now I am in Genoa, Italy. 29 December 1932 at Genoa, Italy.

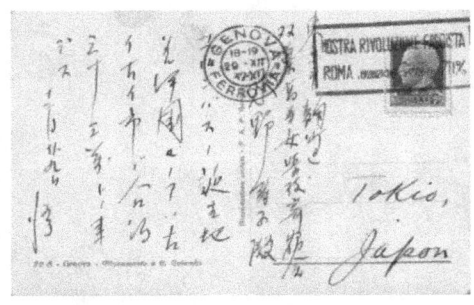

To Hisako: I arrived at Genoa in Italy, which is the place where Columbus was born. 29 December 1932.

 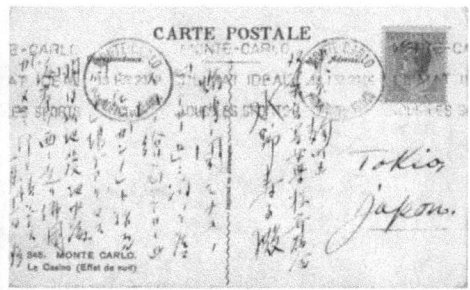

13 January 1933 To Hisako: The gambling country "Monte Carlo in Monaco", it is all about gambling. The place is called "Casino". Tomorrow I will travel west, driving along the Mediterranean Sea, will visit Cannes, France. 11 January.

 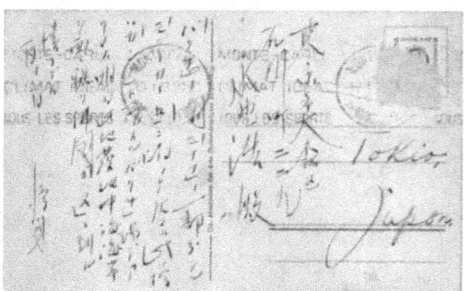

To Hiroshi: I visited some places from Paris, Monte Carlo, which belongs to the country named Monaco. There is a lot of gambling that takes place in the building called "Casino" but I enjoy looking at Mediterranean Sea more. Tomorrow I will be at Cannes, France. 13 January 1933.

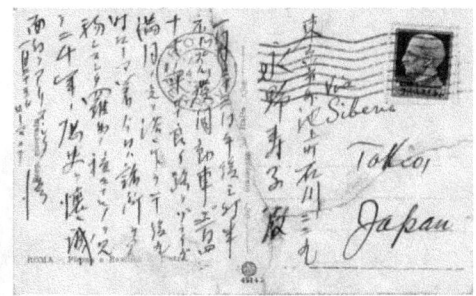

To Hisako: I left Naples by car, drove some 240 kilometers – it was nice drive with quiet and flat road. I arrived at Rome, 9:00 pm in the moonlight. It was a full moon. I had some sightseeing today, it was very interesting to see the Roman Empire's ruins from 2000 years ago. 23 January 1933, Osami in Rome.

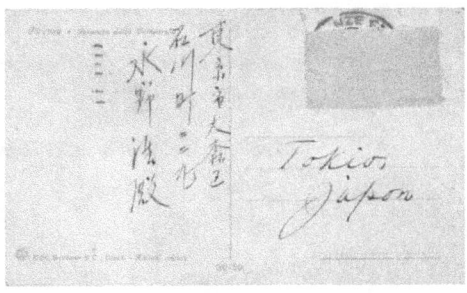

To: Hiroshi

From: Firenze, Italy

Date: Unknown

Front: From the city of Florence which has been the center of European art since the 13th Century, holding the wealth of Europe's best artistic achievements. February 8th. Osami

Both Michelangelo and Dante were born in this city.

HE GAVE THE ORDER

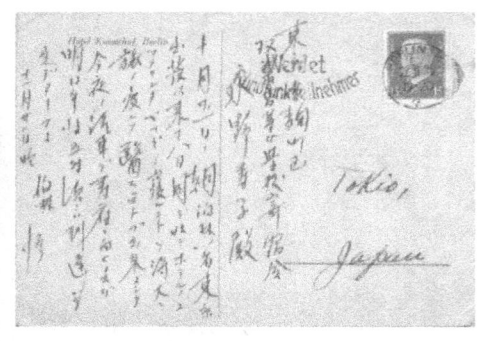

To Hisako, November 21st: I am in Berlin. Since I left Tokyo, first time to sleep on a comfortable bed in a nice hotel. I felt very relaxed and got my energy back. Tonight, I will go to Geneva. I will arrive at 5:00 tomorrow morning.

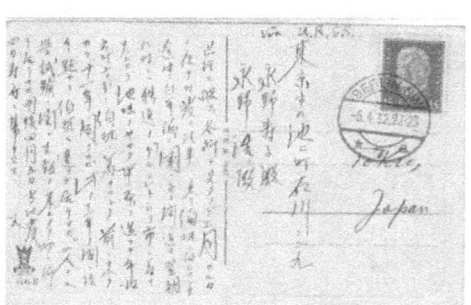

"Hope you are fine. 5 April. Osami" Brandenburg Gate, Berlin

To: Hisako, Hiroshi
From: Berlin
Date: April 5, 1932

"As I saw much of Paris, left by rail for Berlin at 10:00 pm. On 29 March, passed through Belgium during the night, arrived at Koln, Germany at 8:00 next morning. Passing via rather impoverished land, reached Berlin at 6:06 pm. It is about 11 years ago that I was here. Berlin has changed in many ways. Anxiously awaiting good results of the entrance exams for both of you. The day after tomorrow, 5 April, will leave here going back to Geneva."   Dad

 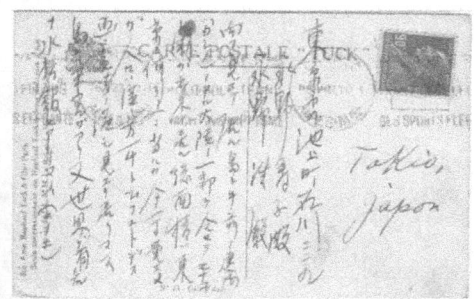

To: Hisako, Hiroshi

Posted in Cannes: 6 May 1932

"The island across and a part of the continent where the building (Casino) stands form the nation of Monaco. I don't know how the space compares with Tokyo but the population is only 11,000. The picture also shows the port of Monaco. This is a palace and a world famous aquarium."

Appendix A2

Travel Tokyo to Geneva

1931 – 1932

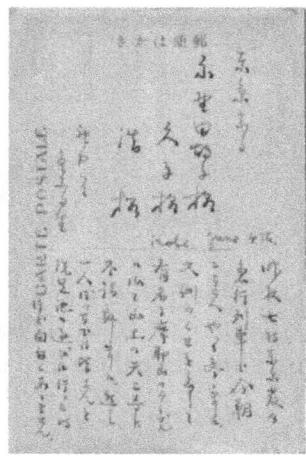

To Tazuko, Hisako, Hiroshi: At Kobe, Japan: I left Tokyo 7:00 pm last night with midnight train and arrived here this morning. As always, you know, I went up the mountain, took the famous "Cable Car," visited and prayed in the shrine which is located on top of the mountain. But, alone it is not as fun as the time when I visited Senzoku Pond with you folks.

To Hisako, January 6, at Ceylon: I arrived at the Colombo Port, which is located in southwest part of Ceylon Island. Before leaving I will visit the temple at Kandy about 72 miles away which keeps Budda's tooth and pray.

 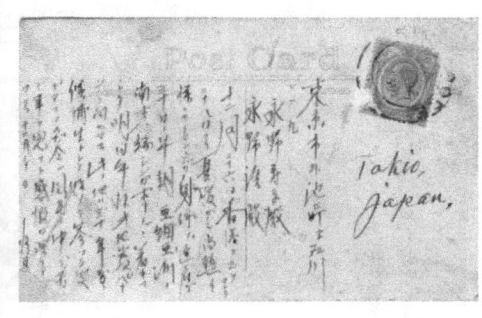

To Hisako, Hiroshi: I left Hong Kong on December 26th; it is so hot even with my summer clothes. I appreciate that I am in good health so I don't get sick. This morning, it is December 30th; we arrived in Singapore, located in the southern part of Asia. Tomorrow we will go to Penang, Malaysia. I remember I came here as a trainee 30 years ago. When I remember my old days here it makes me emotional.

To: Hisako, Hiroshi

From: Hong Kong

Date: 27 December 1931

"On the 22nd at 1:00 pm, left Shanghai. Many Japanese people came to see me of. Arrive Hong Kong at 6:00 am on the 25th. Here again, heavy entertainment for both lunch and dinner every day. Went today around the 37 mile coast of the Hong Kong Island. Also climbed up the Victoria Peak which is the highest point on the island. Had a great view. Tomorrow at 4:00 in the morning, will leave for Singapore."

To Hisako: I appreciate nice weather, safely arrived Geneva, 24 January 1932.

To: Hiroshi

From: Geneva

Date: 28 January 1932

"A smooth trip after completing the schedule in snow-covered Manchuria. Arrived at Geneva on 24 January, evening."

Appendix A3

Travel Tokyo to Washington DC, 1921
Vacation America, July – August 1922
Travel Washington DC to Tokyo, 1923

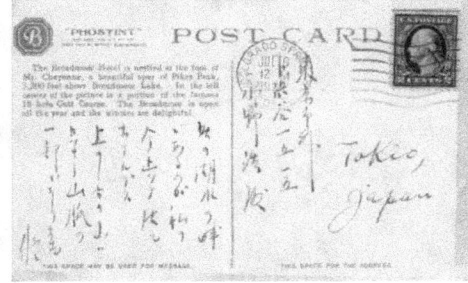

To Hiroshi: It is autumn, I am sitting by the lake, I am ready to climb up to the mountain. I see very beautiful mountains which is called Rocky Mountains, 16 July 1922.

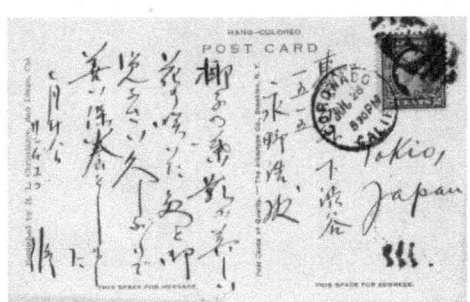

To Hiroshi: There are many palm trees, many colorful flowers, I feel so relaxed now. I had a great vacation which I haven't had for a long time. July 18th at San Diego, 18 July 1922.

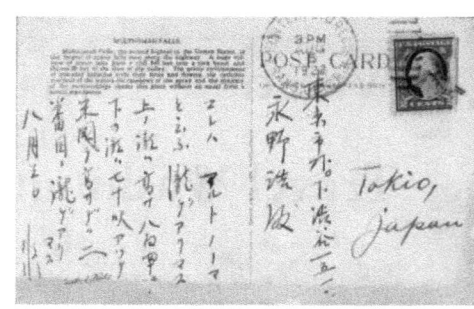

To Hiroshi: This is the famous water fall called "Multnomah Falls". A huge volume of water falls from the cliff 840 feet into a rock basin and thence 70 feet to the floor of the valley - the second biggest falls in USA. 3 August 1922.

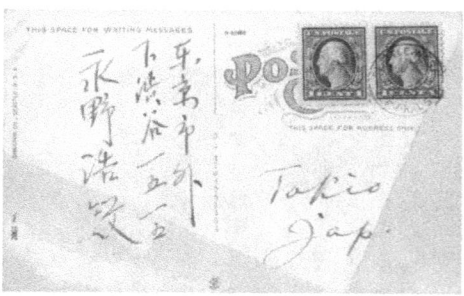

To: Hiroshi

From: Seattle, WA

Date: 8 August 1922

This is a pier of the port city of Seattle. I am right now at about the middle point of my journey from Washington, D.C. back to Tokyo. August 8. Osami

To Hiroshi:

In Mexico City. March 1, 1923. This is the main boulevard of Mexico City. It has a spring-like climate throughout the year and is very beautiful. Such beautiful cities are difficult to find even in the United States.

To Hiroshi

From: Geneva, Switzerland, 22 February 1924

Left Paris at 5:00 pm on February 20th and arrived Geneva at 10:30 am of the 21st. The beautiful mountains and lakes are most enjoyable. Next, I will be heading for Germany via Bern and Zurich.

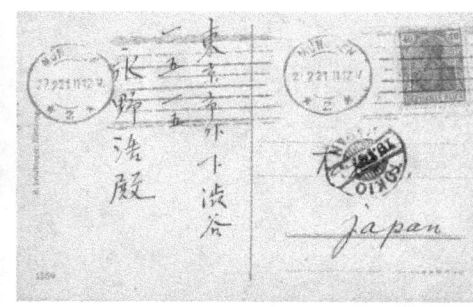

To: Hiroshi

From: Munchen, Germany

Date: February 1, 1927

After crossing the Lake of Boden (after better known as Boden-see or Lake Constance), landed in Lindau at 5:00 pm on the 25th of February. Here begins the land of Germany. Osami

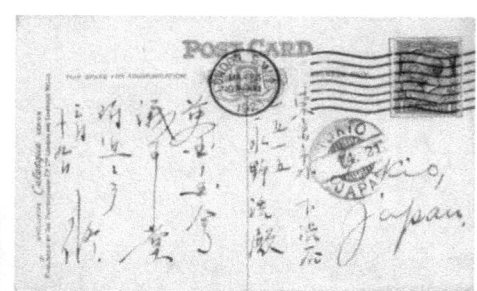

To: Hiroshi

Posted in: London 23 March 1921

"... near the British Parliament" 19 March   Osami

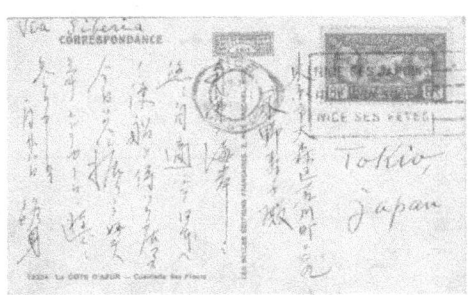

To: Hisako

From: Nice, France

"Relaxing on a beach of southern France waiting for a steamer going back to Japan. A beautiful day today for a change. Spent some time in Monte Carlo today."

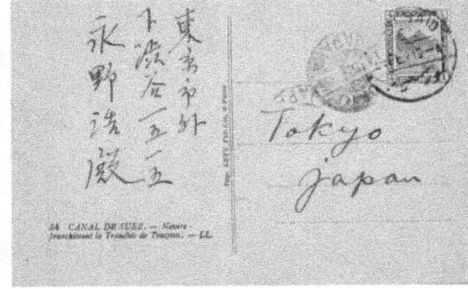

To: Hiroshi

From: Port Said, Egypt

Date: February 2

We are just about exiting the Suez Canal and entering the sea of Mediterranean. Greetings to all. Keep well. Dad

HE GAVE THE ORDER

 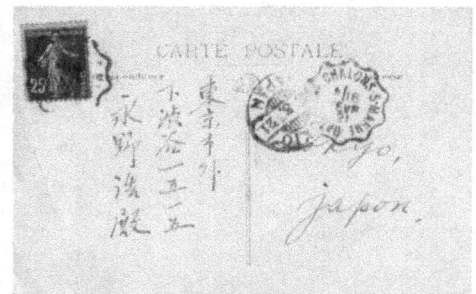

To: Hiroshi

From: Chalons, France

Date: 16 February

Front: Visited Verdun. There is the place with great view, it makes me think a lot.

Appendix A4

Travel Tokyo to London
1935 -1936

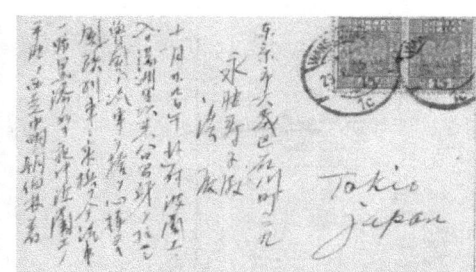

To: Hisako, Hiroshi
Posted: Warsaw, Poland, 29 November 1935
"23 November, 1:00 pm: Entered Poland and finally 'shed' the Russian train in which had to spend 8 days since Manchuria. Now transferred to a comfortable international train speeding, in a pitch dark night, to the West through the vast Polish prairie. Tomorrow morning will reach Berlin."

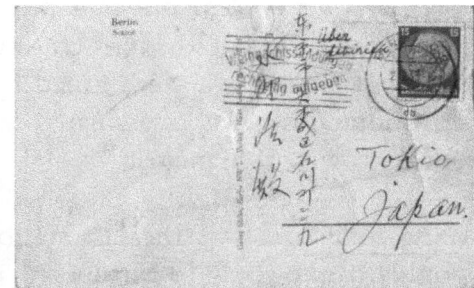

To: Hiroshi
From: Berlin, Germany
Date: 1 December 1935
On November 30th arrived Berlin – my 4th visit to the city. Leaving Berlin now by rail and will reach London tomorrow. December 1st, morning. Osami

 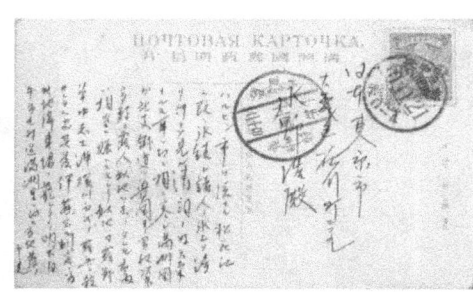

(NK) Date: Kotoku (Manchurian) Year 02.Nov.20 (1935) Additional stamp: Nov.21, Showa 10 (1935) Tokyo Central Post Office

(NK) This is a Manchurian post card "posted" in Harbin city but probably put on board a military plane to Tokyo where is was stamped again and the postage paid in Japan. It was often customary for traveling government, military officials at that time.

Addressed to: Hiroshi

"Shoko River (Chinese name: Songhua) in Harbin City is already frozen and people are walking on it. The weather is clear but it is bitterly cold. Since Manchukuo purchased the North China Railways from Russia, many Russians left but the city is still boisterous. This place is where the Japanese heroes Oki and Yokokawa were killed by the Russians during the Japan-Russo war. This where (Marquis) Hirobumi Itoh was assassinated late. At 9:00 tomorrow, the 20th, scheduled to leave here for (the border town of) Mancuria."

(NK) Manchria was the last station bordering Russia and linked to the Siberian Railway--then the popular route going to Europe.

To: Hisako

From: London

Date: 1936

A HAPPY NEW YEAR! On New Year's Day, 1936. Osami

Appendix A5

Travel to Tokyo via America

11 March 1933

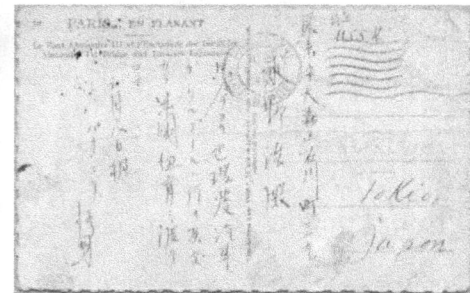

To Hiroshi: Today we leave Paris and go to Cherbourg by train; after that I will travel to New York in America. March 8th morning in Paris – Osami

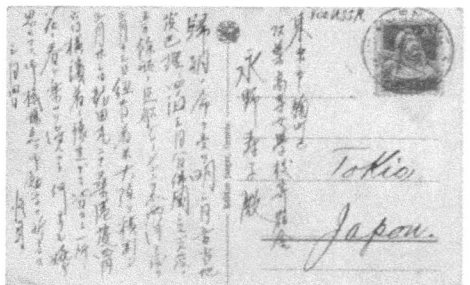

To: Hisako   From: Geneva   Date: 4 March 1933
"As received an order to return to Japan, will leave here tomorrow 5 March for Paris where will stay for 4 nights. Will then take from Cherbourg, France a 50,000 ton giant called S/S Bremen to cross the Atlantic for New York arriving there on 13 March. Will cross the continent catching S/S Tatsuta Maru from San Francisco, arrival Yokohama 6 April. It will be my greatest pleasure to celebrate the spring season with all of you. Wishing you well and success at school. Osami"

To: Hiroshi   On board S/S Bremen   Date 13 March 1933

"March 8: left Cherbourg at 4:00 pm. The sea has been quite rough every day, affecting even this 51,000 tonner. The wind and waves are causing delays by about 10 hours. Will get to New York on the 13th night. On board S/S Bremen in the Atlantic. Osami."

Appendix A6

Travel: Geneva – Tokyo round trip, 1932

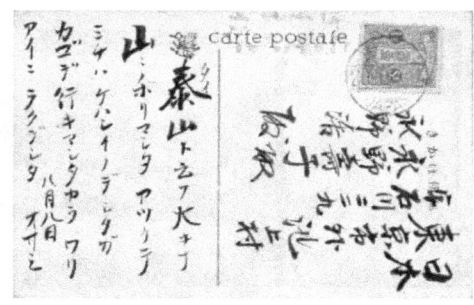

To Hisako, Hiroshi: I went up the big, big mountain "Taizan". It was very hot and hard trail, but I went with sedan chair, so it was OK. 8 August 1932, Osami

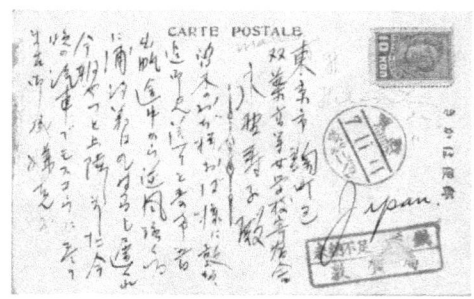

To Hisako: Please say hello to your uncle and aunt in Sogi. When I was in Tsuruga Port they sent me many (?). When we start sailing, I realized we had to head on strong wind – would arrive late. Finally we arrived at the Vladivostok in Russia. We will go to Moscow by train now. Hope you are always as happy as I know you. 19 November 1932

To: Hisako & Hiroshi   From: Moscow   Date: 19 November 1932

"Departed from Vladivostok on November 8th traveling continuously through snow-covered Siberia. Finally reached Moscow in the early morning of the 19th. Train was delayed by snow by 36 hours, thus, spent 11 days on rail – this is my record long trip by train. During the trip, the coldest spot was minus 30 degrees C. Tonight, am leaving for Berlin. November 14.   Osami in Moscow.

To: Hisako Nagan c/o dorm, Futaba Girls High School, Tokyo

From: Geneva

9 January 1933 Milano A city of music

To: Miss Hisako Nagano c/o Futaba Girls High School Dorm, Tokyo.
From Geneva, Switzerland

Front: ... to the right of the bridge exists a lake from where water flows into the River Rhone shown in the picture. City of Geneva is divided into two parts by the river with numerous bridges connecting the city. All the mountains behind the city are French territory. The white mountain is Mont Blanc – the highest in Europe. The right end corner shows a part of a small island of Rhone where a statue of ROUSSEAU stands.

Back: After a day's delay, safely reached Geneva at 5:00 pm on November 23rd. The surrounding mountains, lakes and the breeze from clean rivers all remain the same as always but Geneva in winder is dismally cloudy or rainy every day and not to pleasing. Presently, the "Japan-China issue" is debated at the League of Nations with rather uncertain prospect. As this is of paramount importance for Japan, we are making our utmost effort. Keep well. 25 November 1932. Osami

Appendix A7

Miscellaneous, 1937

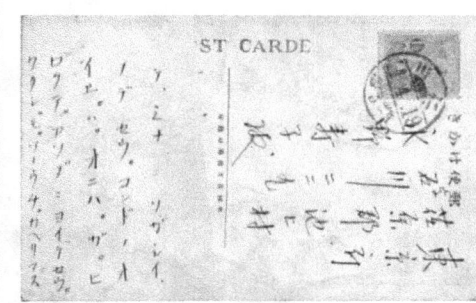

To: Hisako
Posted in: Inchon, Korea
Date 14 April 1937
"… assume (you are keeping) busy. The garden of our new house is big and nice for you to play. I'll come home soon" [written in an infant form]

To: Hisako
From: Kagoshima (Japan)
Date: 19 February 1937
"Away from the severe cold, spending time in southern Satsuma where rape-flowers are in full blossom." Osami

To: Hisako

c/o Futaba Girls High-Dorm, Tokyo

Date: July 1, 1937

"Sorry could not write for a while. Have been extremely busy under a heavy training schedule from early morning till night. Had to go on board many ships one after another observing their exercise: boarded planes from time. The efforts and dedications of the crew are truly impressive. We are all too tired at night to do anything. You'll soon have a summer vacation. Take care and study well". Osami Nagano on board INS Nagato

Appendix A8

Commemorative Postcards

![Steamship Cruise map]

Steamship Cruise map

To: Hisako Futaba Girls High – Dorm

From: Saheki (Japan)

"On the 29th of October, Showa Year 11, reverently attending to His Majesty the Grand Field Marshal on occasion of the Special Naval Drill and the Imperial Fleet Review – Osami"

(NK) The three admirals with the photos are:

Left: Adm. Takayoshi Katoh, Comander, the 2nd Fleet

Center: Adm. Sankichi Takahashi, Commander-in-Chief, Combined Fleet

Right: Adm. Koichi Shiozawa, Commander, the 4th Fleet

(NK) The printed calligraphy of 4 large letter at the bottom is written by Adm. S. Takahashi which reads "Immovable as Mountains". This is a very important motto of the Japanese Imperial Navy at the top leadership meaning that "Navy must maintain a highest capability yet shall not utilize such capability too lightly." This later leads to a head-on against the highly "action-oriented, rapid-fire" Army of Japan.

Addressed to: Hisako

Dated: Showa 11, Oct. 29 (1936)

(NK) this is a Commemorating postcard stamped as:

"Showa 11. Special Naval Drill and the Imperial Fleet Review' on October 29, 1936"

Ministry of the Navy October 29, 1936

HE GAVE THE ORDER

Appendix B

Nagano Family Tree

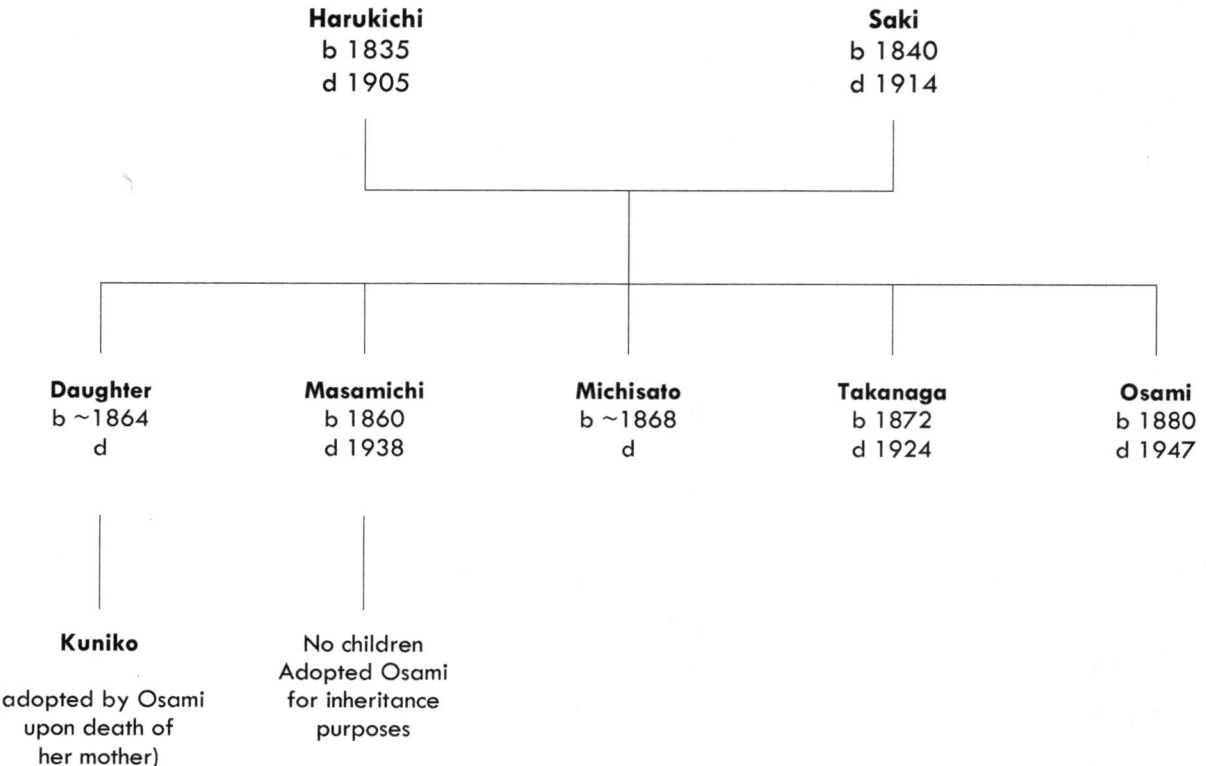

Osami Nagano's Wives, Children and Grandchildren

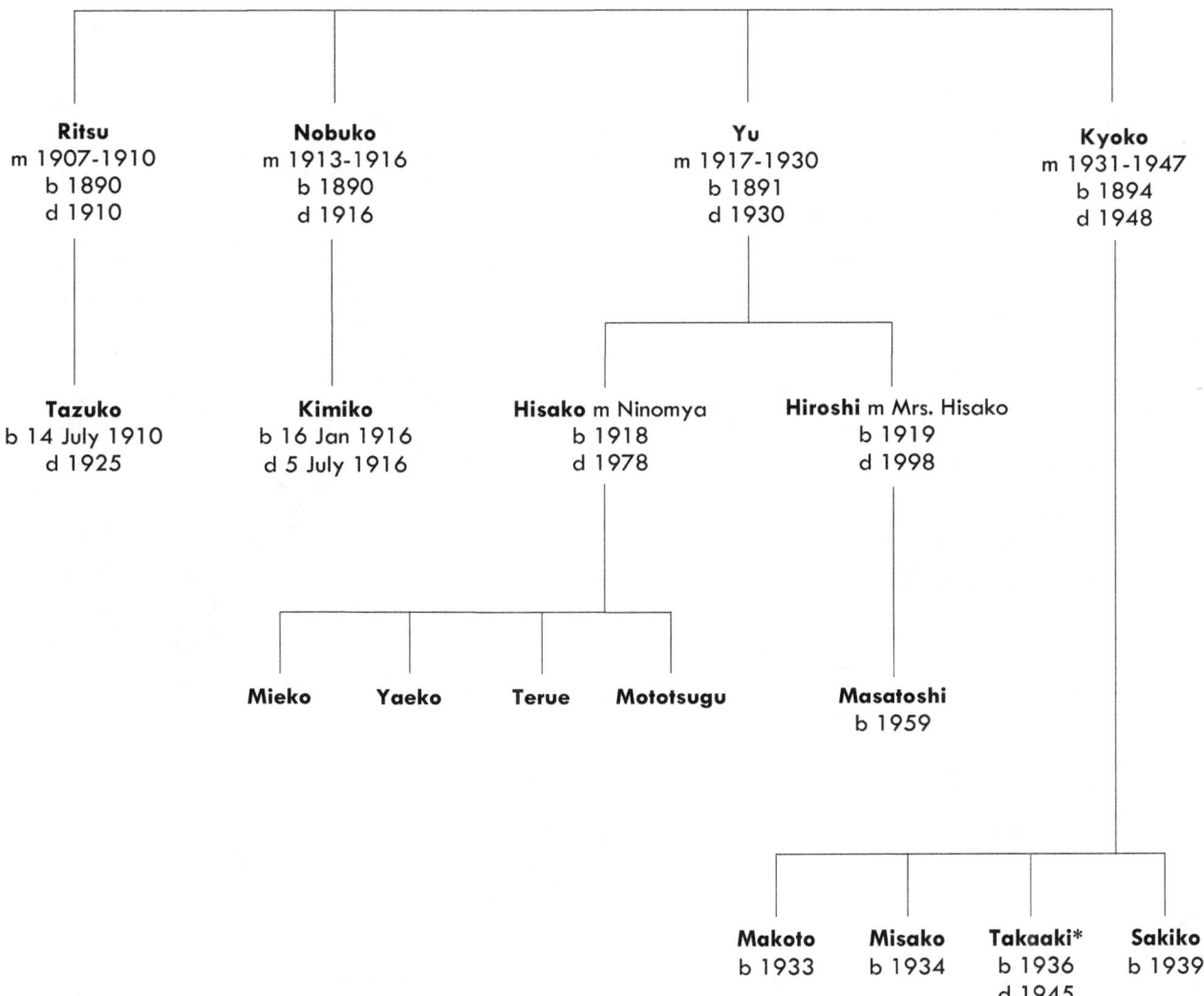

HE GAVE THE ORDER

Appendix C1

Washington Naval Treaty 1922

TREATIES

I. A TREATY BETWEEN THE UNITED STATES OF AMERICA, THE BRITISH EMPIRE, FRANCE, ITALY, AND JAPAN, LIMITING NAVAL ARMAMENT

The United States of America, the British Empire, France, Italy and Japan;

Desiring to contribute to the maintenance of the general peace, and to reduce the burdens of competition in armament;

Have resolved, with a view to accomplishing these purposes, to conclude a treaty to limit their respective naval armament, and to that end have appointed as their Plenipotentiaries;

The President of the United States of America:

Charles Evans Hughes,
Henry Cabot Lodge,
Oscar W. Underwood,
Elihu Root,
Citizens of the United States;

His Majesty the King of the United Kingdom of Great Britain and Ireland and of the British Dominions beyond the Seas, Emperor of India:

The Right Honourable Arthur James Balfour, O. M., M. P., Lord President of His Privy Council;
The Right Honourable Baron Lee of Fareham, G. B. E., K. C. B., First Lord of His Admiralty;
The Right Honourable Sir Auckland Campbell Geddes, K. C. B., His Ambassador Extraordinary and Plenipotentiary to the United States of America;

and

for the Dominion of Canada:
The Right Honourable Sir Robert Laird Borden, G. C. M. G., K. C.;
for the Commonwealth of Australia:
Senator the Right Honourable George Foster Pearce, Minister for Home and Territories;

for the Dominion of New Zealand:
The Honourable Sir John William Salmond, K. C., Judge of the Supreme Court of New Zealand;
for the Union of South Africa:
The Right Honourable Arthur James Balfour, O. M., M. P.;
for India:
The Right Honourable Valingman Sankaranarayana Srinivasa Sastri, Member of the Indian Council of State;

The President of the French Republic:
Mr. Albert Sarraut, Deputy, Minister of the Colonies:
Mr. Jules J. Jusserand, Ambassador Extraordinary and Plenipotentiary to the United States of America, Grand Cross of the National Order of the Legion of Honour;

His Majesty the King of Italy:
The Honourable Carlo Schanzer, Senator of the Kingdom;
The Honourable Vittorio Rolandi Ricci, Senator of the Kingdom, His Ambassador Extraordinary and Plenipotentiary at Washington;
The Honourable Luigi Albertini, Senator of the Kingdom;

His Majesty the Emperor of Japan:
Baron Tomosaburo Kato, Minister for the Navy, Junii, a member of the First Class of the Imperial Order of the Grand Cordon of the Rising Sun with the Paulownia Flower;
Baron Kijuro Shidehara, His Ambassador Extraordinary and Plenipotentiary at Washington, Joshii, a member of the First Class of the Imperial Order of the Rising Sun:
Mr. Masanao Hanihara, Vice Minister for Foreign Affairs, Jushii, a member of the Second Class of the Imperial Order of the Rising Sun;

Who, having communicated to each other their respective full powers, found to be in good and due form, have agreed as follows:

General Provisions Relating to the Limitation of Naval Armament, Washington Conference 1922 from reference Buell, Raymond Leslie, *The Washington Conference*, D. Appleton and Company, New York, 1922

The raw numbers for battleships and aircraft carriers were as follows:

Capital Ships

Nation	Weight (long tons)*	Per unit basis
USA	525,000	1.0
Britain	525,000	1.0
Japan	315,000	0.6
France	175,000	0.33
Italy	175,000	0.33

* no one ship exceeds 35,000 tons
maximum gun caliber: 16 inches (40.64 cm)

Aircraft Carriers

Nation	Weight (long tons)*	Per unit basis
USA	135,000	1.0
Britain	135,000	1.0
Japan	81,000	0.6
France	60,000	0.44
Italy	60,000	0.44

* no aircraft carrier exceeds 27,000 tons
no gun exceeds 8 inches (20.32 cm) and no limit on number of guns on carriers

These tonnages were just the beginning. The actual Treaty covered ships to be scrapped, and took into account the age of the ships and ship building capacity, all of these elements are the subject of three chapters in the Treaty, abstracts of which are given in Appendix I. The chapter titles are as follows:

- Chapter I, General Provisions relating to the Limitation of Naval Armament
- Chapter II, Rules Relating to Execution of the Treaty, Definitions and Terms
- Chapter III, Miscellaneous Provisions

Most importantly, the Treaty detailed which ships were to be scrapped to stay within Treaty limits. The results were as follows:

United States – ships to be scrapped

- 28 battleships – Immediately (12 that had just been built)
- 18 battleships - From 1922–1942

Britain – ships to be scrapped

- 20 battleships - Immediately (plus 4 presently or projected to be built)
- 42 battleships - From 1922–1942

Japan – ships to be scrapped

- 16 battleships – Immediately
- 10 battleships - From 1922–1942

France – ships to be scrapped

- 0 battleships - Immediately
- 7 battleships - From 1922–1942

Italy

- 0 battleships - Immediately
- 6 battleships – From 1922–1942

Appendix C2

London Naval Treaty 1930

Treaty Provisions

(Contracting parties: US, UK and Japan)

London Naval Treaty General Provisions (1930)

- No replacement capital ships built during period 1930-1936 (ship-building moratorium) as provided in Washington Naval Treaty (1922). Exclusion for France and Italy to build replacement capital ships permitted under the Treaty
- Disposal of capital ships
    - United States – *Florida, Utah, Arkansas, Wisconsin*
    - United Kingdom – *Benhow, Iron Duke, Marlborough, Empire of India, Tiger*
    - Japan – *Heyer*
- Spells out scrap procedures
- Article 3 – redefines aircraft carriers
- Article 4 – covers carriers < 10,000 tons, shall be built by US, UK or Japan
- Article 7 – limits submarines to 2000 long tons (2032 metric tons)
- Article 8 – no limits on ships < 600 tons
- Specifications for ships
    - Ships greater than 600 tons and less than 2000 tons
- Article 9 – rules for replacements are listed in Part II, Annex I
- Article 10 – communicate of signatories to Treaty partners of construction information
- Article 12 – special vessels
    - Japan – construct replacement for aged ships
    - Japan may replace *Assma, Akayakience, Izumi* by new vessels of *Kiesuo* class and *Kuma* class vessels
    - *Kuma* class vessels replaced may be used as training vessels
- Annex I – replacement rules
    - Replacement rules for ships 16 to 20 years old and in the range of 3000 to 10,000 tons and submarines 13 years old or older
- Annex II – disposal rules
    - Rules for experimental ships
    - Rules for training ships

- Part III – limits on auxiliary vessels

SHIPS	UNITED STATES	UNITED KINGDOM	JAPAN
Cruisers (heavy) guns > 6.1 inch (155 mm)	180,000 tons per unit 1.0	146,800 tons per unit 0.83	108,400 tons per unit 0.60
Cruisers (light) guns < 6.1 inch (155 mm)	145,500 tons per unit 1.0	192,200 tons per unit 1.3	100,450 tons per unit 0.69
Destroyers	150,000 tons per unit 1.0	150,000 tons per unit 1.0	105,500 tons per unit 0.72
Submarines	52,700 tons per unit 1.0	52,700 tons per unit 1.0	52,700 tons per unit 1.0
Exception for construction over limits if any contracting party feels threatened by non- contracting party			

Table 1. Auxiliary vessels limitations

- Part IV – rules of engagement
    - Submarines conform to international law regarding merchant ships
    - A capital ship shall not sink a merchant ship without warning
- Part V – Treat in force to December 31, 1936
- Many provisions of Washington Naval Treaty of 1922 remain in force
- Agree to meet in 1935 to renegotiate the Treaty

Appendix C3

London Naval Treaty 1936

Contracting Parties, US, UK and later Germany and Soviet Union Treaty Provisions

LONDON NAVAL TREATY (1936)

- Part I - Treaty spells out scrapping provisions
- Overage ships
    - Capital ships >26 years old
    - Aircraft carriers >20 years old
    - Light surface vessels
    - Constructed 1920 – 16 years
    - Constructed after December 1919 – 20 years
    - In general – 16 years
- Submarines – 13 years
- Construction schedule
    - Capital ships <35,000 tons
    - Guns <14 inches
    - In some cases <16 inches
- Aircraft carriers <25,000 tons
    - Guns <6.1 inch (155 mm)
    - No light surface vessel >8,000 tons shall be laid down prior to January 1943
    - Exceptions
    - Submarines <2,000 tons
- Part III – communication among contracting parties regarding annual construction program
- Part IV – lists exceptions to acquisitions in time of emergency
- Part V – Treaty remains in force to December 31, 1942 but means of renegotiating Treaty in 1940

Appendix C4

Naval Combatant Strength, Pacific Ocean, 1 May 1941*

| | United States | | Royal Navy | Royal Netherlands Navy | Total Potential Allies | Japanese Navy (7 Dec.)** |
	Pacific Fleet	Asiatic Fleet				
Battleships	9	-	1	-	10	10
Carriers	3	-	1	-	4	10
Heavy Cruisers	12	1	4	-	17	18
Light Cruisers	9	2	13	3	27	17
Destroyers	67	13	6	7	93	111
Submarines	27	28	-	15	70	64

1. Table 1: Relative strength American, British, Japanese navies.

Ref: Morison S. E., *The Rising Sun in the Pacific 1931-April 1942*, Little, Brown and Company, Boston, 1988, p. 58.
* Data compiled from *Pearl Harbor Attack,* Part 15, prepared by the Office of Naval Intelligence, November 1945.
** Figures furnished by the Japanese Navy Minister to the United States Strategic Bombing Survey, November 1945.

Appendix D

Meiji Constitution

Excerpts

Article 11. The Emperor has the supreme command of the Army and Navy.

Article 12. The Emperor determines the organization and peace standing of the Army and Navy.

Article 13. The Emperor declares war, makes peace, and concludes treaties.

Appendix E

Nagano Medals, Orders, Decorations

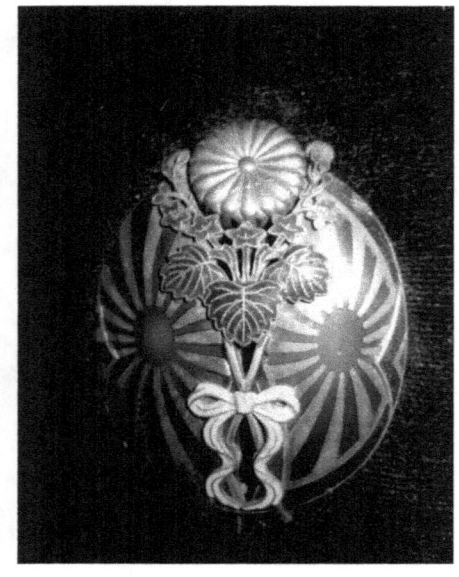

Gensui Badge (Marshal)

(Gensui Kaigun Taisho)

First Order of the Sacred Treasure
(5th class)

Order of the Sacred Treasure (2nd class)
Grand Cross Breast Star

Order of the Rising Sun (2nd Class)
Badge and star

Order of the Golden Kite (5th Class)
Russo-Japanese War medal 1904-05
Taisho Enthronement Commemorative Medal 1915
WWI Japanese Siberian Russian Bolshevik Revolution 1914-20
WWI Inter-Allied Victory medal
Showa Emperor Hirohito Enthronement medal 1928
Manchuria Incident medal 1931-34
China Incident medal 1937-45
2600th National Anniversary Commemoration medal

"Simplicity, Honesty, Honour"

Japanese Delegation to the Conference on the
Limitation of Armament, 1921 Washington, DC

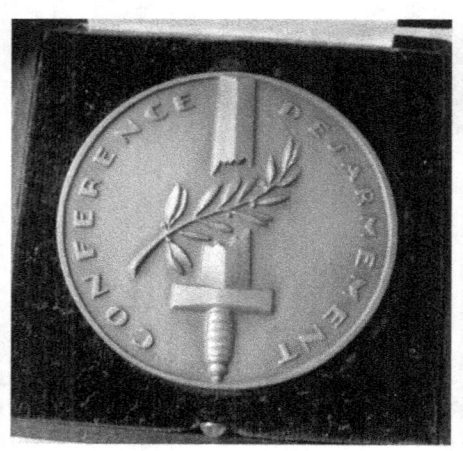  

Geneva Disarmament Conference 1932

Manchukuo Imperial Visit to Japan Commemorative medal 1935

Imperial Sea Disaster Rescue Society honorary membership badge

Navy Staff College Graduation badge 1911
(September 30, 1911)

(discontinued in 1922)

First National Census Commemorative medal 1920

Grosskreuz des Ordens vom Deutschen Adler (Germany)

Grand Cross of the Order of the German Eagle

House of Savoy. Order of St Maurice and St Lazarus Knight Grand Cordon (Italy)

Order of the White Elephant (Thailand)

Grand Cordon of the Order of
Wen-Hu the Striped Tiger
(Chinese)

Order of United Glory
(Manchukuo)

Appendix F

Soviet-Japanese Neutrality Pact
April 13, 1941

Pact of Neutrality Between Union of Soviet Socialist Republics and Japan

The President of the Supreme Soviet Socialist Republics and His Majesty the Emperor of Japan, guided by a desire to strengthen peaceful and friendly relations between the two countries, have decided to conclude a pact on neutrality, for which purpose they have appointed as their Representatives:

The Presidium of the Supreme Soviet of the Union of Soviet Socialist Republics –

Vyacheslav Mikhailovich Molotov,
Chairman of the Council of People's Commissars
And People's Commissar of Foreign Affairs of
The Union of Soviet Socialist Republics;

His Majesty the Emperor of Japan —

Yosuke Matsuoka,
Minister of Foreign affairs, Jusanmin,
Cavalier of the Order of the Sacred
Treasure of the First Class, and

Yoshitsugu Tatekawa,
Ambassador Extraordinary and Plenipotentiary to
the Union of Soviet Socialist Republics,
Lieutenant General, Jusanmin, Cavalier of the
Order of the rising Sun of the First Class and
The Order of the Golden Kite of the Fourth Class,

Who, after an exchange of their credentials, which were found in due and proper form, have agreed on the following:

ARTICLE ONE

Both contracting parties undertake to maintain peaceful and friendly relations between them and mutually respect the territorial integrity and inviolability of the other Contracting Party.

ARTICLE TWO

Should one of the Contracting parties become the object of hostilities on the part of one or several third powers, the other Contacting Party will observe neutrality throughout the duration of the conflict.

ARTICLE THREE

The present pact comes into force from the day of its ratification by both Contracting Parties and remains valid for five years. In case neither of the Contracting parties denounces the Pact one year before the expiration of the term, it will be considered automatically prolonged for the next five years.

ARTICLE FOUR

The present Pact is subject to ratification as soon as possible. The instruments of ratification shall be exchanged in Tokyo, also as soon as possible.

In confirmation whereof the above-named Representatives have signed the present pact in two copies, drawn up in the Russian and Japanese languages, and affixed thereto their seals.

Done in Moscow on April 13, 1941, which corresponds to the 13th day of the fourth month of the 16th year of Showa.

> V. MOLOTOV
> YOSUKE MATSUOKA
> YOSHITSUGU TATEKAWA

Appendix G

Summary of IMTFE Trial Results

LAST NAME	FIRST NAME	BIRTH	DEATH	TITLE/ GOVERNMENT POSITION	SENTENCE	DATE RELEASED
ARAKI	Sadao	1877	1966	General - Minister, War, Education	Life in prison	1955
DOHIHARA	Kenji	1883	23 Dec 1948	General	Death by hanging	
HASHIMOTO	Kingoro	1890	1957	Colonel	Life in prison	1954
HATA	Shunroku	1879	1962	Field Marshall	Life in prison	1954
HIRANUMA	Kiichiro	1867	1952	Minister – Prime	Life in prison	1952
HIROTA	Koki	1878	23 Dec 1948	Minister – Prime, Ambassador	Death by hanging	
HOSHINO	Naoki	1892	1948	Minister – Finance	Life in prison	1955
ITAGAKI	Seishiro	1885	23 Dec 1948	General – Minister, War	Death by hanging	
KAYA	Okinori	1889	1977	Minister – Finance	Life in prison	1955
KIDO	Koichi	1889	1977	Marquis – Lord Keeper of the Privy Seal	Life in prison	1955
KIMURA	Heitar	1888	23 Dec 1948	General	Death by hanging	
KOISO	Kuniaki	1889	1950	General – Minister, Prime	Life in prison	1955
MATSUI	Iwane	1878	23 Dec 1948	General	Death by hanging	
MATSUOKA	Yosuke	1880	27 June 1946	Minister, Foreign	—	Died in prison during trial
MINAMI	Jiro	1874	1955	General	Life in prison	1955
MUTO	Akira	1892	23 Dec 1948	General	Death by hanging	
NAGANO	Osami	1880	5 Jan 1947	Admiral – Minister, Chief of Staff, Navy	—	Died in prison during trial
OKA	Takasumi	1890	1973	Admiral	Life in prison	1954
OKAWA	Shumei	1886	1957	Author	Removed to mental hospital	Declared non compos mentis at trial, 1948
OSHIMA	Hiroshi	1886	1975	General – Ambassador	Life in prison	1955
SATO	Kenryo	1895	1970	General	Life in prison	1956
SHIGEMITSU	Mamoru	1887	1957	Minister, Foreign – Ambassador	7 years in prison	1950
SHIMADA	Shigetaro	1883	1976	Admiral – Minister, Navy	Life in prison	1955
SHIRATORI	Toshio	1887	1949	Minister, Foreign	Life in prison	Died in prison
SUZUKI	Teiichi	1888	1989	General	Life in prison	1955
TOGO	Shigenori	1884	1948	Minister, Foreign – Ambassador	20 years in prison	Died in prison
TOJO	Hideki	1884	23 Dec 1948	General – Minister, Prime, War	Death by hanging	
UMEZU	Yoshijiro	1882	1949	General	Life in prison	Died in prison

Index

A

Abe, General Nobuyuki, 64, 85, 144
Anglo-Japanese Treaty 1901, 55
Anti-Comintern Pact, 68, 69, 75, 84, 123, 141
Anti-Treaty faction (aka Fleet faction), 33, 40, 55, 56, 57, 58
Araki, General Sadao, 63, 65, 66, 79, 144
Arita, Hachiro, 67, 91, 96
Arnold, General Henry "Hap", 130, 136
Asama (cruiser), 12, 22, 23, 28
Atlantic Conference, 109

B

Balfour, Earl Arthur J., 54, 55
Bassett, Captain F. S., 21
Benes, Edward, 34
Bonin Islands, 48, 49
Brannon, John G., 120, 122, 133, 135, 136, 138, 139, 144
Briand, Aristide, 20

C

Calles, Plutarco Elias, 23
Caroline Islands, 12, 37, 41, 48, 49
Chamberlain, Neville, 63, 90, 123
Chiang Kai-shek, 70, 76, 77, 78, 79, 81, 91, 96, 98, 105, 107, 141, 144
China Incident, 92, 94, 96, 97, 98, 102, 103, 104, 107, 109, 110, 111, 114, 115, 116, 119, 141, 185
Chou En-lai, 76
Chungking, 80, 105, 141, 144
Churchill, Winston, 90, 97, 109, 123, 144
Ciano, Count Galleazzo, 124
Control Way, 66, 67, 69, 141
Coolidge, Calvin, 19, 23, 25, 56, 144
Cooper, Gary, 22, 29

D

Denby, Edwin, 21
Dooman, Eugene, 113
Draft Convention, 35, 36
Draft Understanding, 105, 106, 107, 108, 112, 115, 141, 142
Dunkirk, 85, 90, 123
Dutch, 5, 41, 91, 96, 105, 110, 121, 141

E

Edo, 5, 6, 143
Eta Jima, 7, 8, 10, 12, 13, 26, 141

F

FDR, 38, 40, 42, 106, 110, 115, 119, 120, 123
Ferdinand, Archduke Francis, 12, 34
Five-Power Treaty 1922 also see Washington Naval Treaty 1922, 20
Four-Power Treaty 1922, 55
French Indochina, 91, 96, 97, 100, 101, 102, 104, 105, 108, 109, 110, 111, 115, 117, 119, 123, 128, 141, 143
Fuchida, Commander Mitsuo, 120, 135
Fushimi, Prince Hiroyasu, 59, 61, 64, 66, 90, 92, 93, 95, 125, 126, 144

G

Genda, Commander Minoru, 120, 135
Geneva Disarmament Conference 1932-1935, 33, 34, 44, 45, 49, 54, 146, 186
Geneva Naval Conference 1927, 54, 56, 57
Gensui, 12, 184
Gibson, Hugh, 35
Goebbels, Joseph, 107, 132
Great Depression, 19, 38
Greater East Asia Co-Prosperity Sphere, 91, 98, 101, 103, 104, 116, 130
Grew, Joseph, 74, 79, 97, 99, 109, 121, 144

H

Hamada, Kunimatsu, 69
Hamaguchi, Osachi, 33
Hara, Yoshimichi, 91, 92, 104, 116, 144
Harada, Baron Kumao, 63
Harding, Warren G., 19, 20, 54, 144
Harris, Townsend, 6
Hasegawa, Admiral Kiyoshi, 74, 78, 79, 81
Hayashi, General Senjuro, 69, 85, 144
Henderson, Arthur, 19, 34, 35, 40, 44, 144
Hirado (INJ cruiser), 14
Hiranuma, Baron Kiichiro, 65, 85, 97, 108, 144
Hirohito, Emperor, 19, 22, 48, 53, 60, 63, 65, 66, 68, 69, 70, 76, 77, 78, 79, 80, 81, 84, 85, 86, 90, 93, 95, 104, 108, 109, 111, 112, 116, 118, 123, 126, 130, 131, 144, 145, 185
Hirota, Koki, 58, 65, 66, 67, 68, 69, 70, 73, 75, 77, 144
Hitler
  Berchtesgaden, 100
Hitler, Adolf, 36, 37, 38, 68, 69, 84, 85, 86, 90, 91, 92, 93, 96, 97, 99, 100, 101, 103, 104, 106, 107, 108, 110, 118, 121, 124, 125, 130, 131, 136, 142, 143, 144
Honshu, 6, 8, 49, 68, 131, 132, 142
Hoover, Herbert, 19, 37, 38, 39, 57, 144
Hughes, Charles Evans, 20, 26, 54, 55, 56, 144
Hull, Cordell, 19, 106, 107, 109, 110, 112, 113, 114, 115, 117, 119, 121, 144
Hurley, Patrick, 39

I

Imperial Japanese Army, 8, 25, 26, 63, 76, 105, 107, 121, 132, 141, 144
Imperial Japanese Navy, 8, 12, 22, 23, 25, 33, 55, 76, 135, 141, 144
Imperial Way, 66, 67, 141
International Military Tribunal for the Far East (IMTFE) also see Tokyo War Crimes Trial, 5, 86, 131, 132, 133, 139, 142, 144, 145
Inukai, Tsuyoshi, 144, 145

Ishiwara, General Kanji, 64, 79
Iwate (cruiser), 14, 22, 23, 28

J

John Doe Associates, 106, 110, 113, 121, 141, 142, 144, 145
    Drought, Father John, 106, 144
    Ikawa, Tadao, 106
    Iwakuro, Colonel Hideo, 106
    Walsh, Bishop James Edward, 106, 113, 145

K

Kainan Middle School, 7
Kato, Admiral Kanji, 56, 57
Kato, Baron Tomosaburo, 20, 54, 55, 56, 58, 144
Kaya, Okinori, 77, 116, 118, 144
Keenan, Joseph, 131
Kido, Koichi, 63, 70, 95, 115, 116, 121, 144
Kinmochi, Prince Saionji, 65, 145
Kiyonao, Colonel Ichiki, 130
Kobayashi, Admiral Seizo, 48
Kochi, 6, 7, 8, 9, 41, 46, 70, 133, 136, 143
Kondo, Admiral Nobutake, 103
Konoye, Prince Fumimaro, 63, 64, 65, 77, 78, 85, 90, 93, 95, 97, 98, 99, 102, 105, 106, 107, 108, 109, 110, 111, 113, 114, 115, 116, 121, 124, 132, 144
Koo, Welling, 37
Kurusu, Saburo, 118, 119, 124
Kusaka, Admiral Ryunosuke, 120
Kwantung Army, 36, 79

L

League of Nations, 20, 33, 34, 36, 37, 41, 48, 54, 65, 96, 141, 144, 168
Lend Lease, 97, 123, 142
Liaotung Peninsula, 5, 12, 16
London Naval Conference 1930, 57, 58, 69
London Naval Conference 1935, 40, 53, 54, 57, 67
London Naval Treaty 1930, 33, 38, 54, 56, 59, 179
London Naval Treaty 1936, 181
Lytton, Earl, 37, 144

M

MacArthur, General Douglas, 38, 131, 142, 144
MacDonald, Ramsay, 34, 57, 145
Maeda, Admiral Minoru, 116
Manchukuo, 56, 63, 67, 68, 69, 76, 85, 96, 97, 123, 132, 142, 162, 186, 189
Manchuria, 25, 36, 37, 41, 59, 67, 99, 132, 142, 143, 144, 154, 161, 185
Mao Tse-tung, 76, 105
Marco Polo Bridge Incident of July 1937, 56, 76, 81, 142
Marianas Islands, 49, 131
Marshall Islands, 12, 37, 41, 48
Maryknoll, 106, 142, 144, 145
Matsudaira Tsuneo, 26, 36, 57, 144
Matsui, General Iwane, 36, 77, 78, 81, 144
Matsuoka
    Beveridge, Isabelle Dunbar, 41, 47
    treatment of Jews, 107, 108, 121
    University of Oregon, 21, 41, 47, 98
Matsuoka, Yosuke, 37, 39, 40, 41, 42, 47, 48, 49, 84, 90, 91, 92, 93, 96, 98, 99, 100, 101, 102, 103, 104, 105, 106, 107, 108, 110, 114, 116, 121, 125, 130, 131, 132, 133, 136, 141, 144, 190
Meiji, 5, 6, 8, 12, 26, 53, 57, 63, 65, 66, 70, 98, 102, 112, 142, 144, 183
Minseito Party, 53, 65
Mitchell, General Billy, 19, 20, 69
Moffet, Admiral William, 19
Molotov, Vyacheslav M., 93, 125, 132, 144, 190
Mukden Incident, 36, 66, 96, 132, 142
Murfin, Admiral Orin G., 67, 74
Mussolini, Benito, 90
Muto, General Akira, 66, 145

N

Nagai, Matsuzo, 58, 59, 62
Nagano
    Arlington National Cemetery, 23, 30, 84
    Boston Harbor, 22
    calligraphy, 8, 26, 60, 172
    Chief of Naval Staff, 93
    Commander of the Training Fleet, 21
    Commander-in-Chief of the Combined Fleet, 76, 83, 134
    Crown Point Chalet, 21
    Great Kanto earthquake, 21
    Harukichi, 6, 7, 9
    Harvard University, 8, 13, 14, 25
    Havana, Cuba, 22
    Hiroshi, 14, 27, 33, 49, 51, 68, 84, 88, 100, 149, 151, 152, 153, 154, 155, 156, 157, 158, 159, 161, 162, 164, 165, 166, 167, 192
    Hisako, 14, 27, 33, 49, 51, 84, 88, 146, 147, 148, 149, 152, 153, 154, 159, 161, 163, 164, 166, 167, 168, 169, 170
    Ishigawa home, 84
    Japan Society of Boston, 22
    Japanese Embassy, Washington DC, 19
    Kimiko, 14
    Kyoko, 49, 50, 51, 84, 88, 89, 131, 135
    Makoto, 37, 49, 51, 72, 84, 88
    Misako, 8, 49, 51, 52, 66, 70, 72, 84, 88, 89, 131, 136
    Naval Attache, 7, 14, 19, 21, 22, 41, 56
    New Orleans, 23, 24, 28
    Nobuko, 14
    Pan Pacific Club, 25
    Ritsu, 13, 18
    sake cups, 69, 84
    Saki, 6, 7, 13
    Sakiko, 49, 52, 84, 89
    Takaaki, 84, 88, 89, 131, 135
    Tazuko, 13, 14, 17, 18, 33, 135, 152
    Washington Japanese Embassy, 14, 23, 27
    Washington Social Register, 19
    Yankee Stadium, 22
    Yu, 14, 18, 19, 27, 49, 84
Nagano, Admiral Osami, 5, 6, 7, 8, 9, 10, 12, 13, 14, 15, 16, 17, 18, 19, 20, 21, 22, 23, 25, 26, 27, 28, 29, 30, 31, 32, 33, 34, 35, 36, 37, 39, 40, 41, 42, 43, 44, 46, 48, 49, 50, 51, 52, 53, 55, 56, 57, 58, 59, 60, 61, 62, 63, 66, 67, 69, 70, 71, 73, 74, 76, 77, 78, 79, 80, 飢82, 83, 84, 85, 86, 87, 89, 93, 95, 99, 100, 101, 102, 103, 104, 105, 106, 108, 110, 111, 112, 116, 117, 119, 120, 121, 125, 126, 127, 130, 131, 133, 134, 135, 136, 137, 138, 139, 142, 144, 145, 155, 168, 170, 174, 175, 184
Nagasaki, 5, 78
Nagato (flagship), 78, 79, 83, 170
Nagumo, Admiral Chuichi, 120, 135, 145
Nanking, 76, 78, 79, 81, 98, 105, 123, 142, 144, 145
Naval Academy, 7, 8, 10, 11, 12, 13, 22, 25, 26, 141
Netherlands East Indies, 91, 96, 99, 100, 101, 109, 115, 116,

119, 141, 142
Neutrality Pact, German-Russian 1939, 84
Neutrality Pact, Japan-Soviet Russia 1941, 90, 92, 93, 97, 101, 103, 125, 130, 190
Nimitz, Admiral Chester, 130, 145
Nishihara, General I., 96
Nisshin (cruiser), 13, 14
Nomonhan Incident, 84, 85, 93, 142
Nomura, Admiral Kichisaburo, 8, 105, 106, 107, 108, 109, 110, 115, 118, 119, 120, 121, 145

O

Oikawa, Admiral Koshiro, 95, 101, 102, 104, 108, 109, 114, 145
Oka, Admiral Takasumi, 108, 111, 114
Okada, Keisuke, 63, 64, 65, 144
Okawa, Shumei, 131, 132, 136, 138, 145
open door policy, 55
Oshima, General Hiroshi, 68, 100, 145
Osumi, Admiral Mineo, 33, 58, 64, 66, 74, 145
Ott, Eugen, 101, 145

P

Pal, Radhabinod, 131
Panay Incident, 79, 80, 81, 143
Pearl Harbor, 8, 42, 48, 53, 91, 115, 116, 120, 121, 129, 133, 134, 135, 136, 142, 182
Perry, Commodore Matthew, 6, 22, 24, 145
Plunkett, Rear Admiral Chester P., 22
Pope Pius XII, 133
Port Arthur, 8, 12, 13
Pratt, Admiral William, 56

R

Raeder, Admiral Erich, 59
Roosevelt, Franklin Delano also see FDR, 40, 41, 48, 79, 80, 85, 90, 97, 105, 106, 108, 109, 110, 113, 123, 145
Roosevelt, Theodore, 12, 54
Russo-Japanese War, 8, 16, 95, 145, 185
Ruth, Babe, 22, 26

S

Saito, Makoto, 37, 63
Second London Naval Conference 1935, 57, 59, 62, 66, 69
Seiyukai Party, 53, 65, 69
Shanghai Incident of 1932, 37
Shikoku, 6, 7, 9, 131, 133, 143
Shimada, Admiral Shigetaro, 74, 116, 145
Shimonoseki, 5
Shogun, 5, 6, 143, 145
Showa Restoration, 53, 66, 143
Simon, Sir John, 34, 36, 121, 145
South Manchurian Railroad Company, 39, 42, 99, 143
Stalin, Joseph, 76, 84, 90, 92, 93, 125, 130, 132, 145
Steinhardt, Laurence A., 106
Stimson, Henry L., 35, 37, 41, 145
Sugamo Prison, 5, 8, 12, 14, 133, 134, 143
Sugiyama, General Hajime, 66, 77, 101, 102, 111, 116, 117, 130, 145
Suzuki, Baron Kantaro, 63, 117
Swanson, Claude A., 48

T

Taisho, 12, 19, 53, 55, 145, 184, 185
Takaheshi, Admiral Takaheshi, 59
Tatekawa, Yoshitsugu, 93, 190
Terauchi, General Hisaichi, 66, 67, 69, 73, 75
Togo, Admiral Heihachiro, 12, 13, 55, 56, 85, 89, 116, 118, 119, 120, 135, 136, 145
Togo, Shigenori, 116, 117, 118, 121, 122, 145
Tojo, General Hideki, 13, 66, 90, 96, 101, 102, 103, 104, 106, 108, 109, 111, 113, 114, 115, 116, 117, 118, 119, 127, 130, 132, 133, 138, 144, 145
Tokugawa, 5, 6, 26, 145
Tokyo War Crimes Trial (also see IMTFE), 84, 86, 132, 136
Tominaga, General Kyoji, 96
Tosa, 6, 7, 143
Toyoda, Admiral Soemu, 74
Toyoda, Admiral Teijiro, 108, 109, 111, 113, 145
Treaty faction, 33, 55, 56, 57, 58
Treaty of Versailles, 20
Tripartite Pact, 84, 90, 91, 92, 94, 95, 99, 101, 104, 105, 106, 107, 109, 110, 111, 113, 114, 117, 119, 123, 130, 143
Tsukada, General Osamu, 103, 104, 117, 118
Tully, Grace, 119, 121

U

Uchiyama, Japanese Consul General K, 22
Ugaki, Admiral Matome, 116, 121

V

Versailles Treaty 1919, 20, 48
Vichy France, 96, 97, 98, 101, 102, 105, 143
Vladivostok, 13, 76, 102, 166, 167
von Ribbentrop, Joachim, 59, 75, 93

W

Wakatsuki, Reijiro, 113
Walker, Frank, 110, 119, 145
Wang Ching-wei, 98, 105, 123, 145
Washington Arms Limitation Conference 1921-1922, 20, 26, 54, 56
Washington Naval Treaty 1922, 20, 21, 33, 39, 40, 55, 56, 59, 60, 67, 85, 143, 176, 179, 180
Welles, Sumner, 113, 119
Wilson, Woodrow, 13, 20, 54, 145
World War I, 12, 14, 20, 34, 38, 41, 48, 53, 54, 97, 141, 143

Y

Yamamoto, Admiral Isoroku Takano, 8, 13, 14, 20, 22, 23, 30, 33, 56, 57, 58, 59, 69, 71, 77, 78, 116, 120, 122, 130, 134, 135, 136, 145
Yasukuni Shrine, 84, 143
Yen, W. W., 36
Yokosuka, 12, 14, 23, 28, 42, 49, 50, 52, 58, 65
Yonai, Admiral Mitsumasa, 65, 77, 79, 85, 96, 145
Yoshida, Admiral Zengo, 74, 79, 90, 91
Yoshida, Principal Kazuma, 7
Yoshida, Shigeru, 7, 66, 145

Z

Zhukov, General Georgi, 85

www.ingramcontent.com/pod-product-compliance
Lightning Source LLC
Chambersburg PA
CBHW080450170426
43196CB00016B/2748